TERAANGA REPUBLIC

TERAANGA REPUBLIC

WOMEN'S AUTHORITY AND POLITICS IN SENEGAL

EMILY JENAN RILEY

INDIANA UNIVERSITY PRESS

This book is a publication of

Indiana University Press
Office of Scholarly Publishing
Herman B Wells Library 350
1320 East 10th Street
Bloomington, Indiana 47405 USA

iupress.org

First Printing 2025

Cataloging information is available from the Library of Congress.
ISBN 978-0-253-07261-0 (hdbk.)
ISBN 978-0-253-07262-7 (pbk.)
ISBN 978-0-253-07263-4 (web PDF)
ISBN 978-0-253-07264-1 (ebook)

I dedicate this book to my mothers. Susan Yeoman gave me life. Audrey Perkins, Peg Herring, Patty Dawson, and Joan Gross continue to sustain me in her absence.

CONTENTS

PREFACE

This research project would not have been possible without the *teraanga* of so many of the people described in this book and those not mentioned. I am grateful to them and to have been able to work for many years in a place that has a beautiful way of welcoming people like myself to participate in their activities, share their homes and families, and be a nosy researcher. Thanks to a Senegalese culture of openness that wishes to be helpful, I could easily call up an important person and be included in a house visit or spend time at their home, where I was fed, given a room to sleep in, and treated to hospitality without question. Of course, the question of hospitality for a white woman is different from that of someone else.

During research, at times I felt like part of a team or entourage. People expected me to be there, and if I wasn't, the next time they saw me they inquired where I had gone. I felt cared for by many of the women, especially when I regained consciousness on a hospital bed while the parliamentarian Mously Diakhaté massaged my legs after I had passed out from food poisoning.[1] Other times, I was reminded of my role as an outsider. For example, once I waited all day to accompany the politician Ayda Mbóoj to an event, only to be left behind because I was in the bathroom—ultimately a sign that I was completely irrelevant to the group. Yet, I could also be useful, even if symbolically. One evening during the campaigns in 2017, Ayda introduced me to a crowd as her personal biographer who had written several books about her. Although I had written only two articles in which she featured heavily, I was keenly aware that my presence had a political utility for her image. And I felt it was my small way of reciprocating her teraanga.

My positionality as a white non-native Wolof-speaking woman gained me a great deal of purchase among these women and their supporters that I am very aware is not granted equally to others. For example, after several attempts to get ahold of Ayda Mbóoj without luck, I ran into her at an event and spoke with her in Wolof for a few minutes and asked for an interview. She said years later that the only reason she granted me that initial interview was because I spoke to her in Wolof. So, although being a white foreigner does have its innate advantages, demonstrating a level of fluency in something other than French afforded me another level of social capital. In addition to these examples, there were a plethora of occasions when I was able to gain access to political rallies and events, people, and spaces in parliament all because of my identity. Senegalese friends were always amazed and a bit baffled that I was able to so easily access spaces in their own home country that would most likely be closed off to them. As an American woman researcher, I was also given a pass in spaces that were predominately occupied by men as I possibly embodied an "honorary male status" (McNee 2000, 6). This status also gave me a pass among Senegalese women for whom dressing up and extravagance were important to their feminine and political image as we will see throughout this book. Not only did I have access to spaces that others might not, I was also privy to conversations because I was seen as somehow outside of their social paradigm and safe to share thoughts and information with. I was considered to be someone who understood certain social conventions without being bound to them. As I was an outsider with some insider knowledge given my years of studying Wolof and visiting Senegal, they felt comfortable speaking about their feelings, especially pertaining to marginality as women. I am very grateful to them for their candor.

Despite sticking out like a sore thumb, I found it was important to always dress the part. I invested in fabrics and had local styles of *yére* Wolof (Wolof clothing) to attend public events. When not with a particular politician, I spent most of my time with people like Ndey Mbóoj, Ayda's niece, and other family members. It felt strange to parade around with the women and then receive a call from a friend saying they saw me on TV. On other occasions, especially during the 2017 campaigns, I was in the back of a packed truck on the opposite side of the camera with the film crew of the national television company RTS (Radio Télévision Sénégalaise) or other campaign members. In these instances, I allowed myself to dress down, often wearing tennis shoes, in order to run alongside the cars and film the candidate and the surroundings. With Aysata Tall Sall, my time was spent watching her campaign from a few cars back or with her campaign surrogates at the Dakar headquarters or in the *caravane*. It wasn't until after the 2017 election that I managed to squeeze in an interview with Aysata just hours before heading to the airport. It was one of the times I was especially thankful for flights to the US leaving at midnight or later.

In the case of Ayda, I accompanied her to funerals and to weddings of supporters where she was named the matron of honor and therefore gave large amounts of money to the family. I also traveled with her to religious conferences or celebrations of a *marabout* who was especially important to her in the holy city of Tuubaa. I spent the night at her homes in Dakar, Bambey, and Tuubaa and got to know her family quite well. With Mously Diakhaté, I visited her neighborhood associations where they talked of financial support from Mously and international donors, and I spent time with her at her homes in Dakar and Tuubaa. I was privy to their public personas as well as more candid intimate moments of self-reflection or gossip with their close friends and family.

I had the privilege of having a front-row seat for their political activities; I was allowed to observe voting in parliament and to attend several closed-door committee meetings as well as television interview tapings. I also had the advantage of spending this time with them before sitting for our long interviews so that much of our conversations were their reflections on the campaigns, political strategy, and their place in the history of Senegalese politics. Given their roles as public figures, I have been able to rely on television and radio interviews for missing biographical information that wasn't featured in our interviews. But most likely because I have stayed in touch with them over the years, I was able to ask. Even during the chaos of the 2024 elections, Aminata sent me updates about the progress of her campaign. Again, it is the spirit of teraanga and their confessions of duty to their religious principles and membership in the Sufi communities that permitted me to benefit from their time, as we shall see.

My original research plan had been to track a small and fleeting movement that took on debates about the economic and social costs of family ceremonies, but more so to examine women's authority over family resources and decision-making. The movement, if it could be considered that, was called *Lutte Contre le Gaspillage* (the Fight against Wastefulness), referring to the amount of money spent for family ceremonies and its negative impacts on families and national economic development, as was communicated by the Senegalese government. In 1967, the Senghor government passed a law mandating an expenditure limit on those ceremonies as a preventative measure against future inflation and to promote economic development in the postcolonial era, saying the law was to "defend the Senegalese citizen from themselves," or rather from financial burden. Feminist sociologist Fatou Sarr argues it was called wastefulness because it was a redistribution of wealth that was out of the hands of men (Sarr 1998). The oppositions of men towards women's expenditures will become clear throughout the book. I was often given mixed messages about the nature and debate of family ceremonies as they were depicted as exhausting, necessary, joyful, and wasteful. There were rifts about how much was too much or questioning the productivity of family ceremonies that were part sober religious practice and part ostentatious exchanges of material items and money. The ceremonies I attended were festive scenes of gift exchange, music, and singing that could last into the wee hours of the following morning. What wasn't up for debate was that women worked tirelessly to fund, organize, and conduct ceremonies or other manifestations of social solidarity. Of great debate within the discussion of women's role in state politics was the productivity of ceremonies and whether it was a symbol of women's inability to take Republican politics seriously.

The Fight against Wastefulness was fascinating to me because it questioned women's behavior on such monumental social occasions as family ceremonies. In addition, it was the kind of debate that was omnipresent yet never really gained tangible traction. The subject would pop up at different and opportune times, such as during the structural adjustment period of the Diouf administration, when international organizations began investing in women's economic and social programs, or in the first decade of the new millennium, when women were fighting for more representation in parliament. These debates went hand in hand with development speech about microcredit loans and women's central role in the fight against poverty or national development, which I interpreted as putting a great deal of the burden of progress on women's shoulders.

Many of the postcolonial administrations attempted to cultivate national culture by legislating private practices such as family spending. The ultimate failure to administer the law has led to its proliferation as a temporal topic of national concern, thus reinforcing a need to question certain values. Shortly after its inception, the law was loosely reinforced and eventually forgotten and has instead been a campaigning tool for politicians to establish themselves as civic minded and concerned with social issues. Opposition to the *parité* law, which grants equal opportunity for men and women in elected positions, has often co-opted the questions of wastefulness to accuse women of being unprofessional, corrupt, or unqualified for political office.

In seeking the opinions of women politicians working on the question of wastefulness within their projects in the Ministry of Women's Affairs, I began to see the same issues raised when it came to opinions on women in politics. This book is an extension of the curiosity about the theoretical and practical links between women's participation in family ceremonies and political affairs. The relevance of family ceremonies to women's political participation is essential to understanding their authority and strategies.

ACKNOWLEDGMENTS

This book was a labor of love, tears, curiosity, and teraanga. I am still in awe of the generosity of time and knowledge that helped me do research for this project and write this book. An enormous thank you to Ayda Mbóoj, Mously Diakhaté, Aminata Touré, and Aysata Tall Sall. They welcomed me into their homes, allowed me to tag along on their campaigns and to their family events, fed me, and shared their knowledge and experiences with me. Their words, ideas, and actions make the foundation of this book.

Just as the book aims to celebrate the invisible contributions women have made to Senegalese politics, I wish to thank the silent partners during my research and writing phases of the manuscript. Beyond the time and energies that Ndey Mbóoj, Awa Ka, Daba Codou, and Mareem Sow expended making space for me on the campaigns and including me in their activities, they became major consultants for so many of the fact-checking and follow-up questions I had over the years. Thank you to my Layene family in Cambérène—Mbaye Seck Ba, Binta, and their children—for your teraanga over the many years and my many visits to Dakar. Thank you to Fatou Sow Sarr for sharing knowledge of the parité debate and for introducing me to many of the parliamentarians featured in this book.

My longtime Wolof professor, Sidy Géy, helped mold my understanding of and love for the Wolof language and philosophy. He helped check the orthography and use of Wolof throughout the manuscript. Gana Njaay, Mor Géy, Arfang Dabo, and Assane Niang were my first Wolof teachers at Michigan State, and I learned so much from them. My doctoral adviser, Chantal Tetreault, not only guided me through the difficult stages of the PhD but continues to be one of my most invaluable mentors and someone I adore. Laura Fair, also part of my

xiii

committee, has remained another positive presence in my life beyond graduate school. I am grateful to her for her guidance in the publication process and for always encouraging me. So many years ago, when I was on the brink of quitting graduate school, she gave me one of the most valuable answers that allowed me to let go of my fear of not being good enough and just pursue my passion. Thank you to all the members of the African Studies Center at Michigan State and the West African Research Center and Association (WARCA/WARA) for your years of support and fellowship. I am grateful to the US Department of Education for the Foreign Language and Area Studies Funding to study Wolof and to the Fulbright Foundation for the doctoral dissertation research funding. Without these institutions, I would not have been able to do the in-depth research that this project required.

In my personal life, my family has been supportive throughout. To my dad and my big brother Timothy, thank you for your support. To Brittany, thank you for being a sister-in-law many would be jealous to have. To my adoptive dads, Tom Hewes, John Keogh, Geoff Dawson, and David McMurray, thank you for your love and kindness. A special thank you to Bo Williamson, who made me call him every Wednesday after my mom died and while I was writing my dissertation to chat and work things out. I wouldn't have finished it without him. To my friend Jenn Vollner, who calls and texts even when I don't. If ever there was a better friend than Jenn, I'm not aware of them. Thank you for your unconditional support. To Margaret Rowley and Robyn D'Avignon, who read my pages in the earliest and latest stages and also cheered me along through the ups and downs of this process: *Amuleen moroom.* Thank you to Ebenezer Obadare for coaching me through the publishing process and for talking through aspects of the manuscript.

To my colleagues in Mexico and my institution, El Colegio de México, I am grateful for the opportunity to work alongside you. I am proud to work with women such as the president of El Colegio de México, Silvia Giorguli Saucedo, and my dear colleague Flora Botton Beja, a trailblazer of our center. Thank you to all of you who have been patient while I learn Spanish and navigate life in such a monstrous city. A special thanks to Amaury Garcia, my colleague, friend, and neighbor who hired me in the Center for Asian and African Studies and who continues to encourage me in my work. A big thanks to my dear friend and colleague Élodie Brun for her friendship and care, and to Jannette Ramírez Arámburo, and Paola Encarnación who have helped me through some tough times. And last, to my grandmother, Nona, who won't get to read this book but was always proud of me for working on it. She showed me what courageous, curious, and ornery women can do, and I am eternally grateful for her guidance and inspiration.

NOTES ON WOLOF ORTHOGRAPHY AND TRANSLATION

Most speakers of Wolof are unaware of a standard form of the Wolof language. This is due to the fact that Wolof is not taught in any official state-sponsored educational programs. My Wolof formation has been the result of work with several native Wolof speakers who taught me according to varying degrees of a standard form. I have chosen to write Wolof the way I was taught in my private classes and with references of Jean Leopold Diouf's book *Dictionnaire Wolof-Français et Français-Wolof* (2003) as well as the textbook *Nanu Dégg Wolof* by Omar Kâ (2009). However, for consistency's sake, I use the commonly written versions of politicians' names that are universally recognized. This includes former president Abdoulaye Wade instead of Abdulaay Wad, which would be the more correct Wolof orthography. Everyday use of Wolof in text messages, social media, and the advertisements I share in this book stems from a nonstandard use of French orthography that is quite different from the orthography I use. Here, I will provide a few examples that appear in the book.

From the advertisement for *Jongué* spice, the tagline reads, "Ba cibir tchin," meaning "straight into the pot." This is an example of the French orthography. The standard Wolof orthography that I was taught would appear this way: "ba ci biir cin."

Here are some common orthographical correspondences:

Standard Wolof spelling	Nonstandard French-based spelling	In context
c	th	ceeb—thieb (rice)
j	dj	jën—djeun (fish)
x	kh	xorom—khorom (salt)
q	kh	aq—akh (offense)
u	ou	muus—mous (cat)
i	ui	gis—guis (see)
ë	eu	kër—keur (house)

Note about translation throughout the text:

The full-text translations and uses of endnotes are a stylistic and readability decision on my part. It was also a choice to include more Wolof full transcriptions as a way to include Wolof as a central figure in local communication as part of my argument, as well as to demonstrate the creative code-switching and multilingual dynamics of my interlocutors. The transcriptions of all texts are my own with the help of my longtime Wolof professor, Sidy Géy, who checked my grammar and orthography. I am also following spellings of Murīd family names and places based on Fallou Ngom's book *Muslims Beyond the Arab World* (2016). I have tried to remain as close to the original commentary as possible by transcribing the interviews as they are verbalized, not necessarily as they would be written. Some of the questions of grammar throughout the text reflect this.

NOTES ON ETHICS AND NAMING

The choices I have made in this book to use the first names and last names of all women are intentional and follow the ways in which I experienced them in different moments and heard them employed by others. For example, I use Ayda Mbóoj's first name more often than her full name because when I was with her in intimate moments of eating together, staying at her home, or traveling in the same vehicle, those around me used Ayda. There were also instances when Ayda's niece Ndey would refer to her as *mère*, literally "mother," but in this case, it was used as an honorific and a sign of respect for an elder. At other moments, Ndey also called her *bàjjen*, the term for an influential aunt from the father's side. In the case of Aysata Tall Sall, I also heard her first name used among her family and friends in my presence and on television. At other times, people used *Maître* to pay homage to her status as a lawyer. During campaign rallies, people shouted out first names: "Ayda, Ayda." I imagine that since Ayda received her doctorate, in formal interviews she is also referred to as *docteur or professeure*, Ayda, in many instances, especially by *griots*, or praise singers, was called *Adja* Ayda to demarcate her as a woman who had been on the *hàjj* to *Mecca* the annual Muslim pilgrimage. For Mously Diakhaté, I often heard her referred to as *Soxna*, a gendered honorific to show respect and referring to her status as a married woman, similar to when Ayda was called Soxna Ayda. I never personally heard anyone call Aysata or Aminata *Soxna* but rather with *Madame*, the French translation, or *Présidente/Première Ministre* in Aminata's case.

POLITICAL PARTIES AND ORGANIZATIONS ABBREVIATIONS

Political Parties

Afrique-Occidentale Française (AOF) [French West Africa]
Alliance pour la République [Alliance for the Republic]
Ànd, Saxal Liggéey [Alliance Nationale de la Démocratie] [Work and Grow Together]
Ànd-Jëf [African Party for Democracy and Socialism]
Bennoo Bokk Yaakaar (BBY) [United in Hope]
Bloc Démocratique Sénégalais (BDS) [Senegalese Democratic Bloc]
Femmes de Bennoo Bokk Yaakaar (FBBY) [The Women of United in Hope]
Garab gi [Convention of Democrats and Patriots]
Jëf-Jël [Alliance for Progress and Justice]
Ligue Démocratique (LD) [Democratic League]
Mouvement de la Réforme pour le Développement Sociale (MRDS) [Reformist Movement for Social Development]
Ndawi Askan wi [Youth of the Nation]
Osez l'Avenir [Dare to Face the Future]
Parti Africain pour l'Indépendance (PAI) [African Independence Party]
Parti Démocratique Sénégalais (PDS) [Senegalese Democratic Party]
Parti Socialiste (PS) [Socialist Party]
Patriotes du Sénégal (Pastef) [Patriots of Senegal]
Rassemblement National Démocratique (RND) [National Democratic Assembly]
Union Démocratique Sénégalaise (UDS) [Senegalese Democratic Union]

Union Progressiste Sénégalaise (UPS) [Progressive Union of Senegal]
Union Républicaine [Republican Union]
Yewwi Askan wi [Liberate the People]

Organizations and Associations

Ànd, Jappoo Jëf ci Jamm [Unity, Solidarity, and Peace]
Association des Femmes Africaines pour la Recherche et le Développement
    (AFARD) [African Women's Association for Research and Development]
Association des Femmes de l'Afrique de l'Ouest (AFAO) [Association of
    Women of West Africa]
Association des Femmes pour la Promotion de l'Entreprise au Sénégal
    (AFEPES) [Women's Business Association in Senegal]
Association des Juristes Sénégalaises (AJS) [Association of Senegalese
    Women Lawyers]
Association des Professionnelles de la Communication (APAC) [Association
    for Professional Women in Communication]
Communauté Économique des États de l'Afrique de l'Ouest (CEDEAO)
    [Economic Community of West African States] (ECOWAS)
Conseil Sénégalais des Femmes (COSEF) [Senegalese Women's Council]
Crédit Agricole du Sénégal [Crédit Agricole Bank of Senegal]
Groupement d'Intérêt Économique (GIE) [Economic Interest Group]
Groupement de Promotion Féminin (GPF) [Women's Promotional Group]
Fédération des Associations Féminines Sénégalaises (FAFS) [Federation of
    Senegalese Women's Associations]
Fédération Nationale des Groupements de Promotion Féminines (FNGPF)
    [National Federation of the Association for Women's Promotion]
Femme Développement Entreprise en Afrique (FDEA) [Women's Develop-
    ment and Business in Africa]
Fonds International pour le Développement Agricole (FIDA) [International
    Fund for Agricultural Development]
Observatoire National de la Parité (ONP) [National Parity Observatory]
Programme d'Appui aux Mutuelles d'Épargne et de Crédit au Sénégal (PA-
    MECAS) [Savings Mutual and Credit Assitance Program of Senegal]
Réseau Africain pour le Développement Intégré (RADI) [African Network
    for Integrative Development]
Réseau Siggil Jigéen [Women Stand Up Network]
Systèmes Financiers Décentralisés (SFD) [System of Decentralized Bankers]
United States Agency for International Development (USAID)
Yewwu-Yewwi [For Women's Liberation]

TERAANGA
REPUBLIC

Introduction

Welcome to the Land of Teraanga

February 4, 2023, Bambey, Senegal

I sat among a crowd of people wearing vibrant-colored dresses and tunics, most likely made for the occasion. We hugged the shade provided by the stadium overhang while a dance troop from the Casamance entertained us. As they swayed in unison, media cameras captured the entrances of customary and religious leaders and state politicians. Some men were in royal attire of red and gold robes; others wore suits and ties. The royal men sat down in throne-like chairs with a reserved sign entitled *buur*, or king in Wolof, their hands resting upon carved staves. One notable guest was Ousmane Sonko, the main opposition leader running for president. A band from Mauritania played guitar and drums while dancers swirled in their ample dress, flapping their arms like cranes taking flight. Organizers passed out sodas with labels that said *teraanga* (from a van with the same name) and had a picture of a beautiful woman enjoying her drink. The symbolism of the soda's name was not lost on me during an event that was constructed upon the importance of teraanga to these very occasions.

In the middle of the stadium was a small stage with a throne and two smaller chairs decorated in plush white fabric and gold trim. The stage faced the crowd but especially the aforementioned honored guests. Ayda Mbóoj, a politician I had spent a decade shadowing, was being crowned a queen. The Fraternal Union of the Mbóoj Family in Senegal and the Diaspora, an organization of members of the Mbóoj family, had voted unanimously that Ayda deserved to be honored by the family because she had represented them well on the national and international stage. Upon arriving at the stadium, Ayda walked around slowly with her entourage of security, griots (praise singers), and journalists while she waved and greeted the crowd. She took her place on the throne accompanied by two younger women who wore matching flowing, indigo-dyed dresses and headscarves, with orange-colored jewelry weaved into their braids. They also wore sashes diagonally across their chests. Ayda wore numerous cloths layered on her body. The most notable of the fabrics was an intricately woven *sëru rabal* (cotton wrap skirt) that was customarily given to a woman during important life moments such as marriage or the birth of her child. Ayda's headdress was an elaborate wig embroidered with gold and silver coins and cowrie shells that had significant meanings such as womanhood and wealth. You could tell she understood the weight of the moment, posing stoically and looking like the queen-in-waiting she was.

Ayda's griot rose and addressed the crowd from in front of the stage as television cameras and selfie sticks of YouTubers and TikTokers surrounded him and the stage. "Today is a momentous day. A day that when we wake up tomorrow, we will continue to reap its benefits. Today we name Ayda Mbóoj the *Lingéer* [queen], the Super Lingéer. There is something that is erased but also something that is created. I say to you, those of you who are embarrassed by their heritage, you should know that no matter if you are bigger than life, you should return to your culture and traditions. It's important. Today, for the first time in Senegalese history, a woman is celebrated by her family. So, we say, *alhamdoulilah*."[1] Next, politicians such as the female mayor of Bambey sang Ayda's praises, commenting on the weight of the occasion and offering reflections on Ayda's accomplishments and how Ayda had inspired her to get into politics.

Following the speeches, the kings and leaders of other parts of the Mbóoj family performed a short ceremony from which Ayda emerged with an additional crown of gold that towered over her headdress, symbolizing her transition to Super Lingéer status. She then took the microphone and made a few pronouncements. "And now to my Askan wi coalition colleagues, you must know that we are, of course, part of the same family. We share the same values, values are what we have. We should apply them socially and politically. Values that you are defending here. The king said to me that we women, we can protect it [tradition], give it importance and a place within government positions by standing up for our people, our family."[2] And last, she paid homage to her niece, someone who had helped organize the event and who had been steadfast in her support for Ayda through her years in politics as well as her link to broader family affairs. "Ndey Mbóoj, you have honored me, but the teraanga [honor, loyalty, generosity] you have given me is almost scary because it's as if you are sending me a message. It's as if you want those who follow me in politics to grow."[3]

The event I depict here marked ten years since I had started following the political activities of Ayda Mbóoj. In fact, I had been present when Ayda inaugurated the very stadium where her coronation took place, during her time as mayor of Bambey, a dry and hot town in the heart of the peanut basin of central Senegal. Bambey, Ayda's hometown, is significant as it was a central part of the contact between the Murīd Sufi community and the French colonial administration during the height of the colonial peanut cash crop and remains an important space of Murīd influence. This theatrical ceremony also took place just shy of a year before the 2024 presidential elections for which Ayda would eventually launch her campaign. Among some of the distinguished guests was Ousmane Sonko, president of the coalition Yewwi Askan wi (Liberate the People), whom Ayda praised in her speech as "part of the same family" that "shares the same values" that she highlights as the key to an ideal and traditional kind of politics. The tumultuous year leading up to the election would see Ayda being disqualified from the presidential race and ultimately backing the Diomaye Faye/Sonko ticket despite both having been imprisoned for different charges. Sonko, the leader of the Pastef (Patriots of Senegal) party, was deemed ineligible based on his imprisonment following a lengthy and contentious trial for suspicions of rape but charged separately for "fomenting insurrection" (Aljazeera 2023). Bassirou Diomaye Faye took his place as the party's candidate and won the presidency on March 24, 2024. Many people in the opposition, including Ayda, argued that Ousmane Sonko's imprisonment was president Macky Sall's attempt to eliminate his strongest opponent. In many ways, therefore, the ceremony honoring Ayda could be seen as a political alignment, especially given that it married elements from the Wolof kingdom of Waalo, to which Ayda was being inducted as a queen, and performances from a Mauritanian band[4] in honor of the marriage between the Waalo queen Ndaté Yàlla Mbóoj and the king from present-day Mauritania. The Joola musical troupe from the Casamance in southern Senegal honored Sonko, a Joola himself and then-mayor of Ziguinchor, the capital of the Casamance.

Ayda's crowning ceremony is a theatrical ritual or "performance politics," a "dramatization of power" (Strauss and O'Brien 2007) in which ritualized symbols presented a "continuity of the past" with an improvisation that created a new political form (O'Brien 2007). O'Brien argues that this sort of political performance "draws on the past to make itself moving as well as comprehensible,

Chiefs and dignitaries at Ayda Mbóoj Coronation Ceremony, Bambey, Senegal, February 4, 2023. *Photo by author.*

while it also projects the imagination of a possible political future, in a moment of liminality" (18). The uncertainty of the upcoming election was palpable, with an unpopular outgoing president, a widely popular opposition candidate whose political future was in question, and a record number of female presidential candidates including Ayda. In this regard, the speeches by Ayda's griot, the oral historian who sang her praises, and Ayda herself, along with the spectacle of the show, communicated an image of a whole new structure of authority, one that was based on a coveted traditional past to deal with present and future challenges—a particularly postcolonial authority in which one could imagine a woman at its helm.

This book considers the processes of women politicians' cultivation of authority in contemporary Senegalese politics. The opening anecdote of Ayda's coronation is a particular moment of a dramatization of power interwoven with references to less-visible daily constructions of authority by women found in their practices of teraanga—that is, women's social labor and its consequences for their political identities. In other words, how did Ayda arrive at this crowning moment among some of the most consequential politicians in contemporary Senegalese politics? What do the strategies of women in Senegalese politics tell us about questions of postcolonial identities, gender and politics, and gender politics?

Ayda is part of a small yet growing number of women in elected state politics who serve in parliament and are mayors and city councillors. Alongside many women, Ayda was an integral part of the movement for women's political equality, called parité, that was voted into law in 2010. Women like Ayda who demonstrate considerable popularity as well as those less visible are—and have been historically—fundamental to the nature of politics in Senegal. Moreover, Ayda and the anecdote of her coronation demonstrate a kind of authority that is created by what Mbembe (2001) points to as a continuous process of bargaining and improvising in order to navigate a "plurality of 'spheres' and arenas, each having its own separate logic," that is the postcolonial reality—an "entanglement," or the overlay of discontinuities that is the postcolony (14). The particular logic that I identify as the main source of women's political strategy in Senegal is teraanga[5]—a philosophy in the Wolof language that symbolizes both the actions of honor and generosity and the characteristics derived from such actions. Put another way, the authority and prestige bestowed on Ayda at her coronation are the result of a lifetime of the particular social labor that is teraanga.

This book is an ethnography of several women's experiences fighting and striving for political office, primarily in the decade between 2013 and 2023, with particular connections to the history of women's participation and advocacy in Senegalese political and developmental life stretching back much further. More specifically, it is about the complex layers of how conceptions of gender both internationally and locally figure into these women's social realities and performances of politics and governance, as well as how they lobby for equal representation. It is also about the who, what, and how of women's political worlds. I ask throughout, how do women construct their social and political realities, and what has been the result? What processes connect those two spheres? Their stories can represent only a small minority of women in Senegal. However, much of the book is also dedicated to the silent protagonists who represent experiences of the majority of Senegalese women as they navigate marriages, development projects and the informal economy, and relationships with the politicians they interact with. The four main politicians in this book are, in one way or another, elites. Whether they come from superior castes[6] like Ayda Mbóoj, hail from politically active families like Aminata Touré, or stem from powerful religious families, as in the case of Mously Diakhaté and

Aysata Tall Sall, these women are part of an elite group that have access to possibilities that most women and men do not possess.[7] In fact, as we will see in chapter 5, elite women in politics are often afforded a fluidity of gender identity, a privilege rarely extended to both sexes. And yet, their particular political strategies reflect these possibilities at the same time that they demonstrate the negotiations they confront as women. This could be understood as what Kandiyoti argues are women strategizing within a set of concrete constraints that reveal and define the blueprint of what she terms the "patriarchal bargain" (1988). Moreover, it is imperative to see "women as active agents in the implementation of patriarchal systems even as they are subjected to them." As Wale Adebanwi notes, "if elite groups are defined by the control of specific resources by means of which they acquire political power and material advantages, then we need to exhaust the range of resources that society makes available for the acquisition of political power and material advantages" (2024, 51; Pina-Cabral 2020). My book considers the biographies of mostly elite women, my observations of their political and private activities, and the documentation of their political personas and testimonies from the women who work with them in order to capture the complexities of how these women work with the resources and realities society has made available to them in order to "do politics" in contemporary Senegal.

Defining Teraanga

Teraanga means to be welcoming, to give hospitality, and to demonstrate generosity, or to receive a guest with care, evoking the idea that we exist for one another (Seck 2010). Similar to the South African philosophy of *ubuntu*, "I am because you are," teraanga concerns the philosophy and actions that represent what Seck (2015) also calls "communities of sharing" (*mbokk* in Wolof). Therefore, when Ayda uses the term *mbokk* to refer to her political allies, she is speaking about her community that is bonded through reciprocities of teraanga. Bass and Sow (2006) demonstrate that an "overlap between the concepts of family and household in Senegal" means that "an individual not related by blood or marriage may be considered and introduced to others as a part of an extended-family household or even a nonfamily household" (90). Diop argues that households can be defined as those who may not reside within the home but contribute economically and socially to it (1985). Candea and Da Col argue that hospitality—one aspect of teraanga—identifies "several levels of collective identity," (2012) or, as Munyaka and Motlhabi (2005) and Akamonye (2019) say of ubuntu, it is not just about human acts, "it is also about being, it is a disposition that concerns values that contribute to the well-being of others and of community." And as clearly as Sebidi (1988) argues that trying to define ubuntu is like attempting to define time, teraanga is similarly elusive. I have argued elsewhere that teraanga is "an encapsulation of the generous and civic-minded qualities and actions of individuals seen in everyday social encounters, both calculated and improvisational, that are mutually constitutive" (Riley 2016). Teraanga is a system of private and public socioeconomic expressions of reciprocity that unify individuals and communities and is the "major point of reference for social morality among Senegalese Wolof society" (Sow 1980). These expressions can come in the form of a material gift, or a verbal gift of praise, taking, for example, the Wolof praise poetry called *taasu*, primarily performed by women during family ceremonies (McNee 2000, 25).

Although disputed, one version of the etymology of teraanga comes from the verb *ter*, depicting the moment when a boat arrives at the sandy shore, as in the saying *gaal gi ter na* (the boat has arrived on the shore). Senegal, also known as *sunu gaal* (our boat), signifies a snapshot encounter or rather creation and suggests a new kind of shared existence that happens upon contact. As the griot from Ayda Mbóoj's coronation mentioned, the ceremony represented an erasure but also the creation of something new: the honor of Ayda becoming a queen represented a new collective—or political family—based on shared values.

If we consider Ayda's speech during the ceremony, she also used agricultural references to emote a desired return to governance through local values. Agricultural references within Wolof also speak to the idea of reciprocity, citing the saying "dafa ma jii teraanga," which means one planted teraanga, symbolizing the establishment of a flourishing relationship between two people, as Seck has pointed out (2015). Her use of the word *sax* (to plant a seed) and the reference to teraanga as the growth of local values represent a similar idea that for Senegal to progress, values such as teraanga should be part of the political culture. Sax and *jii* are agricultural references to symbolize the creative nature of teraanga to form sustainable bonds. Consequently, Ayda's political party is named Ànd, Saxal Liggéey (Work and Grow Together)—a party she created after years of serving under Abdoulaye Wade and the Parti Démocratique Sénégalais.

Teraanga is a road map of how to be in this world, oftentimes in order to access the next world—an unwritten instruction manual of how to be generous and respected. As Assane Sylla (1978) notes, "Tarànga is the virtue of an individual who knows how to welcome guests with generosity and cordiality," or how to demonstrate authority while embedding oneself among others. As this book will demonstrate, the attempts to define teraanga, grievances of the loss of a teraanga of yesteryear, and the critiques of its current state are the manifestations of anxieties as well as aspirations for modern Senegalese identities. Societal musings about what teraanga truly means is symbolic of a general human desire to understand one's own condition. Reiterated by Sylla, when considering the Wolof moral subject "confronted with questions that overwhelm him, the thinker seeks answers which can reconcile him with himself, with his society, with his God" (23). My analysis of testimonies, anecdotes, and observations of teraanga in the everyday as well as on momentous occasions is an attempt to capture the diversity of experience and thought in a moment of postcolonial modernity. In this regard, it is also useful to think of teraanga—particularly as political strategy this book sustains—as what Mbembe (1992) describes as a "regime of social complicity" (48). Although this regime is built upon ideas of reciprocity, it is also constructed with uneven relationships of hierarchy, prestige, and inequality. Teraanga is the connecting link in the entanglement of these complex subjectivities, including extended families, political activism, religious fellowship, and Republican governance. I therefore posit that we can understand women's roles in Senegalese state politics and teraanga only as their political strategy by discussing what I identify as the historical processes intrinsic to their praxis. These include what Diouf (2013) calls the "Islamo-Wolof model," (7) or the Wolofisation (O'Brien 1998) and urbanization of Senegalese society; the commercialization and gendering of teraanga in relation to the domestic space; and the marketization of women's social labor and the sociocultural connections to changing economics. In this introduction, I will lay out how these elements construct women's political identities and strategies.

The Islamo-Wolof Model and the Wolofisation
of Senegalese Society

Senegal is a nation-state located at the extreme western part of the African continent. It is a country known for its stable democratic institutions, cultural exports, and tolerance in terms of religious and ethnic diversity. Senegal is at once a geographical place and a dynamic expression of the collective imagination of its people. It's a country where 95 percent of the population are Muslim, with a small Catholic population; most Muslims in Senegal are Sufi, divided into four main orders: the Qādiriyya, the Tijāniyya, the Murīdiyya, and the Laayeen (Ngom 2016). The Sufi system, according to Babou (2007), is "shaped by actions and behaviors that aim at freeing the human body from the grip of worldly preoccupations" (5) in order to cultivate a oneness with God. Although

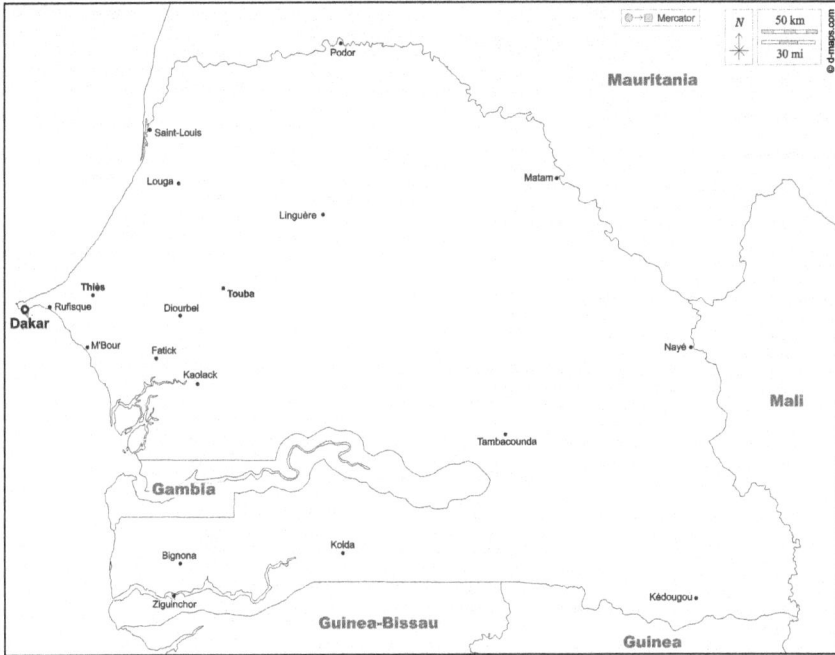

Map of Senegal. Source: https://d-maps.com/carte.php?num_car=1279&lang=en.

these Sufi communities within Senegal have distinct histories, their practices fall under these objectives.

The linguistic mapping of Senegal is quite fascinating. Given what many call Wolofisation—the domination of the Wolof language in mostly urban spaces that goes beyond ethnicity—Senegal has long named Wolof as its lingua franca. However, Wolof is just one of six officially recognized languages in Senegal, along with Sereer, Pulaar, Soninke, Mandika, and Joola, and there are most likely about sixty-five different languages spoken within Senegambia (the area of present Senegal and the Gambia before colonization). Fiona McLaughlin (2008) argues that two distinct linguistic eco-zones exist in Senegal: the northern part between the Senegal River (bordering Mauritania) and the Gambia, dominated by three languages: Wolof, Pulaar, and Sereer. The Casamance, south of the Gambia, is defined by "higher degrees of multilingualism" (145). In 2008, when her article was published, the population of Senegal was eleven million, at which time 44 percent of people were ethnically Wolof, yet 90 percent spoke Wolof as a first or second language. More recent statistics put Senegal's population at eighteen million[8] (2024), 23 percent of whom live in the capital city, Dakar. In a published study looking at statistics from—the most recent national survey—45 percent of the population lived in urban areas (Lombard, Sakho, and Valton 2019). Ten years later, that number has surpassed half of the population, which has become more urban and younger, and the number of Wolof speakers has grown. Keese (2015) points to several phenomena that have led to Wolof's dominance: the French chose Wolof sites such as Saint Louis and Dakar for their colonial administration headquarters and therefore interacted with Wolof elites; Wolof merchants and Sufi marabouts were key to the colonial economy of peanut crops that traveled between these urban centers; and the eventual migrations to cities of all ethnicities once the monocrop economies dwindled. The very phenomenon of Wolofisation has raised questions about ethnicity as a fixed identity (Keese 2015; O'Brien 1998). McLaughlin (2008) argues that in addition to harmony among ethnic groups and the widespread adherence to Sufi Islam, the presence of Wolof as an unofficial national language of Senegal has led to a shared national identity (80). And yet, given that French is the internationally recognized official language and the language in which state institutions operate, the two languages are "at odds with one another" in cities even while Wolof is peppered with French borrowings, creating a new type of urban language (McLaughlin 2009, 75). Fallou Ngom (2016) writes of the Murīdiyya attitude of the Wolof view of themselves as a "macro-ethnolinguistic group into which others have blended ... that has been largely de-ethnicized." He further argues that "the acceptance of ethnic diversity in the Wolof society predates Islamization and colonization" (144). Ngom has found within Ajami sources (Wolof written in modified Arabic script) a de-emphasization of "caste, ethnicity, and race (a word the Wolof language does not have) and stress moral rectitude and piety as the primary basis of judgment of character" (144).

The Wolofisation of Senegalese society has also led to the adoption of particularly Wolof ideologies as representative of national identity writ large. Considering Senegal as the Pays de la Teraanga (Land of Teraanga)[9] or the national soccer team as the Lions of Teraanga demonstrates a normalizing of Wolof language and culture. Other attempts at formalizing a national cultural pedagogy by the state can be seen in the promotion of narratives of *cousinage à plaisanterie* (joking cousins), which "insists on the similarities and horizontal connections between [Senegalese] communities while also delegitimizing separatist imaginations and circulating a pluralist representation of the nation which is not limited to a Islamo-Wolof 'center'" (Smith 2006). Smith also sees the phenomenon of joking cousins as a "product of a crisis of the historically republican nationalist discourse which confronted the social dynamics of the

Wolof-Murīd and Casamance conflicts" (909). In other words, the state's appropriation of certain cultural phenomena aims to normalize them for questions of national unity and political gain. Individual politicians are no different. Despite the fact that many of the politicians I interviewed were not ethnically Wolof, they spoke Wolof and were able to operate within the political sphere dominated by Wolof language and philosophy.

Senegal has had a rich and at times traumatic history of contact, of arrivals and departures, whether slaves from throughout West Africa shipped from Gorée Island off the coast of the current Senegalese capital of Dakar, or traders from throughout the continent making their way to the ocean via trade routes along the Senegal and Casamance Rivers, or, more recently, boats taking migrant hopefuls across the ocean. Movement, encounter, and (re)creation are part of the history of the area. Senegambia has also been a place of spiritual and cultural hybridity, from the importation of Islam in the eleventh century to the formation of local and transnational Sufi Muslim communities. As Sufi communities such as the Murīds have grown within Senegal, they have formed extensive religious and economic networks across the world. In fact, the history of Sufi elites accommodating aspects of the French colonial administration (Robinson 2000) can also be interpreted as the Wolof tradition of teraanga: incorporating foreign elements into the self to form new identities. And as I explore in chapter 5, the master narrative of the Murīd founder, Shaykh Ahmadu Bamba, focused on what Ngom (2016) called "sanctified suffering"—the spiritual blessings received from the suffering endured (148). Through the teachings of Ahmadu Bamba that married Islamic teachings with Wolof philosophy, the Murīd saw the conflict with the French and suffering in general as "central to his mode of *jihād* of the soul . . . necessary to expunge imperfections in his heart" (151).

Teraanga is also an identity that results from the accumulation of small and large gestures of reciprocity. In one instance, *teraanga* meant a very specific gift, and in another, it is employed a way of honoring someone's generosity, as well as generosity itself. At the same time that Ayda mentioned being honored (*teral*) by Ndey Mbóoj, she was also taken aback by Ndey's generosity, referring to the time it took to organize such an event and coordinate with family members that had traveled from throughout Senegal, the Gambia, and Mauritania. Teraanga could also be a verbal nicety spoken by a friend or a bus ticket paid for by a stranger, or even the car behind you in the tollbooth paying your way so you and everyone behind you are not stranded and subsequently waving goodbye with an air of care. This last example is admittedly a personal anecdote. However, teraanga is made up of public and private gestures and material things meant to demonstrate affiliation, care, and honor. This is similar to the Arabic word for hospitality, *karam*, which Shryock (2008) argues demonstrates the "nobility of character that makes generosity possible" and is, as a virtue, "a genealogical endowment and a moral obligation akin to piety" (108). The importance of nobility is also present in the Wolof cosmology of relationships between the royal classes and their subjects where one's nobility is articulated through instances of giving (Diop 1981). In the case of gifting displayed during family ceremonies, Beth Buggenhagen, in her study on Muslim Wolof families in global Senegal, notes that "women saw gifts not as a measure of what they had been given at that moment or in previous moments, but as a measure of how the giver valued their social relationship" (35). She argues further that the quality of the exchange has more to do with the perceived intent of the giver than the items given.

Wolof Society and Hierarchies

Wolof society is structured by caste and order, where access to resources and social mobility is predetermined for individuals. Traditionally, one's work (caste), position in the social hierarchy, and relation to others have been dependent on whether one was a *géer* (superior)—often agriculturalists—or servile artisans called *ñeeño* that included griots (praise singers/genealogists/musicians), *uude* (leathermakers), *tëgg* (ironmakers), and *ràbb* (weavers) (Diop 1981). In terms of the exercise of power, the *buur*,[10] the nobility or the ruling class, held the greatest power, and their subjects were called the *baadoolo*.[11] Each of these groups had a group of slaves (*jaam*). The monarchic power structure was composed of five different orders: *garmi* (principal rulers), *jambur* (part of the administration without possibility of succeeding the throne), *baadoolo* (the monarchy's subjects), and *jaami buur* and *jaami baadoolo* (slaves of the sovereign and of people, respectively) (Dieng 2008, 21–22).

The Mbóoj family, or the *mbóojeen*, are considered one of the royal families that ruled the Waalo Kingdom of northern Senegal. Griots are of the lower classes that serve the géer and the royal families by providing entertainment, spoken-word praises of the royals, and recitations of family genealogies, among other functions. The oral traditions of praise poems—songs recounting individuals and their family's history of kindness and displays of solidarity—is among the repertoire of griots. As Lisa McNnee (2000) points out, the Wolof proverb that goes "teraanga moo dox sunu diggànte, ndee du lu ñaaw" [it is honoring each other with gifts that is between us, but not anything ugly] signifies that "teraanga not only binds them together but is necessary for relationships to function" (26).

Teraanga as Social Hierarchy and Gendered Practice

The proverb also speaks to the kind of hidden, obligatory, and inequal aporia of something like teraanga—an irresolvable contradiction or "double, contradictory imperative" (Derrida 1993). Derrida also says the contradiction of hospitality and the guest is that it is obligatory but needs an air of free will and spontaneity. I often heard people describe teraanga as something in between obligation and voluntary kindness. Insisting that teraanga be a spontaneous and unconditional practice often obfuscates the power dynamics inherent in it. As Maurer (2009) puts it, "gifts can serve as an ideological cover for exploitation or expropriation, or, in other words, business as usual, but with a friendlier face" (258). Others would argue that teraanga is a bright spot in the battle against capitalism that intends to eclipse local forms of moral economies, such as what Seck (2015) proposes in line with teraanga as a "political economy of reciprocity" (Temple 2008).

Despite the positive attributes of a moral philosophy such as teraanga, its practice reflects Wolof social hierarchies that are fraught with social inequalities. I argue that in Wolof society, teraanga not only reinforces social hierarchies but is arguably the basis of its very expression. This very much aligns with Judith Butler's theory of gender as performance—"an expression of social practice that reflects and simultaneously constitutes the larger social order" (1999). While speaking about the Wolof performances of taasu, McNee (2000) argues that "teraanga regulates discourse, it regulates the taxonomy of discourse genres, for these genres are determined by the performance context—which exists because of exchanges. The Wolof system of genres defines performance contexts according to gender and gendered performances" (61). It is specifically in the context of ceremonies that taasu performances "name and celebrate sexual difference" (64). At the same time, as Ivy Mills (2011) points out, "In the complex terrain of contemporary cultural politics . . . the communal and familial teraanga has its limits" (1). And even as teraanga symbolizes "the nation as an honorable subject that is committed to civility and open to outsiders" (1), M'Baye (2019, 4) points out that these limits mean that homosexuality and the LGBTQ population are seen as a threat to the honor that teraanga represents. In a critique of the modern Senegalese subject, Alassane Khodia Kitane (2010) asserts that "the foundational principles of Senegalese morality such as *teraanga, jom* (pride), and *ngor* (honor) have been perverted to mean success" (16) and that the instrumentality of such values is at the root of Senegal's political and moral crises.

Within the Wolof system of castes and orders, teraanga plays a crucial role in the expression of power dynamics between them; as Dieng (2008) notes, "The

"La Teranga" drink advertisement from the company Punch. *Photo by author.*

relationship between the *géer* and the *ñeeño* was centered on the exchange of goods, gifts, and prestation which benefited the inferior group, the *géer* needing to justify their preeminence at every turn" (19). Therefore, the mutual dependence between the two groups meant that those of the inferior groups were sustained by the generosity of the géer, and the prestige of the géer was constructed by their generosity given. This is most visually represented by the dynamic of a géwël being paid by someone of superior caste during a family ceremony or a political rally in which the géwël sings the latter's praises and is publicly compensated. The ambiguity of generosity as obligation or individual will is therefore an important part of Wolof philosophy, which sees the choices of individuals as entangled within collective goals.

A particular focus of this book is locating the aspects of teraanga that represent power dynamics within changing gender relations and their import for women's political praxis. Although teraanga is not etymologically gendered, in practice it is. Because I identify teraanga as being the core component in the history and nature of women's participation in state politics, naturally we must also examine how teraanga is both a product and reflection of what Marame

Gueye (2011) argues is a "gendering process" rather than seeing gender as a historical given when thinking about women's political praxis—that is, understanding the ways in which teraanga and political performance have become particularly gendered.

It is in this regard that I have elsewhere outlined what I call the teraanga ethos (Riley 2019) in order to place women's political process among a myriad of highly gendered performances of generosity, hospitality, and honor. In order to understand these phenomena, I find Marilyn Strathern's definition of gender to be the most illuminating: "by gender I mean those categorizations of persons, artifacts, events, sequences, and so on which draw upon sexual imagery—upon the ways in which the distinctiveness of male and female characteristics make concrete people's ideas about the nature of social relationships" (1988, xi). Strathern furthermore states that these categorizations have often seemed evident and that "their inventive possibilities cannot be appreciated until attention is paid to the way in which relationships are construed through them" (x). Imagining teraanga as a cultural artifact through which normalcies of gender behavior are reflected allows us to explore the ways gender is integral to modern Senegalese politics. The opposition to women in politics and public space in general is therefore framed within the connection between women's sexuality and culture, with culture as a product of the domestic sphere, and therefore women's participation in politics is seen as creating disorder and corrupt public institutions (Diaw 2009). McNee (2000) echoes this assertation by arguing that performances such as taasu at political rallies "highlight the gap between the public and private . . . the genre floats between the domestic sphere and that of national politics, it disrupts the otherwise clear demarcations between the sexes, the public and the private, the individual and the community" (82). Thinking back to Ayda's coronation ceremony, her mention of teraanga as the generosity of her niece as master organizer donating her time and money to the event and the drinks labeled teraanga as a material representation of hospitality and femininity highlighted the gendered labor of women and its sexual imagery. The silent meanings of Ayda's relationship with Ndey are also indicative of the power dynamics inherent in teraanga. As Strathern (1988) says, "To ask about the gender of the gift, then, is to ask about the situation of gift exchange in relation to the form that domination takes in societies" (xii). It is also important to consider that gender "intervenes with other systems of social and economic relationships. A woman is not just a woman. She is also a rural, Wolof, casted woman living in neocolonial Senegal" (Imam, Mama, and Sow 2004, 34). Although Ndey was donating her time and money to this particular event, and had done so for other events over the years as well, she was also financially and socially dependent upon Ayda's generosity. Despite being from the same family, Ndey was inferior to Ayda due to age and status as an unmarried woman. Therefore, their relationship hinged upon these reciprocal moments during the ceremony and also quotidian favors, exchanges, borrowings, and debts. Ayda's visibility as a politician and her prestige among the Mbóoj family federation were dependent upon the work of Ndey, and Ndey's own reputation and possibilities are tied up with Ayda.

Commercializing Cultural Artifacts

In their book *Ethnicity, Inc.* (2009), John and Jean Comaroff argue that in many instances in African societies, "ethnicity was commodified, made into the basis of 'value-added' corporate collectivity, and claimed as the basis of shared emotion, shared lifestyle, shared imaginings for the future." Something similar has happened to teraanga in Senegal, where teraanga has become commodified through a similar process of literally branding products such as instant coffee, cafés/restaurants, car dealerships, mining companies, disposable water, and others with names including *teraanga*. In the physical and media landscape of an urban space like Dakar, commercials, billboards, and grocery stores are packed with images like a woman holding products called teraanga. Cleaning products with scenes of domesticity litter grocery stores. Television shows called *Njeg ak këram* (A Woman/Wife and Her Home) debate how women can make their homes more inviting to guests or interview géwël women called Lawbé—often masters of seduction—about how women can utilize beads around their hips and incense in order to entice their husbands. As Strathern (1988) says, "The basis for classification (of something as female or male) does not inhere in the objects themselves but in how they are transacted and to what ends. The action is the gendered activity" (xi). Women are taught from an early age that they must engage in these gendered performances in order to attract men and satisfy their husbands. In the case of polygamous unions, the acts of teraanga within the home and with a woman's family-in-law serve to either avoid a co-wife or compete with one. Although men give and perform teraanga through giving money to friends and acquaintances or sessions of *àttaaya* (tea) among friends or guests, in cases of formal hospitality, the àttaaya is served by women. Women's labor of teraanga is constant in a way that it is not for men. I explore these realities further in what I call the semantic field of teraanga, which encompasses feminine ideals of *joŋe* or *jongé* (cognate for woman) or *feem* (feminine tricks) that smatter daily discourse and are associated with teraanga practices, in line with Seck's argument that teraanga is represented through "key grammar of daily behaviors" (2015, 26) that are oftentimes gendered. I detail these further in chapters 1 and 2, lending a close reading to the complex relationship between teraanga and these feminine ideals in order to understand their centrality to women's political practice.

The Marketization of Women's Social Labor

Beyond the materiality of teraanga, development programs have sought to "align value with values" (Perutz 2008, 2) by seizing on the moral philosophy of teraanga and targeting women's associations as vectors for a women-driven informal economy. Principles such as solidarity and mutual aid that had historically been expressed through modest money pooling to help women and their peers with unexpected or planned expenses became marketing strategies for how to turn loans into profits. Associations or solidarity groups were formed into state-sponsored *Groupements de Promotion Féminine* (GPFs), and therefore explicitly gendered, or *Groupements d'Intérêt Économique* (GIEs). In some cases, competitions for extra funding have been given to the associations based on their performance in terms of savings. If, as Ralph argues, "masculinity . . . is institutionalized as a kind of prerequisite for access to foreign capital" (2015, 101), it could be said that femininity is a prerequisite for access to state and nongovernmental microfinance. Marieme Lo has shown that female entrepreneurs in Senegal and Mali operating in the informal economy are often "confined to survival activities, with limited possibilities for capital accumulation" (2011, 160), which steers them toward marketing not only material culture but cultural values. In her study, Lo examines women's development of a "cult image" by naming associations and enterprises based on values such as honor, pride, and respect in order to "circumscribe impediments inherent to the precarious nature of the informal economy" (162). She astutely ties the recognition that "creditworthiness requires a certain way of being and acting and the projection of a positive self-image" (166) with women's successes in microenterprises. I explore similar phenomena in chapter 3 by examining the language in newspaper archives that demonstrate the exploitation of teraanga and other aforementioned Wolof values for economic gain. What I also consider is how these feminine spaces of microenterprises and associations have also created a fleet of female leadership that became the springboard for the parité movement.

Teraanga as Politics

Ayda's coronation was the culmination of a career in politics that has been defined by her mastery of teraanga, resulting in a community of followers. I saw the same people at her event in 2023 that I had first met in 2013 and attended countless events both explicitly and implicitly political with. They were family members as well as neighbors turned loyal supporters. They were predominantly women Ayda had supported both financially and socially—maybe a phone call when an elderly parent was sick or financial contributions as well as her presence at a funeral. The majority of my time with Ayda and her entourage was spent attending weddings, naming ceremonies, and funerals; referred to under the umbrella term *family ceremonies*, these are the most visible spaces in which teraanga is given and received, and where women organize and conduct ritualized exchanges. They are the spaces where women have historically exercised power and cultivated authority and prestige. Given that my doctoral fieldwork was about the complexities of family ceremonies, I spent a great deal of time attending them. I was then struck by how much Ayda's political practice took place in similar spaces and mirrored her participation in ritualized exchange. If a member of Ayda's party was in need, she went personally or sent someone from her team to visit them. In between legislative sessions in Dakar or trips with the ministry, Ayda was back in Bambey, making social calls. In return, her supporters remained loyal, sang her praises in public, and reciprocated by not only voting for her but showing up for events, political rallies, and her life moments. When Ayda's mother died, community members attended the funeral en masse to show support for Ayda as well as for the legacy of her mother, a formidable community politician in her own right, employing the same personal style of politics. Therefore, for Ayda and all the women politicians I spent time with, teraanga is their politics. Investing in the life events of others is their politics. Putting in the groundwork of visiting, hosting, giving, and praising others is their politics.

Family ceremonies are the major sites where Senegalese families gather to celebrate births, new unions, and the lives of loved ones who have passed on. They are also opportunities to create affiliations within and between families and reaffirm those bonds. For the women who mostly control the planning and organization as well as the performance of ceremonies, these events are especially crucial spaces for the manifestation and cultivation of honor, reputation, and worth. Women's social labor over years of saving, organizing, and establishing themselves as respectable women through various day-to-day reciprocities such as those I described with Ayda come to fruition during ceremonies. Women's social hierarchy in Senegal is highly dependent upon the mastery of social visits, hosting guests, and providing monetary and emotional exchanges between friends and strangers. Ayda's coronation was an example of the prestige she had developed while taking part in these exchanges that link economic and social debt. The historical centrality and evolution of family ceremonies parallel the significances of women's role in Senegal's economic and political transformations.

Generally speaking, in the context of Senegalese society and the cases in this book, the site of gift exchange, as an act of teraanga, in its public and private forms is a site ripe with gendering and processes of power negotiations. And as McNee (2000) points out, family ceremonies are examples of spaces where Wolof women share experiences "within a loosely woven 'women's world'" (63). These include women as the representation of men's wealth; the negotiations between older and younger women that have to do with their dependence on men; pluralistic references of women's inheritance and general access to resources; and the strong presence of polygamy and competition for access to resources and social relevance. What I demonstrate throughout this book is that these phenomena have contributed to the formation of particular political subjects and their way of doing politics (maa ngiy politique, or "I am doing politics," as many women would say) as well as the impetus for their advocacy for making space for themselves in state politics.

Making connections between women's authority and their power over resources is not a new trend. Much of women's history, from the kingdoms to their roles as *signares* to the present, is marked by their particular control over resources and how they represent them in society. Fatou Kiné Camara (2008) shows us that within the Wolof and Sereer kingdoms, the king was not to be without his female counterpart, the *lingéer*, who exercised real power (95). Camara delineates that a woman crowned as a lingéer did not earn this title as the wife or mistress of the sovereign but according to the fundamental law or constitution of the kingdom (96). Because lingéers were "princesses by blood," and because at the time succession was based on the matrilineal line, the authority of the lingéer had more historical import as it was passed down to her sons. The lingéer's authority and the first wife (*aawo*) of the king had significant authority over their own resources as well as those of other women and royalties from a province they administered (Dieng 1993, 15). As historian Boubacar Barry (1985) notes, "Princesses, by way of lavish parties they put on, gifts they gave nobles of important title, significantly contributed to the authority of the brak [king] and played an important role to the succession of the throne. The lingéer especially plays a large political role in Waalo history because she is above all the guardian of family goods, *meen* (matriarchal line) of which good management should determine success throughout history" (80). In West Africa, through marriage, localized interpretations of authority and access to wealth (Burrill 2015) as well as rights and duties (Cooper 1997) are adapted, negotiated, and contested. Therefore, women's involvement in festivities and gift giving has been a central way of deriving personal power and influence as well as assuring the future of one's family. According to Ayda's family members I spoke with and the program they handed out during the event, Ayda is a descendant of the brak Njak Kumba Ndjaten and the lingéer Kumba Njaay Mbagnik of Waalo on her father and mother's side. Ayda's niece Ndey Mbóoj, an amateur historian of the family, put the program together. It is important to note that the women Barry mentions are women of noble status, whereas Diaw (1998) argues that women of the baadoolo (commoner), who are the majority, are plagued with a double bind of being both women and lower class and therefore "confined to a role of production and reproduction of economic subsistence, of survival mechanisms" (14). In the contemporary period, the derivation of authority from ceremonies is arguably less tied to questions of predetermined social status such as caste and has more to do with other expressions of power dynamics that respond to the social and economic crises of the past century. Investments in kinship and social networks such as family ceremonies have become the norm (Buggenhagen 2012) due to several factors: the interplay of African, Islamic, and French republican legal systems and ambiguities of inheritance; decades of postcolonial mismanagement (Cruise O'Brien, Diop, and Diouf 2002) leading to staggering unemployment due to structural adjustment programs beginning in the Diouf administration; the phasing out of government positions and state employee salaries; and emigration in search of work in the "absence of productive possibilities" (16).

The question of whether Senegal is a matriarchal or patriarchal society is complex and important for understanding the changes to women's and men's accesses to resources and authority. As Josephides (1985) and Strathern (1988) argue, the central preoccupation of societies is the unequal access to the pool of human labor (18). The response, according to Bass and Sow (2006), is that it depends on obvious factors, such as the differences among ethnic groups, and less obvious factors like class and caste, equally depending on a long and complex local history. Diop notes that "prior to Islam among Wolof upper castes, family status, land, and slaves were inherited through the female line, while upper-class men were believed to transmit courage and other social values including honor, power, and authority" (1985). Following the arrival of Islam, "the patriarchal values became even more pronounced, and the patrilineal systems became stronger" (87). Camara argues that the Family Code—adopted in 1972 and revised most recently in 1989—"trades African matriarchy-based laws for patriarchal rules co-opted from French civil law" (2008). As Ruth Evans's work on widows in Dakar shows, the "triple heritage" of Indigenous, Islamic/Arabic, and European/Christian cultures (Bass and Sow 2006) appear in questions of family law and inheritance (Evans 2015, 80). Despite giving women some control over their resources or promised inheritance in the event of a husband's or father's death, these competing systems allow for male-dominated houses to interpret the rules that benefit them and their male heirs. This has meant that according to Islamic law, female heirs receive half of what their brothers gain, or widows often receive less than their male children (82). A specific discrepancy regarding inheritance and household economic responsibility between Islamic law and the Family Code is that the former stipulates that men must provide for the woman who has control over her own resources while the latter requires women to contribute to the economic wellness of the household. An imam interviewed by Evans argues that because of this rule, which means women in theory hold on to the wealth they earn outside the home (in practice, the reality shows otherwise), women gain less in inheritance as a balancing for the years of not contributing to the household economy. The reality is that women contribute a great deal through unpaid domestic work and investing their earned money to household expenses. The Agence Nationale de la Statisque et de la Démographie (ANSD) estimates that unpaid domestic work accounts for 28.3 percent of the Senegalese national gross domestic product.

These complex realities matter because the changes and ambiguities of inheritance have meant that women are often in competition with one another for access and rights to men's wealth and are required to seek alternative means of supporting themselves and their families. As often becomes the case, if women's reproductive fortunes are tied to having male children who will look after them, then their relationships with the young wife (or wives) of their sons often become spaces of competition. The young wife as an extension of her husband's wealth and honor becomes the medium through which his mother also receives his aid in the form of daily and ceremonial teraanga. We will see these tensions throughout chapters 1 and 2. Whether it is a widow who was left with very little, a young wife seeking to maintain her relationship with her in-laws, or a mother saving to pay for her daughter's wedding, women have increasingly turned to rotating credit associations, solidarity groups turned microenterprises, in order to pay for them. In chapters 3 and 4, we will see how these associational spaces and practices of teraanga then become central to the parité movement and women's political praxis. I explore these points in the ethnographic chapters 5, 6, and 7, which describe the political activities and philosophies of the main politicians I investigate.

The devastating effects of Senegal's devaluation of its currency in 1994 and structural adjustment policies beginning in the mid-1980s have also left many to invest in social capital such as the circulation of wealth during family ceremonies. Investing in human capital has been a strategy for many women in Senegal to ensure the well-being of their families in the absence of state investment and salaried state employment that was predominantly men's work. The prominence of women-focused development associations has been at the center of the process of neoliberal reform in Senegal since the 1980s (Doligez, Fall, and Oualy 2012). Since then, there has been a feminization of both poverty and development by the influence of international organizations aiming exclusively to bring women and children out of poverty and economic dependence (Alidou 2005). As a result of these policies, women became the centerpiece of development projects in Senegal as men were increasingly unemployed or migrating outside of Senegal and sending remunerations home, not to mention women being particularly good at gathering. In a resource-poor country such as Senegal, which has only recently begun to exploit natural resources, remittances from Senegalese migrants made up 9.6 percent of the country's annual GDP as of 2021, according to the World Bank (2024). In 2020, most likely due to the COVID-19 pandemic it spiked as high as 10.6 percent. While the importance of migration and its economic benefits is not an explicit aspect of this book, it does loom large in the background of women's access to and mobilization of resources. Beyond the small benefits women gained from their economic activities in the informal economy, remunerations from family members have been a major factor in how women are able to reinvest in social capital.

The strong critiques of women's involvement in family ceremonies and ultimately the opposition to women in politics are situated in the frustrations of these economic disruptions as well as the aspirations of a postcolonial and modern state. In the decade following independence in 1960, excessive spending and the inflated expectations of gift giving—and therefore teraanga—were seen as a matter of draining private and public funds at a time when national development was crucial both socially and economically. For the Senegalese state, citizens were expected to take personal and public part in the productive and consumptive practices of the developing nation and avoid wasteful expenditures for family ceremonies. Excessive spending was deemed counterproductive. Moreover, the undertones of the 1967 law I mentioned in the preface idealized a traditional past. The postcolonial state desired to return to a normal state of realistic economics by means of reaffirming the moral imperatives of the economy and traditional practices. Debates about family ceremonies and social production were therefore a project in establishing the nature of value (Buggenhagen 2011) and the qualities of the nation-state.

In 2011, during Ayda's tenure as minister of women's affairs, the theme of the annual International Women's Day Celebration was Promoting Women's

Self-Reliance and the Parity Between Men and Women, and one of the sub-themes of the event was the Lutte Contre le Gaspillage (Fight against Waste-fulness). Ayda journeyed across the country, meeting with women's groups, nongovernmental organizations (NGOs), and local government officials and speaking about the issue of family ceremonies and women's fight for equal representation in politics. The two subjects of the *Quinzaine* together suggest the pervasive idea that in order for women to be taken seriously in national politics and for women's associations to receive development funds, something would need to be done about the expensive and unprofessional practices of family ceremonies. In one speech to a women's group in a rural community, Ayda mentioned that she herself struggled to limit her expenses due to the pressures of her family when it came to the naming ceremony of her first male grandchild, noting that she did not provide expensive gifts only because of the public spotlight of being a minister. Therefore, Ayda was aware of the expecta-tions of being a model of generosity and the importance of social capital as well as being a liberal capitalist subject who represented the state. In a postcolonial and neoliberal environment where the development complex invests heavily yet conditionally in women's productive capabilities, the conundrums con-tinue. As we will see in chapters 3 and 4, development projects provide funds for money-generating activities to women's associations in order for women to be self-sufficient while raising awareness about investing too heavily in activities, such as family ceremonies, that had been the very sites of the production of so-cial capital that kept families afloat. In essence, this promotion of self-reliance discounts the reality that women's authority comes not from individual pur-chasing power but from their ability to create communities of sharing through teraanga.

The Teraanga Republic

The documentation of Senegalese political history has been marked by charis-matic male political and religious figures (Cruise O'Brien 1975). It has also been a story of what Aminata Diaw (2004) calls the *présence-absence* of Senegalese women in politics. Despite the integral role women have played in men's cam-paigns, they have remained mostly absent from the historical imaginary of Sen-egalese politics and positions of authority, which Diaw further argues, "the very basis of the modern state is constructed upon the exclusion of women to public space" (2009, 50). As Yuval-Davis (1997) puts it, "Women did not just 'enter' the national arena: they were always there. . . . However, it is true that including women explicitly in the analytical discourse around nations and nationalisms is only very recent" (14). Similarly, Beck (2003) refers to Senegalese women's important role as organizers of male-driven campaigns a "hidden public" as they are simply valued as *sama jigéen,* or "my woman/women," by male leaders, despite being association leaders with considerable power in strategic neighborhoods throughout the capital and country. They are active and political in public campaigns yet hidden behind the decisions and achievements of men. They organize rallies, feed attendees, and provide entertainment. Additionally, they serve as the visual representation of the party by wearing matching outfits, *musóor* (head wraps with party-specific colors), and T-shirts with the candidate's portrait. Building on Peter Ekeh's notion of a "dual public"—"the coexistence of a modern nation-state with a Wolof civil-society that lacks the means to create a relationship of mutual dependence and moral accountability that one might find at the local level or the village public sphere" (1975, 91–112)—I argue that the female politicians in this book operate in the connecting space that links these mutual dependencies based on a moral philosophy of teraanga with governing strategies of the modern state. The systems of mutual dependence and moral accountability of teraanga are cultivated in women-driven spaces and are how women in politics translate their private political and moral authorities to the realm of the modern nation-state. Women's engagement with teraanga is their means for bridging the so-called division between the private and the public. During an interview in which she was asked about women's capabilities in the political arena, Aysata Tall Sall—one of the main protagonists of this book and a longtime politician—answered thus: "Women's responsibilities for housework could be transplanted to the management of public affairs" (Camara 2024). Therefore, the potential contributions women can make to politics are often framed as a translation of skills and attitudes from within the private domestic space.

Marcel Mauss (1990) argued in his famous study that the gift is a "*fait social total,*" the guiding principle of social organization. And David Graeber (2001) said that value is created by "the way in which actions become meaningful to the actor by being incorporated in some larger, social totality" (xii). Seck uses the term "*fait de teraanga*" (2010, 228) to conceive of a social organization that is guided by the principles of teraanga—or as he says, "a relational space both domestic and public" (228)—the way in which a majority of Senegalese understand and assign value to their world, in contrast to the "*fait républicain*" (French Republic)—a different kind of social organization based on principles of abstract identities fixed within encoded laws. Considering the "fait de teraanga" in the context of Senegalese politics, women who are particularly adept at the art of teraanga—fortifying their relationships through financial and social prestation—have garnered significant support and success in state as well as local politics (Riley 2019). I argue that this is an art of governance that relies on the principles and practices of teraanga and negotiating its complexities—what I call the Teraanga Republic. I equally argue that it is women who specifically operate within the Teraanga Republic, as we have seen with the political strategies of Ayda Mbóoj. These strategies have emerged as part of both women's engagement in the Senegalese political economy and their marginalization from it.

Seck (2015) suggests that the modern Senegalese subject, in this case women in politics, constructs an amalgamation of social practices that are locally relevant and have been part of their means of social and economic survival—namely, the construction and maintenance of relationships through specific values. And they place themselves at the heart of what they see as the real economy that governs Senegalese society—that is, the principles of the Teraanga Republic as a space that connects the values of traditionally private conduct with public politics are symbols of women's negotiations of flexible identities typical of a postcolonial subject. And as McNee (2000) argues, "Theoretically, modernization and development do away with the need for a gift economy, often equated with premodern or 'archaic' culture. However, attempts to develop Senegal according to the 'rational' model often stumble against the Wolof notion that investments in relationships are safer than investments in objects" (31). Therefore, it is in fact women's social maneuvering of these contradictions, by way of reciprocal relationships in their everyday engagements with teraanga, and their negotiations of gendered identities that have contributed greatly to their successes in local and state politics. In other words, I suggest that it is the connection between women's private involvement in the social reproduction of families that creates their political possibilities and that these negotiations tell us a great deal about the postcolonial anxieties and plasticity that they affront. In fact, this art of governance, the Teraanga Republic, is inspired by the parallel forms of conduct—or, as I understand it, a "political economy of teraanga" (Seck 2015, 26)—in which women have operated for a long time as a result of their overwhelming marginalization in the state political economy. In my research with Senegalese female politicians, I make the same distinction between power and authority as Nwando Achebe (2020, 3) does in her book *Female Monarchs and Merchant Queens in Africa*. According to Achebe, power is "the capacity or ability to direct or influence the behavior of others or the course of events" whereas authority is "the power or right to give orders, make decisions, and enforce obedience." There is no question that women in Senegal have always had power in terms of economic production and innovation or in terms of influencing political opinions and decisions. The question I treat in these pages is how women in relation to state politics create new forms of authority and make space for themselves in decision-making positions.

I conceive of the concept of a Teraanga Republic in two connecting ways. First, historical processes have bound women's relationship to teraanga and its shifting definitions. These processes include the strong legacies of women exercising an authority tied closely to exchange in the precolonial period; the reliance on authority over family ceremonies and women's associations when colonial interpretations of gender and labor allowed for men to gain wages and sought to tie women to work within the home; and the neocolonial development policies that confined women to small-scale enterprises tasked with developing the nation. I contend that these aforementioned processes promoted a parallel political economy of teraanga that has allowed for alternative economic and governing strategies driven by women partly due to these limitations and in spite of them. And even as they operate within parallel governing styles, they also remain embedded in democratic processes of the Senegalese state. This then gave way to the parité movement (formalizing gender quotas) that has concretized their strategies so that Senegal has one of the highest rates in the world of women in elected positions. These strategies have also had their downsides, including opposition to women in government and the moral defeats when women's participation and political advancement have stagnated.

Second, the Teraanga Republic sees teraanga as the major point of reference for social morality and organization of Senegalese society and an urbanizing Wolof-speaking population, and as the particular mode of relationality exercised by women in the context of their families and marriages. As a national culture has been built around the idea of teraanga, so, too, has it become commercialized around highly gendered notions of hospitality, tourism, and authentic African values. Items such as coffee, water, and bouillon spices not only are named teraanga but feature women doing the work of brewing, serving, and cooking. As mentioned above, restaurants throughout Dakar are named teraanga, and the tourism industry uses as its calling card for the outward-facing definition of teraanga as hospitality. Outside of the ethos in which local people live teraanga in their daily lives, the concept has become part of how Senegal is presented to the world—what Maya Angela Smith (2019) calls "global Senegality" (27). As such, teraanga has been one of the most exported ideas of Senegalese identity in France, Italy, Spain, Brazil, and the United States. From Teranga African Restaurant in Cincinnati, Ohio, to Teranga Harlem in New York City, to Restaurante Teranga in Barcelona and Madrid, the ties to hospitality are strongly marketed, and the concept has become well known globally in similar ways to ubuntu, yet on a much smaller scale. In many ways, the commercial consumption of teraanga among the Senegalese themselves is also arguably a caricature of how teraanga is mobilized, talked about, and debated. Arguably, the marketing of teraanga has reinforced Western translations of gender relations in the Senegalese context into a national effort to establish an image or brand that is—literally—inviting. The anecdote I provided in the beginning of this introduction, of a label with a woman enjoying her drink called "la teranga" being handed out during Ayda's coronation, is a good example of this. I argue that while part of this national project is the reification of women as representatives of domestic comfort and traditional African values, women in or aspiring to political office are engaging with these definitions of teraanga to create new possibilities of identity and authority.

As much as women are able to negotiate political possibilities around teraanga, so have critiques of them, such as debates about whether women should hold political positions in Senegal that have partially focused on the disruption of state politics by domestic politics. Articles published by private and government-sponsored media sources, and also people I spoke with, deemed women's profound involvement in family ceremonies as excessive and irresponsible, an example of precisely why women are not qualified to be leaders. In other words, politics was deemed men's business and the nurturing of familial and social relationships—most publicly expressed through ceremonies and teraanga—was women's business (Buggenhagen 2011). Ayda was celebrated during her coronation for being a woman who has been able to bridge these notions of public and private conduct; however, she has received her fair share of criticism, which I demonstrate in chapter 6. In this context, I am therefore interested in taking stock of the various elements of women politicians' performances of politics as well as the debates about their moral character and what this means for the current realities and imaginaries of a modern Senegalese nation. Do the women's social obligations complicate their qualifications to operate in the political scene of a modern Senegalese state, or are they in fact the root of their successes? What are these obligations, their productive elements, and what do women's practices of politics look like? Where do the critiques of women's social and economic investments in family ceremonies come from? In other words, might their associational networks, nurtured by performances of exchange, which some deem wasteful, in fact be a major factor in their political emergence? And can women's business in this context problematize the gendered ideas of public and private, if not the conceptual mobilization of gender as a determinant of authority?

Postcolonial Anxieties

These debates about teraanga highlight several anxieties about postcolonial identity and politics in Senegal. One preoccupation highlighted by Ayda's ceremony is that of the question of governance based on traditional social beliefs and behaviors versus a capitalistic and democracy-focused society of individuals who no longer consider the importance of others to their own well-being. During the speeches, notions of values, culture, and tradition came up repeatedly as a way to both evaluate and critique the dispossession of the current state of politics as well as imagine the possibility of a return to a nostalgic past. These nostalgias are also quite present in public space, as one can see while driving along the streets of Dakar; cars, trucks, and boutiques have Wolof words and sayings colorfully painted on them: *yërmandé* (empathy), *yar ak tégiñ* (correctness), *niité* (humanness), and *teraanga* being an especially present one, as if to remind themselves and others of essential Wolof values. After several years passed following the majority of this research, I returned to find new and shockingly aggressive bumper stickers that read *noppil* (shut up) with a silhouette of a man with his index finger held up to his mouth. This contrast of positive Wolof values and their seeming opposite highlights what Mbembe (2001) calls the entanglement of postcolonial reality as it denotes "the whole cluster of re-orderings of society, culture, and identity and a series of recent changes in the way power is exercised and rationalized" (66). At the same time, subjects in the postcolony are "marked by their ability to manage not just a single identity, but several flexible enough to negotiate as and when necessary" (104). And D'Alisera (2001) argues that objects such as bumper stickers are used by people to "make and maintain their worlds . . . the act of display as physical manifestation of experience" (93). And Yamaguchi (1991) says that objects are "the artistic creation of new sensitives toward the world" (61). The postcolony characterizes the multiplicities of government and identities that are "the product of several cultures, heritages, and traditions of which the features have become entangled over time and so, what may look like 'custom' cannot be reducible to it, while it also partakes of 'modernity' without being wholly included in it (Mbembe 2001, 26)." And as Hadiza Djibo (2001) notes, the "assimilation of Senegalese and Nigérian women in the Western world is not automatically, nor immediately liberating," which requires we also consider that "traditional institutions were far from a time of oppression and alienation for women" (18) as theories of modernity and women's emancipation have us believe. It is in these amalgamations of identity and historical imaginaries that the debate about teraanga and women in politics takes place. The very questions of what governance is, what it should be, and who should have the authority to partake in it are wrapped up in these diverse dimensions of identity and reference in a postcolonial space such as Senegal. The historical changes of women's representation of tradition and culture as well as their visibility/invisibility to state politics is a perfect example of this postcolonial reality.

Conversations, testimonies, and social critiques in this book center on the question of value (the material importance of a thing or action) and values (the social importance of said thing or action) to a collective experience. There are debates about what value teraanga holds, whether it is too much—speaking specifically about gifting during family ceremonies—and whether it continues to retain its standing as the symbol of Senegalese national culture. As Fabian Muniesa says, "Value and values are vernacular concepts" that "not just through rote social processes, are [created] through active 'vernacular deliberation'" (Souleles, Archere, and Thaning 2023). Throughout this book, the testimonies of women politicians demonstrate a preoccupation with determining what values are important and what value they are assigned. The debates about teraanga and women's political strategies are situated within a particular Senegalese vernacular that is rooted in a romanticized yet restorative precolonial tradition, colonial and postcolonial disenfranchisement, and more present global aspirations that pull from the former. Evaluations of what and who hold value are also highly gendered. For example, the state salary—again highly dominated by men—is greatly desired within Senegalese society, and yet women's control over resources and their complex networks of exchange, despite contributing to the economic sustainability of Senegalese families, is less valued, even as it is the bedrock of Senegalese sociality.

Structural adjustment programs affected women disproportionately in many ways, one of which was through the cutting of salaries. In his reflections on the postcolony, Mbembe argues that the "process of decomposition of postcolonial African states" was the continuance of colonial policies that followed "a trinity of violence, allocation, and transfer" (2001, 39). The salary of state employees is a particularly strong example. The allocation of salaries—which were not simply based on wages paid for hours worked—were the colonial and postcolonial form of creating a subjectivity of obedience and social complicity between the state and society. As Melly argues, "the esteem achieved by the 'salaried man' in postcolonial Dakar was owed, in part, to colonial formulations of urban status that privileged bureaucratic work and that employed techniques of spatial segregation to emphasize and enforce hierarchies and exclusions" (2018, 34). The transfer of the salary was then the communal social tie that was "the complex system of reciprocity and obligations binding members of a single household, even a single community, and these obligations and reciprocities governed relations" (46). In the case of Senegal, "state employees represented less than one percent of the working population," and yet "their remuneration accounted for more than fifty percent of state revenue" (Tidjani 1998, 280). In addition, the salary had become the cornerstone of financial well-being and prestige for many families while also deepening the gendered divisions of labor. Men's identities became inextricably linked to the prestige of the salary and the benefits it allowed them such as the possibility to marry multiple wives or send their children abroad to study. For women, the salary and its transfer meant representing their husband's wealth during family ceremonies by dressing to impress or giving generously, accommodating kin by providing food and money, participating in associations, or accommodating family members in need by hosting them within the family home. Therefore, one of the particular violences of the structural adjustment programs was the significant decrease in state employment, leaving many men out of work and without the salary that many families had come to depend on. However, because families depended on these contributions of direct and indirect wealth sharing, it fell to women to continue these practices in the absence of a steady flow of income. In order to perpetuate the reciprocities and obligations to the wider family unit, women had to get creative by joining associations and eventually taking part in development projects. Associations in this context meant money pooling or revolving credit groups that allowed members to invest regular sums of cash for an eventual payout or loan of a greater amount.

Another important aspect of value and values that surfaced through testimonies and debates was that of the differing interpretations of value between capitalist-democratic and sociopatrimonial forms. In other words, the "consequences of the social dissemination of the value-form under capitalism" means an "impersonal and abstract domination of everyone—regardless of their class position—by the [capitalist] value form" (Souleles, Archer, and Thaning 2023, 165). Therefore, the deliberation about what value teraanga holds is also about what kind of relationships people want for their society. In chapter 4, I consider the debates about the neoliberal policies that Elyachar (2005) describes as having incorporated social processes and local values into a free market rationality, therefore dispossessing people of their right to decide what matters and what has value. I do so in the context of transformations of women's associations into development organizations and eventually into platforms for political activism. I argue the women of this book recapture the values that were co-opted by development policies of the 1980s and '90s by reappropriating them for political strategy. They do this by playing to the "intimate connections

"Guardiennes des Valeurs (Women Guardians of Values)," cartoon by Samba Fall that appeared in *Le Soleil* newspaper, August 29, 1990.

between different actors of the social system" (Toulabor, Mbembe, and Bayart 2008, 10) and positioning themselves as actors who have risen from the bottom to the top while remaining situated within the communities that raised them. I particularly examine this in chapter 5.

Patronas and Hustlers: Toward New Forms of Patronage and Clientalism

Another aspect of this book concerns the connections to be made between the history of women's participation in politics via their strong associational networks and the gendered national and international development projects that prioritized these networks and contributed to current political strategies that place gender at the forefront. It is misleading to consider the emphasis on sexual difference as a historical given or part of an African traditional cultural precedent instead of as historical influences from Islam, French colonialism, and neoliberal development complexes, as Oyěwùmi defines in her concept of "historical feminism" (2011, 3). As Bayart (1993) notes, "colonization, independence, and national integration are simply moments in the process of social stratification" that leads to inequality and domination (62). Equally, gender is not simply a question of natural inequalities between the sexes but is rather, as Strathern says, the ways in which distinctions of male and female become concrete in our ideas of the naturalness of social relationships. Therefore, gender can be seen as one kind of stratification such as the male-dominated state or "Big Manism" politics. As Bayart also remarks, "The task of the big men amounts precisely to the achievement of a synthesis of composite influence, whilst assuming multiple roles in various functions" (218). In the case of this book, women's political strategies are entangled in complex negotiations of not just gender but also class and caste, where Big Womanism is its own negotiation between feudal systems of authority and the structures of French republicanism, which in some ways is not that different from Big Men.

Many contemporary critiques of women in politics center on their representation of a patrimonial past that conflicts with the ideals of a modern democratic state. The phenomenon of patron-client networks in African contexts has been well documented, from seeing patronage networks as a kind of political culture to promotion of national political participation as a form of reciprocity (Boone 1992; Bienen 1974) to recognizing the exploitative nature of these relations (Flynn 1974; Fatton 1987). Political patronage has been considered a form of domination, linking the ruling political class that controls state resources with those in need of them—what Bayart (1989) calls the "reappropriation of the state." Boone argues that "the domestic, social, and political pressures following independence created a scope of direct government involvement in the economy," which essentially made the "state a resource" (1992, 16). Boone also argues that development projects were code words for targeted clientelism where "the new forms of government intervention in the economy strengthened the internal revenue base of the state, multiplied opportunities for patronage and clientelism, and allowed regimes to channel economic resources to targeted social groups via 'development projects'" (17). In fact, with every new Senegalese administration, new institutions have capitalized on the voting power of women, and the influence of women's associations, by investing in their economic activities. This includes the structural adjustment programs of the Abdou Diouf era (1981–2000) and its focus on development projects in partnership with the increasing presence of NGOs. In fact, between 1985 and 1992, the adjustment support from the World Bank accounted for almost two-thirds of all development assistance (Creevey, Vengroff, and Gaye 1995). Additionally, it encompasses Abdoulaye Wade's era (2000–12) of state-sponsored small grants to women's associations that defined a reciprocal relationship with the state. Since 2012, the Macky Sall administration seems to be increasing the partisan utilization of women's associations as a source of *militantisme* (fervent support) that was particularly poignant during the 2017 election.

In fact, in patrimonial societies such as Senegal, "the state was indeed the personal domain of one or a few leaders" (Pitcher, Moran, and Johnston 2009, 127). And as Ayda's coronation demonstrates, her role as a figure of authority stems from the celebration of her personality as generous and situated in the context of her subjects. In my experiences of following women in politics, it was common to hear praise from supporters along these lines, making a point that the politician was revered for their generosity that both distinguished them as a noble (despite their background) and tied them to the wellness of their followers. However, as Camara (2008) argues, the sovereign's power was not absolute but privy to a constitution. That is to say that their authority among party supporters or association members derived from their benevolence or a perception of it but could also be challenged in its absence.

Thus, given the recent emergence of women in state politics, state and non-state institutional support for women's associations and development efforts the nature and origins of patron-client networks are changing. These phenomena are what I call patrona-client networks: women-driven networks that target and benefit from women's economic activities, while holding on to the hierarchy of a patron and their clients. Or matronage networks to borrow the phrase from Miriam Kilimo (2022) to signify the role of women driving transactional relationships. Women are strategically questioning the border between public and private by not only "showing that the private is public" (Diaw 2009, 44) but also demonstrating that the private can be a part of the public, in essence using the social capital gained from teraanga among private networks and ceremonies to create political power. If we consider Pitcher, Moran, and Johnston's (2009) critical look at the definition of the *neo* of neopatrimonialism in African contexts, it is crucial to remember how a scholar like Weber understood patrimonialism in the first place. Weber defined patrimonialism as a "specific form of authority and source of legitimacy" (1947) or "political relationships mediated through, and maintained by, personal connections between leaders and subjects, or patrons and clients" (Pitcher, Moran, and Johnston 2009, 129). More importantly to this definition is how those with authority in patrimonial contexts create and maintain this authority among their subjects and what new formations of patronage look like now. The crucial factor, they argue, is a relationship based on reciprocity in which despite being uneven, the relationship between leader and subject is one of shared benefit and dependency. Therefore, although Ayda arguably gains more financial and social authority and prestige from her supporters, she also solidifies her dependency on them through the continual benevolence she must show them.

Therefore, in order for the personal and public to be mutually constitutive, "the collective requires the political authority to exercise its powers responsibly" (140).

Bayart argues that we should not overstate the principle of reciprocity as representative of idealized relationships that obfuscate domination and in-equality. However, his assumption that reciprocity is tandem to equality is misguided, and as I argue throughout the book, it is not an erasure of inequali-ties that forms the political economy of teraanga; rather, it is a way of thinking differently about whom those inequalities serve and in what ways. In fact, the evolution of teraanga as an economic and political strategy was in many ways born from the technocratic policies of development projects that forced women to transform ideas of solidarity and mutual aid into economic benefit. The con-nection between economic investments in development since the 1980s and the number of women representatives explains not only these increases but possibly also the discursive reasons why women are running for office in the first place. Many parliamentarians I spoke with noted that for them, politics was a way to have access to funds for what they called "development," meaning funded projects for women's entrepreneurship, building schools, or donating material to the community. Aysata Daouda Dia, a representative from Keur Massar on the edges of Dakar, said she got into politics because "you can't do development without politics, and you can't do politics without develop-ment." For her, many development projects stalled because of a lack of govern-mental initiative and the difficulty of procuring funds from private sources or government-run sources that had high-interest loans. Whereas the first women to form political parties or run for or be appointed to office were mostly wives of politicians or women of the upper classes, newer waves consist of women who began as sellers in the market or with small enterprises often backed by nongovernmental organizations and state-sponsored loan programs. In fact, the first woman in parliament was proudly hailed as nonliterate in French in order to show that anyone could be a representative.

In chapters 5 and 6, I demonstrate just how Ayda and other political leaders form dependent bonds with their supporters. Just as Edmann and Engel (2007) argue that there must be a deeper study of not just how neopatrimonialism op-erates in formal institutions but how informal relationships structure political and economic power in Africa.

Throughout this book, women politicians' discourses of teraanga and soli-darity denote their awareness of the stereotype of politicians as looking out only for themselves, as well as a philosophy where they understand themselves as linked to others. And although their wealth is potentially gained through similar access to state resources, their notions of redistribution, reciprocity, and personal gain are articulated differently. Given women's intimate relationship between the postcolonial state and its development projects, politics are an avenue in which women gain authority and resources that are then put toward their development. They also express positions that involve codependence from both ends of the hierarchy. Those on the supposed lower end of the hierarchy due to age, caste, or social and economic status at times make clear that they also benefit from their alliances with these politicians in very personal ways, often because they feel that the woman or someone in her family was caring toward them or their family. It also involves their relationships to their religious faith and their community. Even as patronas of their own associations focus on economic and spiritual development, they are also *taalibés* (disciples) of Sufi Muslim leaders. They have been dependent on male political leaders of their parties for decades and in many cases still are. The influence of religion on the political identities of politicians in a secular state such as Senegal is an important aspect of what distinguishes the Teraanga Republic from the French Republic, which seeks to erase personal identity based on affiliations of religion, class, gender, and so forth. Similarly, the women in this book conceive of their faith and practices of piety as informing how they practice politics in terms of the ethical framings of their actions. The philosophies and performances of teraanga draw from Indigenous (Wolof and other ethnic groups) and local Sufi interpretations of ethics that are based on discourses and displays (actions) of generosity, care, and kinship as well as of suffering and sacrifice.

Therefore, throughout this book, I consider questions about what patronage networks or relations look like when women are the patrons and have considerable access to political power and resources. What of questions of corruption? Or moral crises? How do women politicians engage with and understand their relationships with supporters and their constituents as well as members of the associations they lead? I am interested in how discourses about governance and corruption are gendered and the different ways of understanding what we mean by these terms. The parité movement in Senegal, and its critiques, is instructive for understanding how women's role in politics reflects the intersections between patrimonial and democratic forms of authority.

The Stars of the Show

This book is based on my work with various women politicians of all ages, classes, and political parties. The main four politicians I spent time with on their campaigns, attending events and ceremonies, are Aysata (Ayda) Mbóoj of Abdoulaye Wade's Parti Démocratique Sénégalais, affectionately named the Lioness of Bawol[12] in the heart of Senegal; Aysata Tall Sall from the Parti Socialiste that governed Senegal for forty years, also named the queen of Fuutaa to the north bordering Mauritania; Mously Diakhaté, a parliamentarian from the party of president Macky Sall, Alliance pour la République; and Aminata Touré, the former minister of justice and prime minister of Senegal. The ethnographies of these four women are central to the perspectives offered in this book. Two other parliamentarians, Penda Seck from Macky Sall's coalition Bennoo Bokk Yaakaar and Mame Mbayam Gueye Bâ from the Mouvement de la Réforme pour le Développement Social, also feature significantly. Throughout the book, the people who contribute to these four women's successes are also central. These include Ayda's niece Ndey Mbóoj, who has loyally helped with campaigning, crowdsourcing from her various development associations, and entertaining guests. It also includes women such as Daba Codou, the president of Mously's neighborhood association and of the women's chapter of the president's party, whom Mously has groomed to run for mayor of Yarax, a fishing community swallowed up by the city of Dakar. Also featured is Mareem Sow, who was a main partisan for Aysata's movement during the 2017 legislative elections. In addition to these politicians and those who support them, the book includes interviews with other women representatives in parliament and members of the movement for gender parity. My process for choosing parliamentarians was more by availability than by design. Based on Fatou Sow Sarr's book *Les Premières Héritières de la Parité*, which provided the biographies of all the women of the 2012 parliament roster, I began contacting members of diverse parties and backgrounds and was dependent upon their availability and desire to work with me. With them and members of their teams, their families, and their supporters, my interviews were in Wolof, French, and English, and I conducted participant observation and supplemented my research of their political histories with newspaper archives. I mostly employed a peripatetic anthropological method of being where they are. Because as Jackson (2001) says this method "should not just be interpreted as a flighty groundlessness" (14), I found the best places to observe practices of teraanga and politics were in the various lived spaces of my interlocutors. And one would be amazed, or not, to see just how quickly these women's spaces moved around. They were everywhere their supporters were, moving from house to house and town to town during the campaigns and at other times. I was constantly adapting and going with the flow; it was necessary in order to keep up with them.

Structure of the Book

In chapter 1, "One Wedding and a Funeral: Social Reproduction and the Gendering of Teraanga," I consider the feminization and commoditization of teraanga by exploring national ideas and performances of femininity and status portrayed and reproduced in mediascapes such as advertisements, consumer products, music, and television shows. These various medias depict a feminine subject within the domestic space that is constructed through gendered forms of teraanga. The chapter discusses these phenomena as a backdrop to a young woman's wedding and an elder woman's funeral through the eyes of a griot woman, which demonstrate generational rifts regarding the importance of family ceremonies to women's reputations.

In chapter 2, "Sénégalaisement and the Politics of Personality," I consider the conceptualizations and mobilities of relationality, power, and gender by examining particular Senegalese feminine styles, or *sénégalaisement*, an amalgamation of specific Wolof virtues and their centrality to women's social negotiations with families, politics, and nation building itself. By way of personal stories from several women regarding marriage and their relationships with their families-in-law, I demonstrate the complex linkages of women's negotiations of power within marriages and politics. The chapter also describes the tensions of these performances of teraanga and negotiations of status and power by discussing the monetization of family ceremonies. Furthermore, it discusses how materialization of social reproduction evokes questions of conflicting ideas about democracy and society.

Chapter 3, "From Associations to Parliament: Development Politics and Parité," gives a detailed background on women's political power throughout Senegalese history, including details of the parité movement and its opponents. With testimonies from important actors of the movement, I demonstrate how women's participation in national politics—as organizers to men-driven parties or as powerful queens—has always been vital to the life of the nation, however obscured that participation may have been. The chapter will show the differences between the Senegalese parité movement and its sister movement in France, which took place in the decade of the 1990s. The distinctive strategies of both movements highlight key differences in the notion of citizenship and political identity.

The politician biographies placed between chapters 3 and 4 introduce in more detail the main four politicians of the book. They also provide a shift toward the latter chapters of the book, which focus on their political, religious, and social engagements with teraanga as political strategy and debate.

Chapter 4, "Patronas and Hustlers: Women's Associations and Patrona-Client Networks," discusses the central role of associations in women's political success and process, and the dynamics they have created between politicians (patronas) and those who hustle on their behalf. It follows the political activities, including the 2017 campaign, of Ayda Mbóoj and the various actors important to her entourage and popularity, particularly the female praise singers, or griots (géwël). I consider the rise of women in politics and advocacy for the parité law instigated partly due to their mobilization of associations and state and nonstate development projects to participate in political parties and eventually run them. I do so by considering the leadership roles of Mously Diakhaté and Awa Ka, the president of several women's associations in her Dakar neighborhood, and their relationships with women in their associations as examples of new forms of female-driven patronage networks. This chapter shows the mutual dependencies of patronas and those who work in their circles, outlining the unequal yet mutually beneficial relationships that are central to women in politics and other forms of authority seeking.

Chapter 5, "Good Women, Good Deeds: Religious Identity and Political Ambition," considers the performances of teraanga to the political process as an expression of social and spiritual connectedness. I make connections between local Wolof ethics, Murīd Sufi doctrine, and women's fight for political power and parité. I suggest that women like Ayda and Mously rely on their Murīd identity and education for political capital and inspiration. I consider their sophisticated negotiations of identities as *good Muslim women* within the Murīd framework and their connections to women's struggle for equal opportunity.

Chapter 6, "Political Economies of Teraanga," follows the political careers and activities of Ayda Mbóoj and Aminata Touré with anecdotal testimony from Ndey Sukkey Géy. The contrasting political philosophies and practices of the two women offer examples of the complexities of the political economy of teraanga. This chapter also shows the differences between someone such as Ayda, who is an expert at gaining popularity through the many forms of localized teraanga, and Aminata, who is seen as impersonal in her political conduct and represents a more Western style of governance. Symbolically, they represent two different realities of the Senegalese postcolonial experience: one that references local and traditional knowledge systems and another that references Western education and, as a result, is seemingly disconnected from Senegalese cultural practices. This chapter puts their ideas and experiences into conversation with one another as well as with public perceptions of them. I argue by way of discourses from and about Ayda and Aminata that perceptions of corruption are complicated by personal interpretations of democracy and governance and public perception of women's roles in politics and society.

In chapter 7, "Is Senegal Ready for a Female President?," I weave Aysata Tall Sall's reflections regarding her 2017 campaign for parliament with events that took place during the campaign. I do so using my interview with Aysata and an analysis of campaign slogans, messaging, party member accounts, and personal observations from the campaign trail. I also juxtapose them with critiques she received following an unsuccessful bid for president in 2019 and her subsequent choice to join Macky Sall's party. I consider the vicious critiques against her in the larger context of the parité movement and the consequences of having built such a movement and arguing for women's participation in state politics in gendered terms. I also discuss the campaigns of Mareem Sow, an associate of Aysata and a member of her party, as well as the personal and political hustle of Ndey Mbóoj, niece and party member of Ayda Mbóoj.

The epilogue, "Is the Future Female?," serves to reflect upon the political events leading up to the 2024 presidential election with a focus on the gendered implications regarding the accusations of rape against the primary opposition candidate, Ousmane Sonko, and the eventual candidacy and victory of his colleague, Bassirou Diomaye Faye.

1

One Wedding and a Funeral

Social Reproduction and the Gendering of Teraanga

In Senegal, family ceremonies such as weddings, baptisms, and funerals are "moments of consequence" (Meneley 1996). They are opportunities for building solidarity among family members and yet the subject of contentious and polarizing national debates. Historically, they have represented the heart of Senegalese cultural and social reproduction as sites in which kin gather to reaffirm their relationships through the exchange of gifts and demonstration of support (Sow 1985). However, the government and the general public have at times criticized family ceremonies as sites of "excessive and wasteful" (Sow 1996) displays of wealth, leading to social and moral degradation (Masquelier 2009) and economic hardship. In 1967, a law passed by the Senghor administration limited spending for ceremonies such as weddings and baptisms as part of a recapturing of traditional values lost during colonial rule, characteristic of the newly independent nation in the model of African socialism. These measures initially embodied the aspirations of the state to "defend the Senegalese citizen from itself" (Mbengue 1967) and from the financial burden these ceremonies had come to represent.

This chapter examines the complex sites of social reproduction such as family ceremonies and the roles they play in women's lives. They are spaces where women's everyday social labor of teraanga comes to fruition, paraded for friends and family to bask in the woman's magnanimity. The chapter demonstrates how theatrical and less-visible practices of teraanga tie women's worth to a particularly feminine domestic space. The construction of a woman's prestige is therefore situated within the semantic field of femininized traits and linguistic creativities reproduced in popular media and daily utterances. Guided by Aminata Diaw's examination of the borders between the private and public as situated in the colonial legacy of linking a woman's identity as a citizen to her sexuality and reproduction of future (male) citizens, I examine the music, advertisements, and television shows popular during my research trips that reinforced the "sequences that draw upon sexual imagery" (Strathern 1988, xi) and represent women's value. Second, I examine how *géwëls* (griots) are important stewards of this reputation-making process (Buggenhagen 2012) through the experiences and testimonies of a géwël woman who demonstrates the centrality of not only teraanga and family ceremonies to women's lives but also the livelihoods of social actors whose roles are rapidly changing.

Reputation Is Everything

"Sunu benn yaay bu dëkkoon fi moo gaañu. Dama wara dem dëj ba [An elderly woman who lives down the street died. I need to go to the funeral]," said Jéynaba Kouyate, the géwël woman I attended family ceremonies with, just as I arrived at her home in Medina, a popular neighborhood of Dakar.

"Can I go with you?" I asked.

"Ñewal, waaye doo gis lu bare [Come on, but there won't be much to see]," she replied, referring to my interest in watching her perform ceremonies such as the wedding to be held that evening—the original reason I was there. But it proved to be an enlightening experience, linking the phenomena displayed during a wedding to one's lifelong legacy.

Jéynaba and other géwël are ambassadors, or "mobile mouthpieces" (Schulz 1997), of teraanga culture. As we sauntered toward the funeral, Jéynaba called out small niceties to neighbors sitting in front of their homes: "Your dress is beautiful, very beautiful. You are a good person. You love your mother, you love your father"—things a common person would never advertise about themselves as it is frowned upon to tout one's own reputation. That is what géwëls are for, Jéynaba told me. For her, contemporary géwël serve as a mirror to society. Accompanying a woman of high status, whether noble or not, to family ceremonies or representing her in death is also an important part of a géwël's job description, which includes offering praise of the woman's stature, noble qualities, and legacy.

The house of the deceased woman had beautifully tiled walls that enclosed the courtyard; a wide skylight allowed light to reflect off the tiles. It was a sanctuary from the bustling noise of the neighborhood. The family arrived, we said our condolences, and Jéynaba belted out, "Ndeysaan, ku baax lawoon, ku xamoon teraanga [Oh dear, she was a good person, a person who knew teraanga (she was so generous)]." All agreed by shaking their heads to emphasize

their sadness. "Cey, Yàlla! [Yes, Lord!]," another offered straight from her dia-
phragm, expressing profound loss and amazement at God's plan in a kind of
response to Jéynaba's pronouncement. Jéynaba then offered a wise proverb:
"Kuy dund kenn gërëmul la, soo dewee kenn du la joy [If while living no one
thanked you, when you die, no one will cry for you]." Everyone in the room
agreed, some saying "Allahuakbar [God is great]," which reverberated throughout the house. The proverb meant that only a person who has spent a lifetime
demonstrating teraanga toward others will be grieved. By commemorating
the reputation of the deceased woman, her funeral was a way to pay tribute to
her lifetime of generosity, without which her funeral would have been poorly
attended—demonstrating that a woman's journey toward a crowded funeral,
and a spot with God in heaven, is paved with teraanga, because only in death
do we come to understand the truth about our own lives reflected in the perceptions of others.

Gendering the Domestic Space

Part of the discussion regarding change and prosperity in Senegal is focused
on the female body and soul. The proper body continues to be up for debate.
Women of high social status, known as *drianké*, who represent the urban feminine ideal (Buggenhagen 2012), and the younger generation of women known
as *diskette* embody material exchange and the importance of teraanga to the
construction of a desirable and revered personality. These female figures also
visibly demonstrate the generational changes in how teraanga is interpreted
and appropriated. Ceremonies performed by female family members and their
new in-laws and rehearsed by young women trying to assert themselves are,
therefore, places where personal identities and one's place in the social hierarchy are worked out. Older women who are veterans of ceremonies aim to
recuperate their investments from friends and family as well as maintain their
reputations, and younger women are at the beginning investment stages.

   Reminders of the significance of teraanga's components are everywhere.
Reputations are nurtured by the constant presence or "mass mediation"
(Shryock 2004) of teraanga—that is, state and commercial discourses that
feminize teraanga as women's duty. On television and radio shows and in publicity and public discourse, women are the representation of all that is hospitable and generous. Television dramas such as *Mokh Poth*[1] (Adoring wife),
produced online, or talk shows like *Jéeg ak Këram* (A woman and her home)
and *Feem ci Keur* (Tricks in the home)[2] explore urban marriages and discuss
topics of the home. The teraanga ethos encompasses not only a vast catalog of

performances related to hospitality and generosity but also a wide semantic field of concepts that speak to the performance of teraanga (Castaldi 2006). Teraanga has been perceived as a national brand since perhaps the 2002 World Cup, in which Senegal beat France following a campaign referring to the team as the Lions de la Teraanga, the symbol of Le Sénégal qui gagne (The Senegal that wins). In the case of the soccer team, Ralph (2015) notes that "one of the most prominent features of economic liberalization in Senegal has been the way it valorizes masculinity in aspirational narratives" (100) and that men's success in the postcolonial period within state and private companies has been their access to foreign capital and its institutionalization. As Ralph also says, "Meanwhile, the crucial role that women play rearing the nation, as well as attending to the educational and economic aspirations of the populace, remains underappreciated and undertheorized" (101). Even as the national soccer team parades teraanga as a national and masculinized reality, women are the ones who mobilize teraanga for economic gains. Although much of women's access to capital stems from the contributions from their husbands, it is reproduced and grown within the spaces of family ceremonies and associations. Their access to exchange circles depends on specific characteristics within the teraanga ethos. Considering the reproductive possibilities of teraanga, Castaldi (2006) comments, "Terànga denotes not only generosity but accountability, while the recognition of terànga as a virtue speaks of the importance of assistance as a form of moral currency that establishes a moral credit line that can be cashed in at times of need. In other words, terànga ensures the flow of wealth among social networks and guarantees voluntary gift giving as a form of social security amidst a steadily deteriorating economy in a chronic state of crisis" (177).

Anatomy of Marital Exchange

Family ceremonies such as weddings and baptisms and the gift exchanges they entail are the most visible spaces of teraanga. Elder women with children of marrying age invest in community rotating credit associations called *mbootaay*, which serve as a way to pool money with peers for an annual or monthly collective payout. This money is often used to host a wedding for a woman's son or daughter and to solicit further investments from other female neighbors and family members. The latter investment is a particularly interesting social exchange where the money given is part of a long trend of reciprocity that extends over years of prestations and counterprestations. Women who are particularly caught up in these circular networks depend on their reciprocal partners to contribute to their ceremonies in order to recuperate their investments in their partners' life cycle events. For example, a wedding is an event for which the mothers of girls save money for years prior. Depending on the group, women meet once a month, each contributing a fixed amount of 5,000 to 10,000 CFA ($10–20), which is given to the secretary and stored in a cabinet at her home. A particularly upscale mbootaay can have monthly amounts of up to 50,000 CFA ($100).

If a man wants to marry a woman, he demonstrates his intentions through a *may bu njëkk*, or a first symbolic gift consisting most often of a combination of cash and material gifts such as cloth and jewelry. The price is often determined by how much he has to give and where he and his family set the bar for future reciprocities. This is important because most official gifting for ceremonies in Senegal follows a system of doubling prices. For example, if a man truly intends to ask for a woman's parents' permission to marry her, he must furnish a *warugar*, or a dowry consisting of double the amount of cash given for the may bu njëkk. Warugar also expresses the Wolof idea of a moral obligation to fulfill his promise to marry and take care of the woman (Sylla 1978). The dowry price is usually set by the parents of the young woman, who also are careful to strike a balance between gaining a sizable sum and obligating themselves to reciprocate more than they can afford at a later time. Dowries can consist of a large sum of money accompanied by a bed or similar home furnishings (Masquelier 2009). A small part of the dowry is given to the father of the bride-to-be, and the large portion is left for the mother to manage. The father uses his part to buy kola nuts to pass out to his friends at the official *takk*, the tying of the marriage that takes place at the mosque among men. The mother is responsible for securing supplies for the wedding such as many platters of rice and chicken or lamb, drinks, and chair and tent rentals for hundreds of guests; she also oversees the presentation of gifts with the help of the family géwël.

Assane Sylla argues teeranga is manifested in the exchange of gifts (1978). Because gift giving between families is paramount to the marriage process, the mother of the bride must go to the market and buy various types and qualities of cloth, beads, and other amenities, called the *waccay*, to present to the *njékke* (sisters of the groom or close female family members), *goro* (mother or father of the groom), and just about every other person in her family and the new extended one. The money for these amenities comes from the dowry, and the items purchased from the market will be used to reciprocate along with double the cash amount. The teeranga in this instance can be described through a whole host of terms indicating the destined party—for example, *wallu mbajen* (gift given to the paternal aunts), *ndawtal* (money given to the mother of the ceremony), and *añu njékke* (money offered to a woman's sisters-in-law) (Sylla 1978).

In order to face this challenge on the big day, the mother takes cash from her part of the dowry and, in advance of the ceremony, divides it up between different aunts on both the maternal and paternal sides—what is called a *lekku ndey* (mother's part), literally meaning "what the mother eats." Each aunt is asked to bring twice the amount given to her by the time of the wedding in what then becomes the *ndawtal*, an act of solidarity with the mother and a symbol of their bond through exchange and reciprocity. No doubt, the mother of the bride has also participated in the ceremonies of the women who show up to attest to their shared loyalties. Therefore, those contributing the ndawtal are expected to return at least the amount given to them; it is more socially acceptable to give twice that.

On several occasions, women described to me the strategy of gift exchange. The mother takes a risk by putting all her bets on recuperating the ndawtal, as she often seeks credit to purchase everything at the market in hopes that she will be paid back on the day of the wedding. The ndawtal, in addition to the rest of the warugar, is then transformed into what the mother will give to the family of the groom, such as the elements of the waccay (often, cloth and cash). As the evening of the wedding approaches, the women from both the bride's and groom's sides form a gift-giving circle (*géew*), which is facilitated by each family's géwël. Gifts follow an assembly line formation from the mother of the young woman to her géwël, who, standing in the center of the circle, announces the amount and its destined owner and then transfers it to the in-laws' géwël, who repeats the amount, pointing to the importance of the mother based on the quantity of the gift. This process, called *joxalante*, also involves gifting and regifting the same items to enact the trading of niceties and material wealth. Favors are returned, although the family of the young man must wait until the baptism of the firstborn to reciprocate in a proper manner. Payments are also added to the gifts to thank the géwël for their praises. Examining the elements of gift giving and the structure of family ceremonies lays the foundation for understanding the critiques of the gift-giving process.

Parasites and Jàmm ak Xéewal—Peace and Blessings

"Ban role la géwël yi jouer? [What role do géwëls play?]"

"Géwël dafay defar [A géwël solves problems/a géwël heals]," explained Jéynaba.

"What do you mean by that?" I asked.

"Géwël day indi jàmm, defar société bi [Géwëls bring peace and make our society]," she insisted.

Jéynaba has duties during ceremonies, but she also describes herself as being a mediator in Medina, her neighborhood in the heart of Dakar. "You just talk until they come to an understanding," she says, citing a recent example of two conflicting families whom she helped reconcile. Talking is exactly what Jéynaba and most géwëls do in Senegal. They are masters of the spoken word, traditionally serving as praise singers and historians to the ruling class, and Diop (1981) considers their category of *sab-lekk* as being "those who live off of their songs" (34). In the past, they followed kings and queens to public events, singing their praises and reciting family genealogy, acting as a kind of *porte-parole* for the ruling class. Géwëls are historians, musicians, genealogists, and praise singers whose importance has endured the test of colonization and liberal postindependence political change (Leymarie-Ortiz 1979).

Géwëls are part of the casted groups of the great Wolof and Tukulóor kingdoms, framing Senegalese society and continuing to do so in many cases, acting as "repositories of the history of their people" (Panzacchi 1994, 193) in a society that has traditionally been thought to be predominantly oral. However, new research has demonstrated the interlacing of oral and written traditions through the discovery of written Ajami poems and texts also chanted among the Sufi communities in Senegal (Ngom 2016; Diallo 2012; Dell 2018). Géwëls followed nobles into battle and created prestige for their noble masters, and today they still create the ambience at public and private events (Hoffman 2000). Géwëls also play an important role in the creation of political personas. Just as Shryock described *karam* (hospitality) in Jordan as "endowed genealogy—which some are given more," the casted relationship between géwëls and the ruling class is also defined by being bestowed with the resources to give teraanga and the géwëls' inferiority as they live off the generosity of the royals. Both roles have a strong place within Senegalese society, and teraanga is at its core.

Jéynaba, a Bambara woman who comes from a long line of Mandinka géwëls from Guinea and Mali, sees her role as helping to stabilize society and ensure a constant environment of positivity, peace, and self-sacrifice for others. Although ethnically Bambara, Jéynaba grew up in Dakar, speaks Wolof as her primary language, and is able to float between Wolof dominant spaces and others. She is often asked to work with Bambara and Tukulóor families. Many families call upon her to conduct weddings and naming ceremonies and lend support during funerals; the family celebrating their daughter's wedding was a Tukulóor family yet also mostly spoke Wolof. On every visit to Jéynaba's home, I found her sitting under a parasol behind a waist-high table selling vegetables she acquired from the nearby market. The vegetables were not particularly crisp, and customers were few and far between; in fact, it seemed her business was dependent upon loyal friends and neighbors. I asked her why she sold vegetables if she was a géwël. She replied, "Leegi amul liggéey. Nit ñi fonkatuñu géwël yi. Bu njëkk ba mënuloo dem deux jours te demuloo ngente. Leegi, mën nga toog benn wàlla ñaari weer te doo dem xew. Parce que nit ñi leegi dañu wañni yàq bi. Dañu sonn, te Senegal amatul xaalis [Now there is no work. People don't value géwëls anymore. It used to be that you couldn't go two days without going to a naming ceremony. Now, you can go one or two months and not go to a ceremony. Because people don't waste as much. They are tired, and Senegal no longer has any money]."

She noted that the number of ceremonies had dwindled because now people were becoming educated, learning not to spend excessively, and choosing to have smaller and more contained ceremonies, often omitting the participation of géwëls—a possible sign that some development efforts and economic troubles have made an impact on social decisions. Although this countertrend threatened her livelihood, ceremonies and the work of géwëls can hardly be called endangered. However, géwëls like her turn to alternative sources for their craft. "Dara baaxul, moo tax bëgg naa liggéey ak Bamba Fall [It's bad, so I'm hoping to work for Bamba Fall]," she said, referring to the mayor of Medina at the time, a prominent politician.[3] This was a trend I saw among géwëls: looking to turn their skills toward attaching themselves to a politician, as it was thought to be more lucrative.

Jigéen, Jongé, Feem: Commercialization of Femininity and Teraanga

Jéynaba and I returned from the funeral to find the wedding in full swing. A popular song at the time, "Jigéen Feem" [Women's Talents] by artist Titi, blasted in the background. Her song engages a female audience in a conversation about marriage and a woman's responsibility for its well-being. You could hear it playing while walking around the city and happening upon marriages being celebrated on streets blocked off by tents for the occasion. *Feem* is translated in the dictionary as a slogan (Diouf 2003); however, in everyday language, it refers more to the many skills or facets of women's behavior and sexualized abilities, especially when referring to her relationships with her husband and those close to him. These behaviors mostly demonstrate her ability to be dependable yet spontaneous and loving. A popular iteration of *feem* is a woman who goes to great lengths to please her husband by showering him with good meals and impressing him with small tokens of affection embedded in her performances as a doting wife. A great deal of this centers on food, its preparation

and display, and her attentiveness to small aesthetic details. Similar to commercials advertising different products to help women spice up their food, Titi
uses the metaphor of spices to indicate ways to spice up the marriage, and the
lyrics speak to a woman's talents and charm for hospitality, sensuality, and attention to detail. This commercialization of terms such as *feem* reflects and is
reflected in popular discourse with sayings such as "ku bare feem," or "she who
has a lot of charm/talents," used when praising a woman for how she pampers
her husband and family-in-law. In the music video, Titi is featured in her home
preparing an elaborate meal for her husband as he simultaneously leaves the
office, marking a clear difference between women's domestic work and men's
salaried employement. Several dress changes and the decoration of their bedroom set the scene of a happy husband and attentive wife as she serves him a
plate of *ceebu jën*, rice and fish, that is more than any two people can eat. Paul
Nugent argues that "advertising seeks to establish links between the individual
consumer, the commodity, and a nation of fellow consumers" (2010, 97). Citing ceebu jën, which is the Senegalese national dish, Nugent argues that food
consumption in Africa is just as much a symbol of nationalism as Benedict
Anderson's famous example of printed media, calling the dish "a kind of culinary lingua franca consumed by Senegalese across the country" (2010, 106).
In fact, as of 2021, ceebu jën was enshrined as an "intangible cultural heritage
of humanity" by UNESCO,[4] citing that "the recipe and techniques are traditionally passed down from mother to daughter." And, as many pointed out to
me, ceebu jën's allure comes also from the time, care, and effort put into it. As
these commercials and songs demonstrate, the dishes, general hospitality, and
successes of the domestic space are enshrined in women's bodies.

   One television advertisement for the bouillon seasoning product Jongué[5]
shows a woman dressed in beautifully designed bright clothing, in a kitchen
filled with plentiful food, while a narrator intones, "Une vraie jongé, c'est recon-
naître ce qui est nouveau, mais indispensable [A real woman is someone who
recognizes novelty and quality]." Recognizing and representing novelty is also
an aspect of feem. During the commercial, a female géwël sings in Wolof, "Safal
ba sës, safal ba fàww, safal ba ci biir cin [Spice it up until you cannot further,
spice it up forever, spice it up all the way into the pot]." The product's tagline
"spice it up all the way into the pot" refers to *jongé* as a process, of which cooking a good meal is just one element. *Jongé* (*joŋe* in the Wolof standard spelling),
often translated simply as a cognate for woman (*jigéen, jéeg*), is a signifier of a
woman's knowledge of teraanga—its uses, meanings, and contexts. *Jongoma*,
another Wolof term for woman, identifies an especially voluptuous and beautiful woman, giving way to the use of the word *jongé*, the active performativity

Jongué bouillon powder advertisement. "Ba cibir tchiin!" or "All the way into the pot!"

of being a woman. *Jongé* embodies dressing beautifully, performing generosity in the form of gifts, presence, and hosting that all add up to what Jongué, the product and concept, represents as it is poured into the pot (see above). I often heard another phrase that referred to women's good behavior in the home: "jigéen ju baax mooy jigéen ju gàtt tànk [a good woman is a woman with short legs]." A woman who has short legs in Wolof is a woman who does not stray far from her home. This refers to the question of women who stay close to home, as it was better to avoid those who gossip too much about her whereabouts and activities. People who talked a lot consequently were referred to as "ku guud lamiñ [those with long tongues]."

Writing about Dakar families, Adjamagbo, Antoine, and Dial (2004) distinguish between "travailler et 'bien travailler'"—that is, "to work and to do good work / work well." To work is to exchange labor in the public sector for wages, whereas doing good work—particularly for women—is to "labor for the radiant future of one's children and to take good care of her husband and family-in-law." In most rural areas of Senegal, a woman, upon marriage, joins her husband's family home, where she cares for her family-in-law by working around the home, cooking, cleaning, and helping the unmarried sisters-in-law and their mother with the daily running of the home they now share. Titi uses the word *séy* (marriage) in her song as a verb to demonstrate marriage as an active and ongoing process made up of the good work of women that supports the work of men outside the home. Young women I spoke with or overheard delightedly teased their friends who recounted ways they had pampered their husbands, boyfriends, or families-in-law by saying, "seysi nga de! [you did it!]" or a similar phrase, "jongé nga de! [you spiced it up!]," or "yaa baax [nice work / you are a keeper]."[6] Grammatically, the suffix *-si* modifies the verb signifying an arrival of that action. In everyday usage, *séy* is turned into *seysi*,[7] meaning "to bring home the marriage" but referring to a woman who is particularly crafty in pleasing her husband. These playful dialectics about marriage and women's work within it are sprinkled into conversation, made as passing comments to friends, or shared upon someone's moment of greetings. Giving gifts, particularly to a mother-in-law or female relative; cooking a tasty and beautiful meal for an important guest; or going out of their way for their husband would merit such a compliment. Also, showing up to a function particularly well dressed would solicit similar praise as a married woman's clothing (the type of cloth, style) can represent the wealth and status of her husband.

Njékke, Mag, Jabar (Female In-Laws, Elders, Wives)

When it came time for the wedding gift exchanges, Jéynaba joined the *géwëlu juddu* (family griot) of the in-laws in the géew. Like many ceremonies, the géew was a temporary space of a tent spanning a small side street in front of the family's home with chairs set up and moved to create a loose circle for the ceremonial activities. Most géew feature the women of the two families sitting facing one another in the front section of the circle. Nonessential guests, such as neighbors and friends, are audience members sitting at the periphery. "This mother has sacrificed everything, and with the help of God, this is the result," the géwëlu juddu shouted to the attentive wedding guests around her as she transferred a gift from a guest to the mother and host. The overflowing sea of friends at the woman's daughter's wedding was a show of support by her peers, effectively representing all of the hard work the mother had put into securing a future for her daughter on the back of her own reputation, which had been years in the making. As host of her daughter's wedding, the mother was in effect reaping the benefits of her years of social visiting, contributions to friends' and family's ceremonies, and kindness in the form of gifts and cash. The géwëlu juddu spoke highly of the mother, reiterating that the daughter would never have been in a position of marriage if not for the years of her mother's hosting, visiting, and generosity of time and resources. Women's hard work over years—saving, organizing, and establishing themselves as respectable through various day-to-day performances of teraanga—comes to fruition during ceremonies. The various géwël, who also served as advisers, consulted with the mothers on how to proceed with the infamous *joxalante teraanga* (Sall 2010), a back-and-forth of gifting and reciprocity originating from the warugar (obligation or material promise) and ndawtal contributions given to the woman and her family by the groom's sisters and aunts. For this family, there was a dowry of 500,000 CFA ($1,000).

In strategizing with Jéynaba, they began the process of presenting gifts to the groom's family. Suitcases full of cloth, gold jewelry, kitchen utensils, buckets for laundry, and cooking materials were dropped into the laps of the bride's family. The exchange of teraanga continued with the mother of the groom and his sisters or close female relatives or friends. The *premier njékke* is the most honored and is given teraanga that can equal amounts of 50,000–100,000 CFA ($100–200) plus cloth. Jéynaba yelled out with stylistic enthusiasm, "Njég, may na fukki junni premier njékke, six-yard wax, xartum, gis nga lii? [The mother gave the premier njékke 50,000 CFA, six yards of wax fabric, and xartum fabric, did you see this?]" She handed it off to the géwël, who relayed the message and passed it along to the premier njékke (the most important njékke), saying to the mother of the groom, "Laay-layla-laa, xoolal teraanga bii? [My God, did you see the amount of teraanga/gifts she is giving?]" Next was the *deuxième njékke*, the second in line of sisters or important female family members, who was given equal money and four yards of wax fabric and *ganila* fabric, the stiff batik-dyed cloth from Mali. Many ceremonies such as this one in Medina have a *groupu njékke*, a group of residual female relatives or friends who are brought into the gift exchange fold to ensure no one is left out.

Njékke, the term given to a woman of the groom's family, is recognized during ceremonies and given gifts to reinforce her importance. Historically, the njékke was the married older sister of the husband and was also symbolically considered the *jabar* (wife) to her new sister-in-law throughout the marriage to her brother. This position allowed the sister-in-law a way for her to act as a confidante and marriage mentor to her new sister-in-law in case of marital issues or to offer general knowledge of how to manage the household. Often, the firstborn female child is named after a woman's njékke, who becomes the child's godparent, watching out for them. As part of her role of mentoring her sister-in-law, the njékke provides advice about the intimate aspects of the husband and wife relationship, revealing house secrets to the wife about satisfying her husband and creating a universe of intimacy. This universe includes a welcoming home environment that is visually beautiful and stimulating, with a pervading smell of incense and special clothing and undergarments intended for her husband's eyes only, as we saw in Titi's music video.

The mentoring role of the njékke has become more symbolic than practical and is now easily bestowed on a friend or rich female cousin instead of the groom's married sister. In some cases, Jéynaba told me, the njékke is even an unmarried friend, casting doubt on the ability to give the wife any educated mentoring about marriage, sexuality, or marital conflict resolution. Instead, the honor is given to a woman, perhaps a politician, whom the family feels can provide financial assistance and prestige to the family and future children. Although the njékke are given gifts and cash at the wedding, at the naming ceremony of the first child, the woman will reciprocate with even larger sums of money and gifts, and the njékke will also provide gifts as the symbolic guardian of the child and to reaffirm allegiance to the mother. When I asked about the relationship between a woman and her female in-laws, Jéynaba spoke to the phenomenon of urban families that no longer live with one another and its effects on the symbolism and materiality of gifting to social relationships.

> The married older sister of the husband [njékke] then and now is not the same thing. You know before it was the grandparents who chose the female family member. And they respected them. We would wash the clothes for our sisters-in-law or mother, cook for them, do nice things for them because we didn't want them to be angry. If they are angry, we say that in the future our children will not be good people. That is what our culture says. But now, if we have money we give it to our sisters-in-law or our husband's younger brothers because we don't want them to be involved in our family issues. Before, if you were leaving your mother's house [to live with the husband's family] they would lay out a mat and give you advice. Your father's sister, your father, and your mother's brother would tell you, "If your husband says to cook him something, then cook him something tasty. You must care for your husband's family, respect them. Whatever they want, you should want." Your mother will say, "Once you go to your husband's home, don't come back here." That is just an expression because wherever your mother is you will go. It's advice for when you go live with them that you get along. Before, this was taken seriously. But now there are a lot of changes. Now what you see is every youth goes to live with their partner alone, in their own apartment. That is why you see so much divorce. Because they go and live in their own apartment and the elders are no longer there to [tell] your husband, "We told you to bring her here but not to mistreat her. You have a wife now; you shouldn't be out

wandering around." You know, advice. Or if you want to go out, they will tell you to wait for your husband. But now they want freedom, what they own is theirs, which is why they prefer to have their own apartment.[8]

Jéynaba laments the shift in priorities of a new modern generation that wishes to live independently from the larger extended family. She expresses grievances that this generation, in their quest for greater independence (financial, domestic, and otherwise), have replaced the quotidian labor for the family that Jéynaba describes with monetary gifts. These prestations allow married couples to form their lives independent from the meddling of their families, which Jéynaba believes leads to greater divorce rates as the couples no longer have their elders to help counsel them through arguments and to remind them of their duties to one another as well as the larger family.

Ungrateful Daughters: Generational Rifts Regarding Teraanga

The wedding in Medina went so late that most guests lost interest after the food was given out, and they returned home. Following the exchange of gifts, Jéynaba and the bride's family and other géwëls packed into a small room of the house for the *yebbi* (cataloging of gifts), to add up the amounts of cloth, buckets, and money they had left to give out to the *bàjjen yi* (paternal aunts), the *groupu njékke* (group of female relatives), the father of the groom, and his brothers. Despite it being late the various géwëls were urging the young bride to pay attention and respect the process of providing gifts to everyone in her husband's family. Her body language suggested a lack of interest, confirming gripes I had heard from elder women that the younger generation was increasingly impatient with the presence of géwëls at ceremonies and felt they had no place.

The bride was tired and wished to finish this step and move on as she still had to be transported to her husband's apartment, where they would live together, just the two of them. The fact that she would not be living with her family-in-law made the exchanges during the wedding that much more important. It would set the tone for her relationship with her extended family. She had slumped into a chair; her once stiff fabric dress had loosened and was equally droopy. She became agitated and asked several times if they were finished.

"Il faut nga practiquer jànq. Naka ngay mëna muñe ci sa séy bi? [You must practice being a young lady. How are you going to survive your marriage if you can't learn patience?]" her aunt said.

"Dama sonn te kenn mënula wax ne mayewuma, may du force [I'm tired, and no one can say I didn't give enough. Giving is not an obligation]," the bride retorted.

Her aunt snapped back, saying, "Teraanga, kenn du ko xëcco [No one can force teraanga]." And the bride stormed off. *Xëcco* means to tug something or someone, to fight over it, or taken without regard for whether it is deserved or not. Negating xëcco (the *morpheme-du*) therefore instructs us that teraanga cannot be simply given or claimed but is dependent upon the personal qualities of the receiver, who is bestowed with teraanga because they are perceived as friendly and generous and have honorable qualities, or their parents were well known for these qualities. Denying the reception and acknowledgment of teraanga given was to negate the giver themselves. Disappointment in the young bride's disregard for the importance of the intention embedded in teraanga is a sign of frustration with her lack of appreciation for custom and privileging her own needs over those of the collective. Jéynaba and another family géwël complained in frustration about the young bride's behavior: "Su jàngul muñ te xam ne *teraanga* lepp la, seyam du yàgg, te leegi mu dellu këru pàppam [If she doesn't learn patience or that teraanga is everything, her marriage won't last, and she is going to be returning to her father's home soon]," insinuating that the marriage would end in divorce because the girl would not have the skills to overcome impatience or exercise *kersa* (discretion) if she only mouthed off in disapproval. *Muñ*, the ability to remain stoic, self-composed, and uncomplaining in the face of challenges (Hannaford and Foley 2015) as well as *kersa*, discretion and deference to elders, are two more Wolof virtues in moments particularly emphasized by and about women. Without patience and discretion, the bride would crumble in the face of obligations to her family-in-law and therefore put her marriage at risk.

These examples show the generational fractures regarding the relevance of teraanga to women's positions within families and communities. Although these obligations can seem oppressive at times, especially for younger women, they are a holistic part of growing up within Senegalese society.

Conclusion

Jéynaba's comments I overheard during the funeral highlight how lives are made up of the mundane and significant instances of teraanga. The wedding of a young woman who struggles to grasp this reality delineates new generational challenges to the dominance of relationships based on teraanga. Jéynaba's experience with a reticent newlywed and the funeral of a reputable woman demonstrate that the social rules of reciprocity place a great deal of onus on married women to work within a political economy of teraanga in order to ensure the stability of their family life. It is complex because reputation depends on the giving and receiving of teraanga, yet, as we have seen with the young bride, the symbolic distinction of how teraanga is given also matters a great deal. In the case of the elder woman whose funeral we attended, her legacy of teraanga, cultivated over time, meant she had a community of people who recognized her goodness. The young bride's dismissal of teraanga could complicate not only the intimate aspects of her marriage but also her membership among her family-in-law that was bound by the exchanges during her wedding, and would continue throughout her marriage.

The commercialization of Wolof values such as teraanga and jongé and newly emphasized links between femininity and *bien travailler*—caring for the family—have both added to the expectations of women to be good wives, daughters-in-law, and mothers and allowed for new strategies. In modern urban spaces such as Dakar where families are physically separated, women must find creative—and sometimes excessive—ways to maintain the harmony of their relationships. Although daily instances of teraanga are crucial to this process, family ceremonies controlled by women offer the most visible and pronounced way to pay back social debts, establish new ones, and link women to their greater social network. This is the reality that the majority of Senegalese women live, including women in positions of power. The examples from this chapter have served to lay a conceptual foundation for the centrality of teraanga in its many forms to understand the social realities from which women in politics source their authority.

2

Sénégalaisement and the Politics of Personality

In the introduction, I presented a snapshot of several ways that teraanga is present in women's lives, and in chapter 1, I focused on the processes in which teraanga becomes gendered and tied to women's private conduct. In this chapter, I dive into the many forms teraanga takes that reflect women's negotiations of authority in their daily lives and into public politics. During an interview with then newly elected representative Aysata Tall Sall in 2017, she shared with me an illustrative point: "There are women in politics, there are African women in politics, and then there are Senegalese women in politics. Regarding all three, I think we have a lot to say." As Aysata astutely stated, it is not sufficient to talk about women in politics or African women in politics without speaking of the particularities of Senegalese women in and out of politics. And in order to understand how teraanga is instrumentalized in women's political pursuits, it is crucial to first explore the ways teraanga is negotiated and instrumentalized in everyday life. In this chapter, I provide stories that contextualize the different factors that make a modern Senegalese woman in order to also appreciate the political strategies they employ. We begin with the example of Ndey Sukkey Géy, director of the Family Affairs Office of the Ministry of Women's Affairs at the time I met her in 2010. She told me this story:

> A representative of President Abdoulaye Wade called me to say that the president wanted me to go to New York City for the annual United Nations conference on women, and I was supposed to be the official representative of Senegal. I was shocked when they only offered four of us to go. So, I asked for an audience with the president to ask for more women to represent Senegal, especially because we are the Land of Teraanga. I showed up at the

presidential palace with a large group of women and said that if we were going to go to New York, we needed to do it sénégalaisement or not go at all. We must go and go big. He agreed. When we took the stage there was a look of joy on [UN members'] faces, and everyone applauded. We were so beautiful up there with our traditional *yére* Wolof [typical Wolof clothing made from local fabrics], we were *sañse* [dressed to impress]. Everyone listened to what we had to say. When we came back from New York, the president asked us all to come to see him. He was so pleased with our representation that he said he wanted to honor [*teral*] us and handed us an envelope full of money. Money is how Senegalese people show appreciation for one another.[1]

I first met Ndey Sukkey at her Family Affairs Office as part of her work regarding the government's efforts to curb ostentatious spending during ceremonies. So, when I met her at her home again in 2017—during my research trip to document the legislative campaigns—I wanted to follow up on the topic of family ceremonies but was also curious about her campaign for mayor of her cité in Géjawaay. The story she tells here is significant in two ways: she points to a specific subjectivity that she calls sénégalaisement, or Senegalese style, a way of doing politics based on local values of beauty and notions of power; and second, the role of money as an important way of honoring social ties.

Sénégalaisement

According to Ndey, sénégalaisement meant going to the United Nations meeting with a large group of well-dressed women in their vibrant, locally dyed and tailored clothing and taking command of the stage with inviting beauty and swift rhetoric. The ways I often heard sénégalaisement pronounced seemed to refer to an active way of being Senegalese *in the feminine*.[2] People would say, "Xam nga, sénégalaisement rekk [You know, Senegalese style]" when responding to a compliment about their outfit or a friendly gesture followed by a note of thanks. Social media platforms show countless daily postings of dressed-up women and men with the hashtag #sénégalaisement. Oftentimes the term is thought of as "Senegalese fashion," both in the sense of clothing and makeup trends and in a shared sense of what it means to be Senegalese through action. Dress, cloth, jewelry, and showing off wealth and status are only part of the dialectical nature of those operating within the Teraanga Republic. Luxurious clothing and prestige are accompanied by public displays of generosity and pointed discourse that communicates one's knowledge of genealogy and historical ties to others. In Deborah Heath's analysis of *sañse* (dressing up), dress is "inflected by accents of identity and difference such as 'tradition' and 'modernity,' religious devotion and heterodoxy" (1992). In all instances, dress is a form of communication (Andrewes 2005), an expression of personal identity as well as a tool to communicate their desires to others.

Political oratory as well as everyday speech acts play a crucial role, as does personal representation through dress. The importance of a discussion on dress is that it is one of the most visual markers of difference (social and economic status as well as ethnic and cultural), affiliation, and identity. In politics, dress is a gateway for women to gain traction in a male-dominated arena. Female politicians in Senegal, just as in Nigeria, use calculated beauty and elaborate dress to create charismatic personas (Weber 1968), demonstrate their "feminine arts" (Bastian 2013), and navigate the political system. Writing about the importance of dress and politics to a female politician in Nigeria, Bastian notes, "A woman hoping to demonstrate her mastery of feminine skills would never be caught in anything but a contained and controlled state of dress." In Senegal, dress is also a communication of teraanga, signaling the gifts of cloth and dresses a woman most likely received during a ceremony. Just as we saw in chapter 1, the cloth received is then turned into a dress that then is a physical manifestation of the gift and honor received and the relationship cultivated in the process. Women's armoires are filled with cloth and dresses, and it is common for them to give them away to friends and visitors as a show of solidarity. Many of the yére Wolof I own are gifts I received upon visiting a friend or politician.

Therefore, through physical manifestations of dress and specific rhetoric, sénégalaisement meant a political and social genealogy tracking the ways Ndey Sukkey had created and nurtured such a group of dedicated women to follow her lead, as well as the power to command the president's attention. We will continue to see throughout the book the different ways women use dress and speech to negotiate political identities.

Sénégalaisement has elsewhere been theorized as "vivre sénégalaisement" to describe particularly Senegalese "ways of getting by, or the art of making do without, or struggling along" (Coulon and Cruise O'Brien 1989), what others have called "se débrouiller" (Simioni 2019), or "manière de faire" (Coulon 1992, 7), innovation in the wake of economic crises or a lack of state support for social security. Vivre sénégalaisement has been understood in the context of poverty and changing ideas of love and marital strategies (Van Eerdewijk 2007). Senegal's postcolonial nation builders favored a style of governance modeled on traditional and patriarchal African culture and social structures (Cruise O'Brien, Diop, and Diouf 2002). Thus they emphasized domestic life, with the mother as the guardian of the home. This social structure was also a remnant of colonial policy, which monetized men's labor in new ways, focusing their work outside the home and leaving the majority of women's labor tied to the home (Sall 2010). The everyday exchanges of teraanga in instances of hospitality, family ceremonies, and socializing—phenomena that had typically been directed by women to assert considerable power among the patronage operations of the king or the more modern-day politician—were then confined to a representative role for men's honor and wealth at such events (Diaw 2004). The popular cartoon turned television series entitled *Góorgóorlu* (to be a man, to make do) demonstrates ways in which "se débrouiller" is gendered. As Simioni (2019) depicts, the original sense of the term *góorgóorlu* simply meant to be a man while the modern conceptions of masculinity require men to be providers. The term is now more associated with hard work and pulling oneself up by the bootstraps in the service of one's family. The main character, Góorgóorlu, is therefore depicted as a master at navigating the political and socioeconomic difficulties of society as he weaves in and out of the family compound, finding creative ways to make a quick buck. His wife, Diek,[3] covers for him when he fails, "finding food thanks to her cleaver ways" (210), solutions available to her in ways her husband cannot access. The clever ways speak to both *lijjanti* (se débrouiller, or quest for solutions) and the feminine tricks of *feem*, discussed in the previous chapter. Góorgóorlu is a representation of the contrasting ways that structural adjustment programs affected men and women and the gendered conflicts that arose within families. And as Seck (2018) calls him the "neoliberal *homo senegalensis*," she notes that "his role as breadwinner is at the core of his gendered identity" (263). In a televised episode from Radio Télévision Sénégalais and reproduced on YouTube (2021), Góorgóorlu is seen worrying about how to pay for the family's daily expenses when a local politician greets him asking for campaign donations. Góorgóorlu refuses with an air of disgust, citing a tight budget. Upon returning home, Diek presents him with a substantial wad of cash saying she would be unavailable for a few days because of duties to her associational and religious groups. The money, she says, is for Góorgóorlu to go to the market and purchase the necessary goods to cook lunch for the family in her absence. Furious, he tells her that that is her job. Cutting to the next scene, Góorgóorlu is laid out on a mat visibly content, while a young woman with a baby on her back is seen doing the chores Diek tasked him with. When Diek returns and asks who the woman is, he indignantly says that a woman's place is in the home cooking and cleaning. The irony is that while Góorgóorlu uses the money that we assume Diek received from her associational money pooling to pay another woman, he remains stagnant, unemployed, and generally useless, yet insists on his authority as the *boroom kër*, or man of the house.

This assumption I make as the reader is part of what Seck (2022) argues is both "reading between the lines or between the frames" (296) in the case of the comic strip white space for the representation of women's strategies and financial contributions to domestic spaces. Both in art and in life, their contributions have often remained silent yet fundamental, aligning with the culture of *sutura* (discretion).

Ndey Sukkey's story about the UN demonstrates women's visible and invisible representations of the state on one of the biggest stages in world politics, which also reflects their visibility back at home. Although thinking of sénégalaisement as mostly a survival technique during times of hardship may be useful—the term has certainly been employed thus—the women in this book challenge the notion of struggling along by showing how they cultivate authentically Senegalese feminine qualities to thrive and demonstrate authority. It is true that women's efforts to make money through development-funded programs or neighborhood associations has long been a strategy for weathering tough economic times; however, for women in politics, what have been understood as survival techniques through an appropriation of certain feminine material cultures are turned into political opportunities and strategies.

In the last chapter, we saw the intricate ways teraanga is performed during family ceremonies as an accumulation of particularly femininized social labor within women's marriages. In this chapter, I explore the ways in which women "ingeniously and imaginatively draw on notions of female virtue to lend moral weight to their activities outside the household" (Schulz 2012, 53). This chapter begins the process of understanding the historical connections that have made new forms of women's authority possible. Through examples from Ndey Sukkey Géy and a young journalist and her aunt who speak about the complex relationships with their families-in-law, we begin to see the emerging connections between women's private negotiations and new forms of authority making and the possibilities for doing politics sénégalaisement. This chapter also examines the debates about democracy and modern governance that stem from women's practices and discourses of family ceremonies and teraanga. The dramatic socioeconomic changes in Senegal are reflected in gift exchanges in interesting ways, including how people understand government and social organization.

"Money Cures Shame"

The second component of Ndey Sukkey's story of the UN is President Abdoulaye Wade's gift of money upon the delegates' return. It is fair to say that Wade was known and often criticized for giving money freely to basketball or football teams when they won important medals or to a Senegalese child who won the highest distinction for reciting the Qur'an during his presidency. Although many disapproved, he was also understood to be offering praise for their accomplishments in a way that most Senegalese are accustomed to do. Ndey Sukkey said it herself: money is how Senegalese people show appreciation for one another. In these instances, giving money during a ceremony or as a token of recognition and honor is called teraanga by many to symbolize a larger connection than a simple economic exchange. There are other ways of demonstrating the potency of money. There is a saying in Wolof—"xaalis moo faj gàcce," which means that money cures shame, shame being a very potent aspect of Wolof culture that is both avoided and engaged for social success (Ngom 2016) and respect (Buggenhagen 2012). The gifting of money is thus used as a preventative measure to ensure that shame does not befall oneself, and withholding money or flaunting it can be used to shame those who are envious. Money can serve as a positive way to express solidarity, and it can also demonstrate power and competition.

Senegalese society is run on social debt that is highly monetized. Ismael Moya argues that in Dakar especially, "there is no domain in social life in which money does not play a continuous role. Money is central to the economy as well as matrimonial and kinship relations, politics, or religious practice" (2015, 156). Because of the centrality of money to all social relations, people are always indebted to one person or another as they nurture their network of friends and family members. It is used to demonstrate affiliation, to honor others, and to assert power. Discussions about money are a dime a dozen. People talk about how money is to be given away to help others and should never stay in one's hands too long. Everyday conversations, religious sermons, and formal gatherings take on critiques of the dangers of money in society, and proverbs such as xaalis moo faj gàcce point to money's importance as a social regulator. Ceremonies and women's participation in them are an easy target due to their flagrant displays of exchange that to many mark a modern conundrum of participating in a capitalist economy in which one's resources are their own and the social realities that obligate the sharing of resources and the tensions that arise. Ndey Sukkey demonstrated these tensions during our interview, where she reflected on the changes to her relationships with her family-in-law.

> Women are tired in this country. Only God knows that she spends so much money, and she can be repudiated by her husband two days later. Her sisters-in-law can take advantage of their problems and make sure their brother divorces his wife. . . . For me, it was my mother-in-law (goro) who made my life difficult. You can't even imagine. In front of everyone, she yelled at me,

and I had agreed to go join my husband and live in her home. . . . The social norm that requires us to give presents to our sister-in-law, mother-in-law, father-in-law, and our husband's friends has existed until now, but it was not based on money. Money was only for the transportation [it is customary to pay for guests' trips home from a social visit or ceremony]. . . . Now we call it *fóot* [items for the home]. The fóot existed before but not to this level because the sister-in-law is obligated to bring soap, powder, perfume, and voilà. She could even add a little money. . . . Now what do you see? Suitcases, gold jewelry. We are now at a point where the mother-in-law even brings furniture. She brings gold. Where did she find all the money for this? That is the fundamental question.[4]

In Mariama Bâ's famous novel *So Long a Letter* (1979), she offers a stinging critique of the role family ceremonies play in limiting women's options for self-autonomy by becoming servants to their families-in-law, equating the gifting of women's material items to a loss in personal pride. She notes that family ceremonies are "the moment dreaded by every Senegalese woman, the moment when she sacrifices her possessions as gifts to her family-in-law; and, worst still, beyond her possessions she gives up her personality, her dignity, becoming a servant to her husband's family, his grandparents, his father, his mother, his elder and younger siblings, his uncle, his aunt, his male and female cousins. Everyone he knows, even his friends. Everything she owns, even her own actions are given away. No sister-in-law will touch the head of any wife who has been stingy, unfaithful, or inhospitable."[5] I heard similar frustrations from many women who felt helpless to refuse to contribute their hard-earned wealth in instances of ceremonies for fear of refusal from their families-in-law, despite their own financial difficulties. Therein lies the proverb. Giving gifts or money prevents the terror of shame, but not always, as we will see later in the chapter.

Ndey Sukkey gave another example of how money can also be mobilized, creating new spaces for women. She told me about going on the offensive, using teraanga to assert her authority and shame her mother-in-law as payback for her mistreatment over the years. She is crafty about it and is careful to remain within the parameters of the Wolof concept of *sutura*—discretion, modesty, and privacy (Mills 2011)—by choosing the right moment, private space, and indirect communication style. This demonstrates an important aspect of the sénégalaisement strategy: knowing how to use everyday obligations and power dynamics to carve out a space of one's own power. As a woman of means and education, Ndey Sukkey is able to push back. Once her political career took hold, she gained the social and economic capital to effectively assert authority over her mother-in-law. She told the story of conflicts with her mother-in-law and her use of teraanga to expose this exploitation.

> One day, there was no one in the house. I was the one cleaning her room, lighting incense. I closed and locked the door. "Sit down," I said. "For how long have you been mistreating me? It's been more than ten years. Have you seen me die? I am not blind; I did not go crazy. Did you think you would see something in me? You are lucky. You and your son are lucky. I could show them [the letter], but when I see my husband I adore you. I'll tell you something: I will never leave this house as long as I am living. I see you going to these marabouts. All my grandfathers are marabouts; I can do the same to you. Just wait and see what will happen. I can show you what I'm made of." And she lost it. She cried out, "Aahh ehh," and when my husband came in she told him, "Ndey Sukkey did this to me, she told me, 'You will see.'" My husband told her, "She's right to do so. Why do you give her grief?" The next day, I went to the market; it also happened to be *tabaski* [celebration of the birth of the Prophet Muhammad]. I bought her a suitcase full of clothes, all the things she liked. I bought her powder and other makeup. I bought gold jewelry. I had just returned from a work trip, and they had paid me, so I put the suitcase on my head, singing and dancing. When I arrived, her daughter had just come from Thies, and I took that suitcase and danced and sang my mother-in-law's praises. I set the suitcase down in front of her, hugged her, and she screamed, "Eh eh eh" and cried. My husband was crying too. His sister came out and told her mother, "You are ashamed today."[6]

As Ndey Sukkey recounted the part of the story about singing and dancing in front of her mother-in-law, she grinned and laughed with a kind of mischievous pride. This theatrical moment mimics the gift giving during ceremonies we saw in chapter 1 in which the géwël parades around the gift-giving circle (géew) flashing gifts before handing them over to the mother of the ceremony. After ten years of being treated as a housemaid in her husband's family home, Ndey Sukkey had been hired as director of family affairs, a position that afforded her access to new resources that she used to shame her mother-in-law. Ndey also told me that if you are someone without a strong personality, you risk leaving your husband because the situation is too difficult. Her reference to a strong personality is significant given that many women in politics are said to be of strong character and personality. The importance of shame in Wolof society cannot be overstated as a means of social regulation and power. "Money cures shame" references the role of money gifted to others as a preventative measure against personal and familial shame. Moreover, money is a central way of showing affection and affiliation, and it is important to maintain relationships and prevent issues of resentment in its absence. In this case the use of money to shame someone is also a potent way to indirectly address injustices felt. Although her actions seem unsubtle, Ndey was careful not to threaten the material livelihood of her mother-in-law nor her standing with her. In fact, at the same time as she was shaming her mother-in-law, she was also assuring that the family would be taken care of, even if she was asserting dominance.

The Art of Subtle Dominance

In her anecdote, Ndey Sukkey referred to rumors about her mother-in-law seeking intervention from marabouts, or occult practitioners—a common but often secretive exercise for a range of desired outcomes, including to receive a positive result when applying for a visa to travel internationally or to help resolve family problems. However, it can also be used for more nefarious purposes, such as inducing infertility in a co-wife in the case of a polygamous marriage or, as Ndey Sukkey hinted at, a mother-in-law who wishes harm upon her or for her to divorce her son. Through prestations of her mother-in-law's favorite items, she is able to flaunt her new economic status and publicly shame her mother-in-law for years of hardship. The excess of money spent and material items presented in the style of *taasu*, a "satirico-laudatory" praise song female panegyric genre practiced by Wolof women (Gueye 2011, 66), mostly reserved for celebrating the kindness and generosity of an individual while also communicating shrouded criticism (*gaaruwaale*), was a way of mocking her mother-in-law for her own lack of teraanga—that is, years of cultivating an unwelcoming environment for Ndey Sukkey in her home. Lisa McNee (2000), who writes about taasu as a style of autobiography for women in particular, believes taasu is a political act of "inserting the 'self' within a historical and social framework" (79). This can be applied both in the case of Ndey Sukkey performing power in her private life to resist oppression and using laudatory praises on the public political stage as a way of resisting exclusion and making themselves seen and relevant in a particularly Senegalese way—a subtle and yet theatrical way that communicates with two different audiences: the global where her beautiful clothing is appreciated as authentically African and the local, which communicates social norms and the teraanga that made her status possible.

Ndey Sukkey's story weaves connections between private forms of power within family dynamics and public sources of authority. The emergence of a political economy of teraanga and its reproduction in women's strategies for political authority is played out daily in marriages, family dynamics, and women and

Samba Fall cartoon depicting the dividing of the ndawtal given to the mother [Here is the mother's part, dignified for a woman of your stature. 500,000 CFA that she must reimburse, +12 bethio (cloth), +12 dial diali (waistbeads), +12 nightshirts + nightgowns +12 bath towels +12 . . .]. Appeared in *Le Soleil* newspaper, date unknown.

men's negotiation of gendered identities, as we saw in chapter 1. Ndey Sukkey's inversion of daily exploitations within her marriage into power moves were examples I heard often. These examples speak to the hierarchical differences women are subject to depending on age, class, and even caste. Ndey Sukkey was able to confront her mother-in-law not only due to her new political position but also because this wealth and status came about after years of suffering in silence as a young and newly married woman of inferior status. Moreover, it is important to add an extra category to Aysata Tall Sall's list of female experience that considers age and class as part of a distinctive woman's gaze. In the next sections, I present the personal experiences of a young journalist named Aysatu Laye as well as the stories she reports that speak to the sticky realities of family relationships and young women's struggles for authority within them.

Money Troubles

"C'est comme une loi, mais binduñu ko fenn [It's like a law, but it's not written anywhere]," said Aysatu Laye, referring to the complex exchanges before and during a family ceremony. She shared another example of gaaruwaale and the level of power money has for women's status as Ndey Sukkey had done.

> My friend you met, Alimatou, when her younger sister Penda got married, she went to live with her in-laws. Their family was wealthy. When she arrived at the home, they were celebrating the naming ceremony of a sister-in-law's new baby. She gave them 3 million CFA [$5,000]. That is how Penda honored her family-in-law. Another sister-in-law, when she showed up, you want to know how much she gave? Seven million CFA [$12,000].[7] The mother-in-law got up to say that "I don't have any bad daughters-in-law, but I thank this one"— the daughter-in-law who gave the 7 million CFA. Even though just a year prior, Penda had given her 3 million, which she said was a small amount.

Gaaruwaale is or a speech form "whose real addressee is not the one the speaker seems to be addressing" (Gueye 2011, 67) and is intended to make a critical remark toward a listening party or as a form of gossip. I remarked to Aysatu, "Alimatou sax ne na ma, dafa fekk ràkkam Penda doon sàcc ay perle ngir mën leen jaay ba am lu muy joxe [Alimatou told me her younger sister Penda had been caught stealing pearls in order to give the amount that she did]."

"Voilà," said Aysatu, "trois millions la ko jox ak dëkk bi ni mu mettee. Dafa metti de. C'est très dur pour les femmes [Exactly—she gave three million ($5,000) despite the poor economic conditions in the country. It's tough. It is really difficult for women]."

Aysatu's aunt Uley added that "boo gisee nit ñi di joxe teraanga, dañu bañ seeni goro di leen xas wàlla mu yàq seen diggànte ak seeni jëkkër [When you see people giving teraanga, it's because they don't want their *goro* to criticize you or ruin your relationship with their husband]." Aysatu's aunt Uley told a plethora of stories of women's struggles and pressures to keep up and be good wives and good daughters by giving teraanga. They welcomed me into their home, and we sat comfortably on Aysatu's bed as she tended to her small baby girl.

I first met Aysatu after I read an article she wrote for a local commentary magazine, *La Gazette*. I was so intrigued that I wanted to meet the author. She was tickled I was interested. The article was entitled "The *gas'pillage'* in Family Ceremonies: A Social Phenomenon That Extracts from Senegalese Daily

Expenses"[8] (Laye 2009). The title is meant to be ironic, taking the French word *gaspillage* (wastefulness) but isolating *pillage*, the French word meaning to pillage or steal, pegging ceremonies as places where money is wasted and stolen. In popular discourse the financial investments made by women of all classes for these occasions are often referred to as wasteful spending, or gaspillage. The movement Lutte Contre le Gaspillage comes from this term, and the debate about gaspillage is usually spurred by the state or development groups who say that women's careless ostentation harms families' prospects of economic and social progress. At the time Aysatu wrote the article, she was under the same impression.

Aysatu's article tells the unfortunate story of Habib, a man she interviewed along with others, who lived in central Dakar. Quoting from her article: "Habib's sister Amy had diminishing hope of finding a husband," marriage being an aspiration most Senegalese women share. "As a local socialite, however, Amy had amassed a great amount of investment in her peers' ceremonies, and a ceremony of her own would be the sole way to recuperate that money. With dwindling prospects of her own marriage, she decided to use her unemployed brother Habib to marry Astou, a girl from the outskirts of Dakar." Had Amy married, the women she invested in would be obliged to reciprocate, and Amy would reap the benefits of her investments, double or triple the original amounts. Instead, she used her brother's wedding as a surrogate.

Aysatu told me that Amy and her friends took a sum of 500,000 CFA ($1,000) to Habib's future sister-in-law Ndey Mbaye, who explained the process of dividing up the sum for the ceremony and the portion to be given to each of her friends and female relatives as an interest-bearing loan. She gave each 500 CFA ($1) before the wedding and expected ten times the amount ($10) at the time of the naming ceremony, which could occur nine months after the wedding. When Aysatu asked Ndey Mbaye why it was done this way, she replied, "We found it here; it has always been this way. It is our culture." At this, Aysatu wrote with indignation, "Culture, or swindling?" (Laye 2009). Throughout the article Aysatu, a single woman at the time, showed her disapproval of the system of ceremonies and women's obligations to their female in-laws, saying, "Amy spends 500,000 CFA for her brother's marriage and yet refuses to pay for her sister-in-law's medical bills when she falls ill," highlighting the irony of the situation. Aysatu's article highlighted the conspicuous consumption of obligatory gift giving at family ceremonies in the name of honor and what she argued was its destructiveness to women's emancipation and social solidarity. At the time, Aysatu was outspoken against these practices, disapproving of the pressure young people felt to keep up with the demands of conducting their marriages as their parents had.

"Senegalese Society Is Large": Teraanga as Social Cohesion

"Xam nga article boobu? [You know that article?]" Aysatu asked during our interview, in her aunt's bedroom. "Sama bàjjen Uley moom laa daan laaj ci terminologie [My aunt Uley is the one I had to ask about all the terminology]," she said, referring to the complex Wolof terms for the wide array of women's roles within the ceremony and the assigned gifts given to them. Uley retorted, looking straight at me, "Moom, moo la yées, xamu ci dara [She's just as bad as you are, doesn't know anything about it]." We laughed at the comparison between me as the *Tuubaab* (foreigner) and Aysatu as the member of a younger generation that had yet to learn all the nuances of exchange and marriage. Bajjen (Aysatu's father's sister) was an important family member who transmitted the knowledge Uley jokingly said Aysatu was ignorant of. They were mentors to their young nieces, giving them advice about sexuality, marriage, and navigating these complex gift exchanges. At that time, that was why she wrote critically about these practices of family ceremonies, the amounts of money required, and the financial and emotional toll they could take on families. As an unmarried woman, Aysatu did not hide her dislike for the practices. But when we met for the interview at her house three years after our first encounter, her tone had changed. I learned she had married her Senegalese boyfriend, who had studied in England, and they had a young daughter together who was cooing contentedly during our conversation. "But if you look at it from the perspective of the mother, her son is all she has. And she worked hard for him. She pays for his schooling, and it is not guaranteed he will have a wife. So, when God provides him an opportunity to get married, the things he used to provide for his mother are now for his wife. He takes care of her needs, and all the mother gets is money once a month. That is all she gets from her son. So, the day of the ceremony is the only chance he gets to reimburse her,"[9] Aysatu says and giggles, signaling she's not a fan of the term *remboursement* but can't think of a better word. Buggenhagen (2012) refers to this reciprocity as ways in which women "ensure a replacement that forms the basis of future wealth and lineage continuity" (31). In cities like Dakar, many women no longer live with their husbands' families. Instead, they share an apartment with their husband and children. Therefore, in the absence of a wife's labor and care in the husband's home, as well as the loss of a son's labor and finances, women perform teraanga by bringing food supplies to the family-in-law's home on regular visits or, if the distance is not too great, portioning the daily lunch to be sent to the family home. Giving teraanga can also take the shape of sending phone credits or money transfers to family members to provide help and show affection. A woman represents her husband's wealth and honor through these performances as a way of sharing his wealth with his family in his absence while also creating a specific reputation as generous and social.

Despite her criticism of ceremonies and what she saw as the distorted role of teraanga, Aysatu acknowledged their importance to the ongoing wellness of relationships, speaking specifically about the relationship that a wife has with her female in-laws as part of the reimbursement for the hard work sisters and mothers put into caring for the boys and men in their family.

> We are always with and grow up with our close ones, our brothers, we care a great deal for them, and we help each other. Like, you are sitting somewhere with your brothers, and they say, "I don't have a cigarette," or they ask for 100 francs, or they ask you to buy them a shirt, or they say, "My girlfriend is coming over," and they want you to prepare them some juice. So, you grow up together like this, and one day, when he has a wife, it would be ideal that she integrates into the family, to know that they are together and share.[10]

In this sense, the small daily sacrifices that a woman makes for her brothers can be paid back through the teraanga given by the brother's wife acting partly as an extension of his wealth and gratitude to his sisters, demonstrating her affection to her new family. In this respect, as Aysatu says, "Amul dara lu graw ci loolu [There is nothing bad about that]," meaning that these prestations are not only harmless but necessary for social cohesion. However, as Uley chimes in, "Booba ci les années soixante, c'était pas grave. Melulwoon comme leegi dafa lay indil problème, dangay wuti par force [In the 1960s it wasn't so bad. It wasn't like it is now, where it causes you problems and you are forced to find solutions]." Finding solutions (lijjanti) seemed like a particularly Senegalese specialty where everyone was always borrowing from someone else to pay another back. Most of the women I spoke with agreed that ceremonies were crucial to the maintenance of established relationships—such as close family members—and the formation of new ones in the case of a woman marrying into a family. They also agreed, however, that ceremonies had become untenable, leaving women to take extreme measures such as going into debt with banks as well as people, stealing, or balancing memberships to numerous money-pooling associations.

Not long after my interview, Aysatu's story took a sad turn. She called and said she was splitting with her husband, even though their baby was not yet a

year old, because he had decided to marry a second wife without Aysatu's consent. Although the Senegalese Family Code states that the right to polygamy
is signed by men and that lack of consent from a man's wife to marry another
wife is not a stated legal reason for divorce, many marriages end for this very
reason.[11] Women often claim irreconcilable differences when a husband fails to
ask for permission or they find out that men have led double lives with separate
families. Within Islam and the Family Code, men are allowed to have up to four
wives. Although many men say they do not plan on marrying more than one
wife, they choose polygamy at the time of a state-approved marriage to keep
their options open. Aysatu said she felt betrayed and suspected that her mother-
in-law had encouraged him because Aysatu had failed at fulling her obligations
of teraanga. This was often stated as a major factor for divorce. As a working
mom, the fact that Aysatu worked outside the home left her little time to tend to
her relationship with her mother-in-law and sisters-in-law by sharing prepared
meals, visiting them bearing gifts, or even attending family ceremonies with
them. When speaking about her mother-in-law she said, "Elle a toujours pensé
dama nay [She always thought I was stingy]," just as Mariama Bâ describes in
her novel, where the main character is accused of the same by her mother-in-
law. Part of the deception Aysatu also felt was due to her husband's unwilling-
ness to defend her against the discrimination she felt from his family. She is
among many women who find themselves in this situation and decide to either
stay and accept the co-wife or leave as Aysatu did. Of course, the ability to leave
a marriage is also about class. A professional woman such as Aysatu had the
resources and education to leave, but many women depend on their husbands
for financial and social security. Similar to Ndey Sukkey, Aysatu was in a position to either leave the marriage or take a stand and risk it because her various
sources of capital afforded her that privilege. Thinking back to Ndey Sukkey's
comment that it takes courage to stay in a marriage, it's clear she was referring
to the great pressures that many women receive from their female in-laws. It
is important to note that the social pressures to remain married or be married
can be equally if not more significant than the economic ones.

Teraanga, *Demokaraasi*, and Social Change

"Tell me what you remember from ceremonies back then," I said to Uley Samb
about when the 1967 law limiting expenditures for ceremonies was in full effect.

"What I remember from that time is that they used to prohibit them [cer-
emonies]. So, when you had a ceremony during that time, you went into your
room. There, you would get out your money and give it to your friend, relative

of a husband, or your family-in-law member and close your door and hide. Because if not, the police would come arrest you and take you to jail. That was about forty years ago. You would close your door to give your in-laws teraanga, fabric, money, and the *ndawtal*."[12] *Ndawtal* is a type of teraanga, a reciprocal gift intended for female family members and friends who share a mbootaay (money-pooling association) to provide financial and social support that enables the ceremony's host to meet the often steep gift obligations.

> The most for a ndawtal at that time was about 1,000 CFA [$2] and six yards of *lagos* or twelve yards of a different fabric. The era that we are in now [2013], the money is a lot, and people give it away and waste it. Now, you can see someone come give a ndawtal of 500,000 CFA [$1,000], or 300,000 CFA [$600], or 200,000 CFA [$400]. The *Ndeyale* [the ceremony's woman of honor] can bring 1 million CFA plus other fabrics such as *bazin riche*, *ganila*, or *brodé*. So, once they have come to give me all the ndawtal and I put it together with the money I have been saving, I go to the géew [gift exchange circle] and give my *goro* 1 million [$1,850] and each other person 300,000 [$550] to 500,000 [$1,000] until the money is gone. When I go to [women's] ceremonies, I owe them double what they individually gave me.[13]

The géew is used to signify an arena where competitive events happen such as wrestling matches as well as ceremonies. The irony of the géew as a battle scene in both cases this was never lost on me. The rules of reciprocity tend to follow a doubling schema, ensuring heightened sums over time as well as continual obligation. Uley gave examples of the trials and tribulations of how women come by such significant sums and what happens if one cannot produce them: "Sometimes, I have to sell my clothes if I can't come up with the money. And if I don't give it, I will be insulted by the woman. She'll say, 'danga ñakka jom [you are disgraceful/shameful/lacking courage]' and have serious issues within my extended family. On the other hand, if a géwël sings your praises in reference to the gifts given, they might say 'am nga jom moo tax nga joxe teraanga [you are dignified, and that is why you gave teraanga],'" said Uley. Her reference to giving teraanga as a preventative measure reflects back to *xaalis moo faj gàcce* (money cures shame) and the role given to teraanga as a reflection of one's honor.

Uley's grievances about the stark contrasts between the modes and amounts of teraanga in the late 1960s and in 2013 tell the classic story of the social and economic repercussions of changing political economies. She is acutely aware of how these transformations affect the relationships she has and their expressions through the medium of ceremonies, which are part of the domestic economy.

What you see now has nothing to do with what it used to be like. There are huge differences. Then, even though you had very little, you cherished it. You know what that means? Cherish it and don't give it all away. If you gave 5,000 CFA [$8] to someone, they would be happy. Now if you give 5,000 CFA [$8], they will return it, or they would refuse it. Before, if they gave you 5,000 CFA [$8] and you tried to give 1 million CFA [$1,700] in return, they would refuse. People weren't like they are now. At that time, those who gave teraanga first were lucky and kept the peace. Then, people were at peace. There wasn't development, and there wasn't democracy. People, whatever you gave them they were happy with it. But democracy has ruined this country. Democracy is bad; it has ruined this country. Now people do whatever they want. They say that "this is my money, and I will do whatever I want with it." That's not how it was. Before, what you owned you managed and invested (teg ci yoon). Now with democracy, no one manages their money anymore. They just say, "This is my money, I worked for it, and I will do whatever I want with it." That is the big difference.[14]

I asked Uley about a phrase she said and what she meant by "teg sa xaalis ci yoon" [put their money into circulation/invested]. She said, "Limit what you give and save the rest. Now people get up in the morning and beg for money to buy breakfast—that's not good. The way we were before was better than now. If we had continued to save as we were, Senegal would be past where we are now!"[15]

The word *yoon* can have several translations: It can mean something or someone with a specific purpose, on a path or journey such as a religious path (e.g., the *yoonu Murīd*, or Murīd order). *Yoon* can also refer to the law or to justice. Uley's reference to yoon in the context of giving money for a ceremony points to a norm or expectation that goes beyond simply exchanging or giving money. Here, we see Seck's (2015) argument that exchange and reciprocity are different—the first having profit as its main objective, the latter concerning a redistribution of shared goods. Therefore, "putting money into circulation [yoon]" suggests an investment in others with personal gain but in a way that allows them to redistribute into a proverbial communal pot. One cannot sustainably participate in these reciprocities if their counterpart sets the bar too high because they are thinking only of themselves and how much money they have. We must be careful to not disregard what Sahlins has said: "Everywhere in the world the indigenous category for exploitation is 'reciprocity'" (1972, 134). These differences are what Strathern (1988) argues are the distinctions between commodity exchange—which establishes a relationship between two objects exchanged, "thus people experience their interest in commodities as a desire to appropriate goods"—and gift exchange, or the establishment of a relationship between the exchanging subjects who "wish to expand social relations" (143). Uley's disdain for democracy is therefore about how it has threatened a collective dynamic by placing the focus on the commodity itself—and an individual's ownership and appropriation of value—instead of seeing it as a gift that seeks sustainability of the family and the nation. In this sense, democracy is a stand-in for capitalism or a commodity economy. In other words, she regrets the loss of a mutual dependence in favor of individual freedoms, what Frederic Schaffer (1998) defined in his work as the differences between the French notion of *démocratie* and the Wolof meaning of *demokaraasi*. *Démocratie* in Senegal, according to the French-literate elite, is about a multiparty system with elections free from manipulation, solidified in the context of a Socialist party that had dominated Senegalese political life and discourse for almost forty years before the 2000 election that saw Abdoulaye Wade and his democratic party win the presidency. French *démocratie* not only favors individual rights but also understands the individual as an abstraction divorced from social (or private) reality (Scott 2005), as we can see in the French women's parité movement in the late 1990s. Something similar can be said for the definitions of neoliberalism, which "subjects citizens to act in accordance with the market principles of discipline, efficiency, and competitiveness" instead of solidarity, community, and the sharing of resources (Ong 2006, 4). Objections to démocratie in popular opinion also focused on free speech and fears that people felt they could say whatever they wanted without social recourse. Therefore, in terms of the ceremonial practices Uley mentioned, the issue centers on the striking distinction between a system of reciprocity that considers individuals' contributions to community cohesion and one in which the individual as agentive obscures its embeddedness within a larger community and its goals. Whereas demokaraasi, according to Schaffer, is used more by rural Wolof non-French speakers to mean unity of opinion in the context of small communities that aspire for consensus, interviewees in his book liken demokaraasi with other Wolof terms such as *juboo* (to come together, to resolve disagreements), *déggoo* (to come to agreement), or *ànd* (to be in consensus, to have solidarity). This is similar to Seck's definition of mbokk. The last definition of solidarity (which will be important in the next chapter) is an aspect of demokaraasi that concerns working together toward a common goal and supporting one another. And just like Mbembe's assertion of the violence of democracy mentioned in the introduction, Uley and others I spoke to considered the detriments of democracy a moral imperative and a concern for the kind of subject it produces. In this vein, the frictions between démocratie and demokaraasi, or exchange versus reciprocity, come down to what Josephides (1985) says is the central preoccupation of all societies: "the unequal access to the pool of human labour" and the control of labor power "that establishes and reproduces relations in which some social actors may exercise political dominance over the community" (18).

Schaffer provides an example in his book that underlines "the hidden inequalities between men and their exploitation of women's labor" (Strathern 1988, 146). Schaffer asks an elderly woman from the neighborhood of Medina in Dakar in the 1990s whether demokaraasi exists in Senegal: "Yes, there is demokaraasi here. The Socialist Party chose a local elder to be the delegate for this neighborhood. Everything he gets from the party, whether it's rice or sugar, he shares with us. Whenever I have a family occasion, he gives me money" (48). Schaffer goes on to interpret her understanding of demokaraasi as receiving goods. I interpret her statement differently in the context of Uley's comment and what I understand her to be saying about teraanga. To argue that the woman understands demokaraasi as receiving goods for personal benefit misunderstands the relationship between money and people in Wolof society. Uley's own romanticization of the teraanga of yesteryear as void of conflict is in fact more about new forms of exploitation of women's labor in the modern democratic moment, which instrumentalizes women's social labor for predominantly men's political authority.

Using the example of the moka (ceremonial exchange) among the Melpa of the Western Highlands of Papua New Guinea, Strathern (1988) and Josephides (1985) argue that "what is concealed in these ceremonial exchanges . . . is the relationship between the prestige gained there and productive labour; in other words the role of moka as the mode of appropriation, and, in a wider sense, as relations of production" (146). In the case of Ndey Sukkey and her political entourage as well as the lifelong reputation making of the elderly woman from chapter 1, the ceremonial spaces in which they and all women operate are the background for their prestige. And these public displays of prestige conceal and support the "hierarchy of domestic relations" (Josephides 1985, 18) that ultimately favor men's production of labor. In this sense, the male politician's benevolence reaffirms that women's value is dependent upon a man's assignation and control over it. This demonstrates, therefore, the falsity of gift exchange and democracy as egalitarian.

Conclusion

This chapter has served to examine the connections between power relations and ceremonial exchange and its implications for political authority. As we have seen with stories from Aysatu and Ndey Sukkey about marriage and exchanges, the definitional tensions of democracy and teraanga reveal struggles over women's authority within and beyond the domestic space. The competition for power and resources played out within ceremonial spaces or the gift framework demonstrates how women's worth continues to be tied to these domestic forms of production. Ndey Sukkey's power play in the face of her mother-in-law was accomplished by manipulating the gifting process made possible by new accesses to wealth and power. Therefore, not only does this competition between women highlight different hierarchies of the domestic space according to gender, age, and class, but it also exposes the unequal opportunities for women to break from this mold. Even as Ndey Sukkey has gained considerable wealth and political influence, she still must channel that prestige through the domestic economy. As we saw in the previous chapter and the introduction, the economic shifts that have assigned women's social labor and production with the task of both creating wealth and symbolically representing that of men (especially in the absence of salaries or stable employment) have also painted ceremonial exchange as problematic and corrupting of public space. These contradictions present both frictions and opportunities for women to make new spaces for themselves within family dynamics and state politics, even while operating within their limitations. As Hodžić (2017) notes, it is important to understand that the social is already "entangled in with the governmental" (5), and therefore the tensions about what teraanga means in the contemporary moment are also about what governance means in the contemporary moment. Therefore, in the next chapter, I focus on how women stretch these margins into new political territories via their economic and political bargaining within associations and development programs.

3

From Associations to Parliament
Development Politics and Parité

A journalist using the name Kiné Tabara wrote an opinion piece for the state newspaper *Le Soleil*, published on the weekend of December 2–3, 2000. In a sarcastic tone, she critiqued the United Nations' decision to hold a Women's March in Washington, DC, two months earlier, to which the Senegalese government sent twenty women as representatives (Dianko 2000). Kiné argued this was expensive and ineffectual. She pondered whether it would be more potent if "women told off their husbands, or secretaries their male bosses, or why women can't learn to say no and to leave in search of their dignity instead of flying across the world to present a letter to Kofi Annan to express their desire for an improvement to women's lives."[1] Speaking directly to women, Kiné proposed they "make a resolution to renounce the '*guente*,'[2] '*ndawtal*' and other festivities or Senegalese futilities." Her solution was simple: "Une femme, un cri [One woman, one scream]." At noon sharp on March 8—International Women's Day—all women in Senegal should let out a simultaneous scream of distress and pain to tell all the men of Senegal that "on est fat-ti-guées [We are tiii-red]."[3] Speaking directly to women in all corners of Senegal, she said that these cries would send a message to the "monsieurs exploiteurs-misogynistes-polygames [mister exploiters, misogynists, and polygamists]" whom women had had enough of and desired that these men would "finally leave us to manage our dear Senegal '*fémininement*' with our own national Marie-Angélique"[4] (Tabara 2000).

This is a gutsy suggestion to put in a newspaper, even if the author was being mostly facetious. It was potentially even more surprising for the state newspaper to publish it. In interesting ways, it echoes the story told by Ndey Sukkey Géy in the previous chapter about going to New York "sénégalaisment,"

76

yet Kiné's comments critique this kind of representation as purely for show, whereas governing "fémininement" sees true activism as collective action. Her comments came at a time when the effects of structural adjustment programs of the IMF, World Bank reforms, and the consequential takeover of the development industry had made their marks on the previous decades and showed no signs of slowing down. Structural adjustment programs were "conditionalities" set by funding institutions aimed at reducing inflation, among other things. Some of the conditionalities included cutting back on state capital and the devaluation of currency to allow business and industry to expand (Tidjani 1998, 279). Women bore most of the brunt of the economic fallout and the responsibility to sustain families and develop the nation. By way of marches calling for equal rights to land and inheritance, or turning neighborhood solidarity groups into microenterprises, women in Senegal worked tirelessly throughout the Diouf administration (1981–2000) and continue to work to this day to fight for their rights while also maneuvering within a national political economy that has mostly denied them membership.

In a published interview following Abdoulaye Wade's victory over Abdou Diouf, consequently ending forty years of rule by the Parti Socialiste, Marie-Angélique Savané was asked why she thought women voted in such high numbers. She replied, "Because women understood that all the social evils fall on them. On top of all of her problems, she takes on those of her husband and children" (Faye 2000). Marie-Angélique Savané—the wife of Landing Savané, leader of Ànd-Jëf/African Party for Democracy and Socialism, to whom Kiné refers as the president of their desired alternative government—has been one of the most influential political activists for women's rights in Senegal. Her movement, Yewwu-Yewwi (For Women's Liberation), beginning in 1984, advocated for women's rights, called out the patriarchy, and educated the public about women's political and economic power in African history through their publication *Fippu* (ending subordination) (Kane and Kane 2018). Their goal was to raise awareness about women's subordination and support the activities of specific women's NGOs and other associations. And like Kiné's comments, the organization aimed to address "salary equity between men and women, the eradication of polygamy, equal legal rights, and the advancement of women in terms of political representation" (22).

Kiné and Marie-Angélique Savané's comments point to the much broader scope of women's frustrations about simultaneously being the saviors of family economies hit hard by structural adjustment programs and yet excluded from contributing to the national economy in any meaningful way. As Marie-Angélique Savané points out, women are the ones who deal with all the social evils that befall them and their families. During the heyday of her organization, Yewwu-Yewwi (For Women's Liberation), structural adjustment programs had affected the economic dynamics of families and the social conceptions of gender and work because of the drastic cuts in state employment. Therefore, as mentioned in the introduction, the particular violence of the structural adjustment programs was a significant decrease in state employment, leaving many men out of work and without the salaries that many families had come to depend on. However, because families had come to depend on these contributions of direct and indirect wealth sharing, it fell to women to continue the transfer of these state allocations in the absence of a steady flow of income. In order to perpetuate the reciprocities and obligations to the wider family unit, women had to get creative by joining associations and eventually taking part in development projects that afforded them the capital to take part in the very "futilities" Kiné mentions.

Therefore, the fatigue and frustration that Kiné alludes to in her commentary piece are about both the burden women have carried to keep families afloat and the critique from men that these very strategies make them unqualified to participate in decision-making for the nation that goes beyond applauding and mediating. Kiné's reference to Marie-Angélique as the leader of a kind of women-led government refers to a cultivated culture of governance among women in associations and solidarity groups that support their communities economically and politically—a political economy of teraanga—that have functioned apart from and despite a male-dominated political economy. In fact, I argue that Kiné's wish for men to simply leave women to their own governing devices has to do with the evolution and sophistication of women's leadership skills within associations and the politicization of development as much as it does with the burden placed upon women to contribute to the economic security of the nation without proper representation. The previous chapter examined the dynamics of ceremonies in producing relationships sénégalaisement within the political economy of teraanga; this chapter examines how women's associations became targets for development programs that pigeonholed women's economic possibilities while at the same time helping to produce a class of women political leaders. And many of the principles of such a feminine identity became co-opted by development projects and instrumentalized by women to gain resources for said projects.

Women's Associations in Context

Associations are mostly about development. We get together to be able to make progress, to make some money to help our families. Groups like the *daayiras*[5] are for women to exchange ideas, help one another. They talk about how to live, how to run a household and take care of a family, how to run a household budget, and how to live in peace with their husband and his family. I think these associations help train women and help them develop. To have a sense of sharing and mutual aid. They loan money together, reimburse that money together, work together. . . . It is from these associations that we distinguish leaders, those who have leadership skills. It is usually their fathers or sisters that propose they join because they recognize their leadership. Many deputies come from this environment. They help other women by founding associations and becoming leaders.

These are the reflections of the parliamentarian Penda Seck. I'll let her introduce herself: "Je suis Penda Seck Dieng Diop. Madame Diop. Je suis mariée [I am Penda Seck Dieng Diop. Mrs. Diop. I am married]." It is customary for a woman to keep her last name in Senegal but to be referred to informally by her husband's last name. Penda Seck was born in Dakar at the l'Hôpital Principal in 1948. She is married with one son who studied in France and now works for the Senegalese Ministry of Finance. She has four grandchildren, all boys. Penda's father was a *gendarme*[6] in the French colonial administration, and therefore she traveled for much of her youth. She started school in Ouagadougou in Burkina Faso, where her father was stationed, and then went on to Abidjan in Côte d'Ivoire, Conakry in Guinea, and Bamako in Mali. "I speak Bambara. I lived in Ouagadougou and speak Mosi. I went to Abidjan and now speak Baoulé; from Guinea I speak Susu. Came back to Dakar at age twelve. Worked at Lycée Limamou Laye, which is the biggest high school in Senegal and one of the most prestigious. Trained as a teacher at the university."

She was part of the first wave of post-parité women representatives in parliament from 2012 to 2017. Her political career started with the Ligue Démocratique (LD), born from the communist Parti africain de l'Indépendance, a major underground opposition party to the Senghor administration. Following the LD's incorporation into Bennoo Bokk Yaakaar (United in Hope) coalition of President Macky Sall, Penda became active with the group Femmes de Bennoo Bokk Yaakaar (Women of United in Hope) that campaigned for the president by holding press conferences and rallies.

Colonial policies that focused on the connections among gender, labor, and space increasingly created a situation in which women's work was linked to the private space in order to legitimate men's work in the public space. Not only did French laws decrease the limited educational and professional opportunities for women, but they also imposed state rules for family planning and reproductive rights of women to control their bodies within the confined space of the home. Much of this was important in order to mark women's difference from men, who dominated public space. Lisa McNee argues that given the context of women's exclusion from most salaried jobs, they "engage more intensely in building exchange relationships with *other* women in order to survive" (2000, 64, emphasis in original). Associations, where many of these "exchange relationships" develop, range from small groups of friends within a neighborhood who gather to socialize and pool resources to mbootaay, associations with significant membership numbers that are often sponsored by women and men of greater means like politicians. With or without state engagement with communities, women's associations serve as protectors of families, their health, and their economic vitality, and they increasingly provide local political representation. However, as Lucy Creevey argues, Senegalese women's formalized associations did not necessarily change this reality but rather allowed women to gain resources that allowed them to deal with the reality of having less authority in both public and private lives (2004, 68). In the next chapter, I give greater ethnographic details of the nature of women's associations, which have, over the years, been the target of private and state-sponsored programs for moneymaking activities, microcredit loans, and cooperatives, called *mutuelles*, from private institutions such as banks or NGOs (Doligez, Fall, and Oualy 2012). Following Senegal's economic crisis of the 1980s and 1990s, these development programs were popularized by international organizations to boost small enterprises. Into the 1990s, the Senegalese state became more hands-on in terms of regulating bank loans and providing specific funds for qualified projects run through women's associations. By 2003, a Ministry of Development and Microfinance was established, and by 2008 microfinance made up 10.25 percent of funds contributing to the economy (2012). Funded associations, especially those for women, took part in short trainings on how to preserve fruit, mill flour, or dye textiles for eventual sale. Associations that sought loans but did not have bank accounts would find project finance in state-sponsored institutions such as the Programme d'Appui aux Mutuelles d'Épargne et de Crédit au Sénégal (PAMECAS) and Crédit Mutuel du Sénégal or Crédit Agricole (state-sponsored institutions) as well as larger banks with microfinance divisions.

These community banks and organizations emerged as part of the structural adjustment programs of the Abdou Diouf era and its focus on development projects (spearheaded mostly by NGOs). The Diouf years proved to be first a ballooning or "technocratization of the Senegalese administrative apparatus" (Diop and Diouf 1990, 150) followed by an NGOization of the political economy due to fallouts from a bloated state budget and deals signed with the IMF and

World Bank. Additionally, Abdoulaye Wade's era (2000–12) of state-sponsored small grants to women's associations defined a reciprocal relationship with the state. And in the current Macky Sall administration, the situation is similar. In an interview, the Senegalese public intellectual and sociologist Dr. Baba Biaye (2017) told me that the state under Wade began to take over what NGOs were doing and began promoting women's associations by controlling where state microcredit funds went as a political move, hoping for a majority in the elections. For access to money, women's associations became dependent on state-organized funds funneled through registered programs such as Groupement d'Intérêt Économique (GIEs) [Economic Interest Groups] and Groupements de Promotion Féminin (GPFs) [Women's Promotional Groups] (Creevey 2004, 67). By implication, Wade's Parti Démocratique Sénégalais (PDS) and the associations receiving microcredit and finance monies also capitalized on the power of women's associations, one outcome being the vote to approve gender quotas in 2010. Since 2012, the Macky Sall administration has followed a similar partisanship utilizing women's associations as a source of *militantisme* (fervent support) that was particularly important during the 2017 election season.

Between the 1980s and the 2000s there was an intense injection of resources into women's associations in the forms of microcredit loans, microfinance, and microenterprise from national and international NGOs, in partnership with the state. These development structures ensured an increase in the separation of labor by gender; they also married the processes of cultural reproduction and production, or, as Perutz calls it, "aligning value with values" (2008, 2). This was done by promoting values of solidarity, mutual aid, and teraanga as profitable. It was up to women to put in the hard work of attending trainings, taking out loans, and sustaining small, mostly informal businesses in order to pay back those loans and, with luck, have a surplus for their families. Many have called this the "feminization of poverty" (McLanahan and Kelly 2006, 134), and I would further argue it is the feminization of the fight against poverty by placing the onerous task of eradicating poverty—a state-created problem—on the shoulders of women. Julia Elyachar (2005) argues that "relational value," which is "the positive value attached to the creation, reproduction, and extension of relationships in communities" (7), is talked about in terms of kinship metaphors and operating through reciprocal exchange. The incorporation of these types of values into a capitalist free market scheme dispossesses the very people who created the value in the first place. Not only are the actors dispossessed of agency, but the very object being given is also dispossessed of its original value. Kiné's plea to men (or rather the male-controlled state) to "finally leave us to manage our dear Senegal 'fémininement'" (Tabara 2000) is both an acknowledgment of this feminization of the development industry and a theory that perhaps the processes that women in Senegal have been employing are a more effective strategy for national progress. This may be particularly relevant when thinking about what Ferguson calls the new "politics of distribution" where "new powers and possibilities" that have opened up for women have seen a "crisis of masculinity" (2015, 36) for men as wage labor has decreased significantly and social grants have gone to women's economic development. Arguably, this crisis of masculinity has been accentuated by men's social limitations of employment, while women have more flexibility to work within the domestic space, in the informal economy, and through associations that have targeted women's social activities.

The boom of investments in women's associations paralleled new forms of gendered responsibility for economic security and general morality. Dakar billboards posted announcements for state- and nonstate-sponsored events with titles such as "The Role of Women and Development" and "The Role of Women and Agriculture." My personal favorite was "The Role of Women in Preventing Vehicle Accidents." Although I could not find the statistic for the number of drivers by sex in 2017, it was curious to me that women should be responsible for road accidents when they were most likely the minority of drivers. Although the driving population in Dakar was diversifying, the large majority of taxi drivers, transport chauffeurs, and public transportation workers are men. Melly (2018) comments that in 2006 when a program called *Sister Taxi* was spearheaded by the Ministry of Family, Female Organizations, Infancy, and Childhood, there were only ten taxis driven by women (58). Beyond billboards and other forms of advertisements, a public discourse emerged that made women responsible for, as Marie-Angélique noted, "the social evils" (Faye 2000) in Senegal. Events put on by state-sponsored organisms such as the Ministry of Finance or international organizations were consistently burdened with being the drivers of social change. For example, the question of domestic violence was brought up in the context of women's role within the family, rather than addressing men and women together. Therefore, women were often left to discuss issues that concerned them and their partners in a vacuum.

In this context of increasing professionalization and monetization of women's domestic economic activities, as a potentially unforeseen consequence of the restriction of women to microfinance and credit programs, the Senegalese state effectively promoted a feminized sector of the macroeconomy, leaving women within organizations to utilize the resources at their disposal. In the words of Mareem Sow, member of Aysata Tall Sall's Osez L'Avenir party, "people are our greatest asset" (Sow 2017)—a kind of social capital with an influx of development funds to build from. However, this labor segregation actually allows for women to transform their political capabilities from leadership roles within development programs into positions of public authority: The path toward the parité movement and women's increased participation in state politics was paved by a technocratization of women's traditional solidarity associations, or, as Escobar (1995) sees it, "conceiving of social life as a technical problem, as a matter or rational decision" (36). This is likely a legacy of what Mbembe (2001) calls "colonial arbitrariness" that "muddled the imperatives of morality, economics, and politics" (31).

This connection between the NGOization (Karim 2014) discourse tying the fate of women's empowerment to the market and a "rationality of governance" that "subjects citizens to act in accordance with the market principles of discipline, efficiency, and competitiveness" (Ong 2006, 4) creates an inextricable link between the economic and the political. And more importantly, what we see in this chapter and the following is how this link plays out within the context of women's political strategy that is born from these neoliberal and postcolonial rationalities that have based their economic and political strategies on dispossessing local values and subjecting them to these principles of competition, efficiency, and savings. When I speak of a feminized sector of the macroeconomy, I refer to the economic structures created by the Senegalese state, and I consider economy as the possible "ways individuals coalesce to produce and reproduce each day and over time the goods and services that make a collective life possible" (Perutz 2008, xii). This kind of sectorization of the macroeconomy both limits women's full participation in wage-labor industrial capitalism and necessitate the creation of space for themselves to develop their own industry, an informal mercantile economy that both commodifies and reproduces gendered urban Wolof values. Chapter 2 described the commercialization of teraanga as coffee and other products or the feminization of hospitality seen throughout popular music and cleaning or cooking products. But Wolof values such as solidarity, care, and teraanga are also used to encourage national development and savings. This does not mean that the development enterprises (Esteva, Babones, and Babcicky 2013) that radically transformed Senegalese society have solved issues of gender disparities but rather that they have shifted a piece of the power pie to a certain class of women who have arguably reinforced these social inequalities. In many ways, development projects have (re)invented women[7] as a hyperfeminized capitalist subject.

Even as it is easy to critique NGOization as the "increased professionalization and specialization of significant sector of women's movements" (Lang 1997), Hodžić (2014) encourages us to think beyond the tropes of NGOs as the demise of feminism and feminist movements in postcolonial contexts. Hodžić suggests that despite the blind feminist critiques of NGOization as "feminist organizing that has turned collective and political women's movements into professional NGO bureaucracies" (227), it is more productive to consider that some NGOs "transgress boundaries and produce new kinds of political engagements, however tentative and fraught" (232). I argue something similar has happened with the parité movement and its evolutions from within both feminist organizations and the NGO-funded associations that I highlight in this chapter. The women see themselves as having matured politically from their work within associations and their NGO partners. So much so that for them, the boundary between development and politics becomes intrinsically linked.

In fact, when women such as Ayda Mbóoj or Mously Diakhaté talk about politics, they often speak of themselves as leaders of development as much as politicians. "Am na ay jigéen yoo xam ne dañu juddu rekk nekk des femmes leaders, am na jigéen yiy def politique de développement, di mobiliser ay nit, di organizer ay nit di leen definiral yoon. Pour man, loolu politique la [There are women who are born leaders. There are women who do development politics by mobilizing people, organizing people, and defining a path for them. To me, that is politics]," said Ayda when I asked her about what politics means in Senegal. Mously uses similar language regarding using her political position of power to help develop opportunities for women in her associations. Therefore, they see themselves as important gatekeepers to women's progress and understand politics as their modality for doing so. A great deal of the women in associations that I encountered in 2017 overwhelmingly spoke of development strategies in terms of having access to politicians or running for office themselves. This tone was a noticeable shift from my previous years in Senegal between 2010 and 2013.

I explore these connections between women's involvement in development programs by way of their associations and, in the next chapter, the emergence of what I call patrona networks driven by women as leaders of these associations, often funded through their positions in the government for the benefit of other women and men. In this chapter, I outline the evolution of women's associations as vectors for development projects that produced a class of women leaders and gave birth to the parité movement. I also focus on COSEF (Conseil des Femmes Sénégalaises- Council for Senegalese Women), a driving force in the movement. I demonstrate how women's participation in national politics, as well as their participation more historically, has always been vital to the life of the nation. I discuss the strategies of the parité movement based on examples of women and authority throughout Senegalese history and the beneficial and problematic uses of gender as a foundational part of the movement.

Solidarity Groups to Microenterprises:
From the Archives

Newspaper sources from the Senegalese National Archives show a diverse group of microcredit, microfinance, and mutual credit organizations targeting local women's informal associations to inject an incredible amount of financial aid from the Senegalese state, international NGOs, and parastatal financial institutions. Reports and opinion pieces, such as the opening epigraph to this chapter, recount the evolution of women's domestic activities into formal institutions and in many ways into politically active spaces.

The Association des Femmes pour la Promotion de l'Entreprise au Sénégal (AFEPES) inaugurated a *mutuelle d'épargne et de crédit* attended by Aminata Tall, the minister of the family and national solidarity. Easier access to credit was linked to "active solidarity" in order to reinforce women's entrepreneurial skills and free them from economic dependence (Thiam 2000),[8] although arguably creating a different kind of dependence. This particular ministry was created to address the "woman problem" and has had its name changed many times, but its focus has mostly remained the same: the orientation of women as responsible for national development. It has been the vehicle for the Senegalese state to transfer international and national funds to women's community associations. For example, the ministry oversees projects such as GPF and GIE, which offer finances for small moneymaking enterprises to be administered via women's groups.

The ministry has often been controversial, and there are increasing calls for its dissolution, especially by politicians such as Aysata Tall Sall and others, who argue that its focus on women only promotes their marginalization and exclusion from the political economy. Led entirely by women, it was often argued that it was a "soft" ministry given to women in order to avoid giving them real responsibility, such as in the Ministry of Finance or of Infrastructure. In 1987, Mantoulaye Guèye was the minister of social development, and in 1991, Ndioro Ndiaye was minister of the newly named Ministry of Women, Children, and the Family. In 1999, the ministry changed again under the leadership of Aminata Mbengue Ndiaye and was called Ministry of the Family, Social Action and National Solidarity. Following the installation of the Wade administration, Aminata Tall became minister of the family and national solidarity, dropping the reference to social action (Thiam 2000). By 2001, Awa Guèye Kébé headed up what was called the Ministry of the Family and Petite Enfance (Children's Affairs) (*Le Soleil* 2001). At an event in 2003 to inaugurate women's cooperatives, Saoudatou Seck Ndiaye, the minister of women's entrepreneurship and microcredit, was in attendance.

Wade then switched out Seck Ndiaye for Mareem Ndiaye as minister, adding *petits et moyens entreprises* (PME, small and medium enterprises) to the title. An interview with Mareem Ndiaye published in *Le Soleil* on April 1, 2004, was laid out like a gossip column, including glamour pictures of the minister as if she were a movie star. An economist by training, Mareem Ndiaye talked about Wade's vision for women to be entrepreneurs and manage businesses: "We want to ensure the emergence of a real female patronage . . . because it is President Wade's idea that all prosperous political economies have to include women" (*Le Soleil* 2004). Over the next decade and more, the ministry changed hands and titles many times. But the minister's words about female patrons and the capitalization of women's associational networks show the progressive nature in which women's associations became increasingly sponsored by microcredit loans, turning what were support groups into market enterprises.

Technocratization of Women's Support Networks

"The official administrative and political power is still almost exclusively reserved for men. Women are for the most part still delegated to the domestic sphere. Even still, they are not powerless. They demonstrate their capacities outside of the masculine structure of power through their organizations such as associations for the promotion of women (GPF). They can act, be entrepreneurs, manage, organize, and exercise considerable influence among their community as well as their family. Unofficial power, but real nonetheless" (Hazard 1991).

This quotation comes from a report and announcement that the National Federation of the Association of Women's Promotion (FNGPF) was receiving 100 million CFA ($185,000) from the Crédit Agricole of Senegal (one of the first local banks) and the International Fund for Agricultural Development (FIDA). The FNGPF had also recently broken off from the state to become its own NGO and, like many other organizations, targeted women's associations. In fact, in an article in 2000, the organization Femme Développement Entreprise en Afrique (FDEA) reported that of 25,000 people who received a total amount of 1,245,745 CFA ($2,315), 98 percent were women and 2 percent were men (Dieng 2000). Thus, by the early 2000s, the investments and profits were women-focused and women-driven. Soukeyna Ndiaye Bâ, the president of FDEA, said that the objective of the organization was to represent "women with considerable businesses in the informal sector who wished to be part of the national macro-economy" (unknown 2000). And yet, the FDEA was established in 1987 as an institution of microfinance that "trains women in micro-enterprises." Madame Bâ, however, recommended that the government, NGOs, and political parties get more involved in integrating women into "a macroeconomic national politics."[9] Women became known as *opératrices économiques* (economic opera-tors) (*Le Soleil* 2000b) or "depositories of virtues and values of our society" (1987) or "an active agent of development" (Samb 1988). Their solidarity groups, historically designed as spaces for women to gather and pool resources but also to gossip or talk about and find solutions to their problems, became monetized and semiprofessionalized. Because of women's roles as guardians of culture and their strong associations, the Diouf administration monopolized on their potential to cure the moral and economic crises facing the country. Founded in 1983, the Association des Femmes de l'Afrique de l'Ouest (AFAO, Association of Women of West Africa), a partner association of the Economic Commu-nity of West African States (ECOWAS, or CEDEAO in French), also framed women as "agents of development that must operate within a framework of solidarity and ideal community values" (Samb 1988). These dynamics turned mbootaay (women's associations) into competitive enterprises. One article read, "A space of solidarity turned towards development" (Gonzales 2001). Practices of solidarity and mutual aid were exploited, creating microspaces for an exclusively women's economy away from the official economy—what I refer to as the domestic political economy of teraanga occupied by women and the political (public) economy dominated by men. And as Karim (2011) points out in the case of microfinance in Bangladesh, "the introduction of microfinance into private life has led to the loss of social solidarity . . . the profit orientation of microfinance policies has begun to rupture deeply held notions of family and community solidarity" (200).

The language—"unofficial power," "masculine structure of power," or inte-grating women into a "macroeconomic national politics"—therefore points to a clear separation of the political and economic realities of men and women. If the "macroeconomic national politics" not only is driven by men but is the political economy that makes decisions on behalf of the general population and interfaces with the outside world, and if women are not operating within a space of official power or macroeconomics, then what does their economic and political authority look like?

The journalist Seynabou Diop echoes this critique of turning cultural and social phenomena into something marketable, writing about the splitting of the FNGPF and criticizing the transformations of associations by saying, "The pol-itics of women's promotion . . . inspired by traditional *mbootaay* or *daayiras* that had nothing but a cultural or religious character, in 1975 they became women's promotion associations (GPF) . . . essentially technocratizing these groups and culture in general" (Diop 1991). By 1985, these GPF became GIE, represent-ing 4,000 women with about 400,000 associations receiving 100 million CFA

(Hazard 1991). By the early 2000s the cash influx and loans remained similar if not higher (Gueye 2000b). In the case of microfinance projects, the number of clients went from about 700,000 in 2005 to just over 1,400,000 in 2010 (Doligez, Fall, and Oualy 2012).

In this entrepreneurial spirit, associations were made to compete with each other for further funding with the establishment of the Presidential Grand Prix in 1990. One article tells of an economic group with a fishing enterprise from Ziguinchor who won the prize in 1996, receiving "five million cfa ($9,295) . . . and a ticket to Mecca . . . from the president during the international women's day events" (Benga 1996).[10] As noted by President Diouf and Mantoulaye Guèye, minister of social development, these funds were necessary "in the only battle that merited waging: that of economic and social development of the nation" (Diop 1991), thus making women responsible for an insurmountable task as the "major part of traditional associations have become GPF or GIE and oriented towards lucrative activities" (Benga 1996). In 1999, the Fédération Nationale des Groupements de Promotion Féminines (FNGPF) [National Federation of the Association for Women's Promotion], headed by Khady Ndao, received vehicles and 580 million CFA ($930,000), with another 500 million on the way from Abdou Diouf (MLB 1999). They in turn named their association Góoru Mbootaay (His Excellency) in his honor (Sarr 1999).

In 1999 and 2000, leading up to the presidential election, the Diouf administration announced a stream of funds to newly inaugurated *crédits mutuels*, or loans for start-up women's associations. Around this time reports about mutuelles became more frequent. The AFAO met to create a regional bank where heads of state of the fourteen member states would contribute funds annually (Sarr 1999), and on January 5, 2000, members of the Dakar regional chapter of the FGPF received 500,000 CFA ($1,000) from the president and manuals written in local languages for training offered to leaders of various associations. The training consisted of financial management skills, literacy in local languages, and trade skills, with help from the German and Dutch embassies and the British Council (*Le Soleil* 2000b). Candidate Abdoulaye Wade, having come in second in the first round of the presidential election, therefore forcing a runoff, was welcomed by a women's gathering with drumming, applause, and whistles. "The solution to your problems is *l'alternance*," (*Le Soleil* 2000a) he said to the crowd. *Alternance* (change in power), or *soppi* in Wolof, was the slogan for Wade's party, signifying an alternative to the dominance of the Parti Socialiste of Senghor and Diouf.

Following his eventual victory, and, in a move to show his gratitude, Wade's new administration followed the precedent set by Diouf, focusing on investments in women's associations, at that point called *mutuelles d'épargne et de crédit* (cooperative savings and loans). Even six years after being elected, in a speech in front of thousands of women, he promised to do more for them, to "consolidate and reinforce the pact of solidarity and complicity" (Dione 2006) using similar language to Diouf as a way to capitalize on values that were historically part of social life and not for sale.

A report about the history of mutuelles d'épargne called them "women's banks" that starting in the 1980s became popular ways for women to help their families through the structural adjustment period, which experienced a "boom of tontines" (*Le Soleil* 1993) or a sudden increase in associations. These "banks" transformed from mbootaay among friends to savings institutions that required stricter reimbursements. The cooperatives allowed for women to work with much larger sums than those from money-pooling among friends. Testimonies from women emphasize issues of indebtedness to others versus a financial institution and skepticism of mutuelles as a way to take advantage of non-French literate women; nevertheless, one woman stated that "if mutuelles had been around longer it would have prevented many divorces that were caused by lack of money" (Talla 2000). Indeed, during this time when men were losing their salaried jobs, it was women who kept the family going from what little they earned in their microenterprises.

At the same time that mutuelles increased, so did opportunities for women to spend their borrowed money. During a ceremony in Podor to establish a mutuelle, the mayor, Aysata Tall Sall, was given 1 million CFA destined for twenty-one women's associations and fourteen GIE in the region (Ndao 2000), and another ceremony was held for mutuelles created in the region of Diourbel, with initial funds of 100 million CFA and 12 million CFA in loans from Fédération des Associations Féminines Sénégalaises (FAFS) to Crédit Agricole. Awa Ndiaye, the general treasurer of FAFS, "saluted the women's initiative to end the practices of excessive wastefulness during ceremonies" (Gueye 2000a). Reinforcing this sentiment, an associational member from Diourbel, who was present at another ceremony for an association to receive 12.3 million CFA, said that "women had become conscious of the benefits of savings. They know saving and taking credit in order to avoid wastefulness" (Marone 2000).

When women were not able to pay back their loans or were not meeting growth standards, the development community began blaming women's prioritization of money for family ceremonies, using language such as "wastefulness" to describe the same activities that had benefited from associational organizing. Oddly, an article in 1988, on the topic of women's weak representation in elected positions, describes the establishment of an "Observatoire de la femme et de la petite fille" to improve the status of women, and yet the cover photo features a critique of women's conduct of family ceremonies as wasteful (Sow 1998). Therefore, the very condition for receiving funds became linked to material and judicial proof of addressing wastefulness, since it was said to impede the progress made by savings and loan projects. Organizations such as Réseau pour le Développement Intégré (RADI), or the Integrative Development Network, had designed the "fight against wastefulness" campaigns to raise awareness about the harmful effects of investing money gained from microenterprises into family ceremonies. With help from Ayda Mbóoj, the minister of women, the family, and social development, the campaign took off and was soon an important topic during the Quinzaine de la Femme to celebrate International Women's Day. When referring to the campaign, Daba Gaye, the legal affairs director of RADI, said, "We realized that all of our other development projects were being obstructed by women's obligations to family ceremonies" (Gaye 2010). In effect, their members were successful in generating funds but still had significant obligations to the family, preventing the money from helping create paying jobs to alleviate poverty. Madame Gaye also indicated that women needed to be emancipated from the social obligations of gifts, participation in family ceremonies, and strict financial obligations to family members. Her statement reflects the sentiment of the columnist Kiné, who wrote that women's obligations to family ceremonies are just as much of a hindrance to their own emancipation as they are crucial to maintaining healthy relationships. For Madame Gaye and many others, women's liberation would come from financial independence and security.

One of the members of Gaye's development groups was Cécile Dièye, a widow with mostly grown children. She first came into contact with RADI as part of her mbootaay, which RADI leaders suggested "il ne s'agit pas seulement des mbootaay mais avec notre assemblée on pourrait faire beaucoup de choses utiles [it is not just about gathering as an association but that our group could do things that were much more useful]" (Dièye 2013), Cécile remembered hearing. They began first with learning how to dye fabrics and then went on to small loans from RADI for other types of training in product management, marketing, and learning about human rights and women's rights specifically. "Après on a passé à une formation sur le genre. Ça suscitait un éveil chez les femmes. Que maintenant on ne se laissera plus dominé, on va réclamer nos droits [After that, we had trainings on gender. That inspired an awakening among women. That we will no longer let them (men) dominate us, and to reclaim our rights]" (Dièye 2013). Cécile lived in a small house in the neighborhood of Boon, notorious for having been built along the floodplains of the city. Many families could not inhabit their own homes during the rainy season due to extreme flooding. Cécile shared her home with her grown children, who had also felt the effects of the economic decline. When I met her in 2013, her husband had recently passed, and the family was struggling to get by. She spoke proudly yet with a profound sadness about her son, who had a promising future as a student of pharmacy at the university but who had to put his studies on hold to help the family earn money. "I had a job as the secretary at the Boon Chamber of Commerce, but ever since Abdou Diouf distributed our society [referring to the IMF and World Bank structural adjustment programs signed off by Diouf], I can no longer find a job even though I looked everywhere. It has been since 1989 or '90 that I gave up and decided to sell dried fish. You see, there are no jobs, there is no money. Unemployment is grueling, and everyone is selling, and we don't diversify as all the products are about the same."[11]

Cécile no doubt learned the trade of drying and selling fish through another microenterprise program. Her reference to a lack of diversity and to women selling all the same products is itself a product of the omnipresent and uniform microenterprise projects that targeted women like her, effectively limiting them to small-scale activities. Cécile's story also tells of how structural adjustment programs slowed or paused women's entry into the labor economy, again forcing them to depend on petty market and family ceremonies and associations to survive.

Since Cécile began working with RADI, she has described ways to hold herself and others in the association accountable for the money they received and spent as a part of the program. She and her peers conceived of and signed a *code de conduite* (code of conduct), inspired by the 1967 law (limiting expenditures for family ceremonies) that stated the limits to how much money they could use for ceremonies. They then agreed upon a fine to be paid to the group if a member violated the terms of the code, essentially policing themselves. If the limit for expenses for a ceremony surpassed 10,000 CFA—as outlined in the law—the woman was sanctioned. Despite the fact that in the more than thirty years since the law's adoption, no allowance was made for inflation and for changing economic realities, these sanctions have penalized the very activities that were the original point of women's associations.

> I think wastefulness is bad. They think that for a country to make itself in the future, it has to have money, but we have to save. When it is a question of sociality and not a ceremony, I can understand that, I can be social. I want to give my mother-in-law a gift, I can buy her a dress and give it to her, that's no problem. It is nothing compared to when I offer her a gift during a ceremony

because I will buy a dress that costs $10 and give her $12.50 in cash. I don't stop there. I must give her ten or fifteen more dresses, money, bowls, scarves, rosaries, even sandals. Just for her. If she has any sisters, I must give to them as well, and if my husband has sisters and aunts I must give to them. And of course, the griots get the most. I am obliged to do all of this. Often when I hear there is a ceremony in the neighborhood I immediately don't want to go. The government needs to put us in jail just to stop us from wasting.[12]

Cécile chuckled when she mentioned being put in jail; however she, like Uley in the previous chapter, lamented the untenable obligations that ceremonies and gifting had become. Uley argued that development had created these dynamics, but Cécile seemed to internalize the critique of women's behavior as a result of their inabilities to make productive decisions for themselves, rather than seeing the problem as a structural issue. As Fatou Sarr (1998) points out, structures such as the *tontine* have tended to evolve parallel to the changes observed in family ceremonies: "Progressively, these associations—born from a need to ensure the reproduction of the social system (births, marriages, and deaths)—will become the precise instruments for economic objectives" (55). The result of this technocratization of women's associations, as well as the punishments for transgressions, has meant that many women's relationships have become transactional, competitive, and framed around maximum economic benefit. In fact, the newer phenomenon of doubling and tripling reciprocal gifting that Uley mentions is strikingly similar to the microfinance schemes, or the Systèmes Financiers Décentralisés (SFD) created by the Senegalese government. At the time, SFD had two main approaches: solidarity credit (also known as collective borrowing) and individual credit. The SFD's strategic messaging to encourage repayment from the collective borrowing groups was self-control and playing to the dynamics of social pressure among the group. When it came to individual credit, the tactic employed was to entice individual borrowers with higher levels of credit upon repayment of a loan (Ndiaye 2012, 108).

In the case of reciprocal gifting during family ceremonies, each woman has a ledger noting how much each individual gave her in order to know the amount she owes them, with interest, for future ceremonies. The same ledger is also used to keep track of who owes her and how much. It functions much like a bank ledger, providing the date, occasion, name, and amount given.

During my 2013 stay in Dakar, I lived in an apartment building in a small neighborhood called Ouagou Niayes. Every evening several of the men of the building gathered on the small stoop to make *àttaaya* (tea) and chat about current events and life. Most nights I joined them. Ndiaga, Djadji, Thierno, and

Benjamin were always curious to see what information I had come up with that day and found my work entertaining. When I came back from a trip to a wedding, I told them about these ledgers, at which they laughed uproariously, making fun of the women who kept their ledgers locked up in a secure location. Benjamin expressed his frustration with this system of exchange. "Senegalese only know how to waste money, the most out of all the West African countries," he said. "Senegal is perpetually partying, and this solidarity we talk about is crap, because it ends up that you have to spend a lot of money that most people don't have. We are after all a poor country," he noted emphatically. My friends' negative opinions about women and exchange were common and also spoke to a resentment of many unemployed young men. Djadji, the youngest of the group, often grumbled about how women were the only ones who receive help; "meanwhile, I have to work in a biscuit factory for Lebanese people who pay terrible wages."

These two examples demonstrate not only the imbalance of where development funds are invested but also the deepening tensions between men and women due to these decisions. A woman like Cécile became dependent on development organizations and solidarity groups—that most men did not have access to—and men like Djadji were left to work for unregulated wages. These inequal opportunities have arguably created the economic and social divisions that are at the root of critiques against women and how they spend money.

By the late 1990s, the discourse and activities coming from the Ministry of Women's Affairs and NGOs began to turn toward questions of women's representation and access to decision-making roles within local and national government. The focus remained on women's associations; however, it shifted to seeing these organizations as a source of female leadership. As Penda Seck noted, "It is from associations that we distinguish leaders" (2017). Women's rights advocates argued that for development projects to function, especially those targeting women's associations, the issue of women's leadership came into focus. That is, "how can women—who are numerically superior in population but represent the most vulnerable of society—play their role in social and economic development?" (Sy 2006). This was the primary question during a training held by RADI called "Women, Gender, Leadership, Advocacy and Lobbying." RADI hoped to instruct other organizations on how to advocate on behalf of their members and for women to have more say in how development funds would be allocated and in other policy decisions. Newspaper stories also spotlight events attended by representatives from various ministries and partner organizations on the topics of women, leadership, local governance, and the idea of parité. Kang and Tripp (2018) have documented the importance of domestically sourced advocacy groups in African countries, especially Senegal, for the successful advocacy and adoption of gender quota laws. They argue that understanding international organizations as driving the fight for gender equality overlooks the contributions of domestic organizations. In the case of most women's groups in Senegal, domestic does not simply mean within Senegalese territory; it includes the home as an important space for organizing. Some of the most involved organizations for gender equality, such as the network of women's organizations called Siggil Jigéen (Women Rise), or most famously the Council for Senegalese Women (COSEF), began with women meeting at one another's homes, through mbootaay groups. Homes have also launched larger coalitions. As Rokhaya Gassama, president of COSEF, states, "Long before it was called parité, it was simply our mothers and grandmothers at home organizing and calling for women to be able to participate in the life of the nation."[13] With help from prominent women who had broken into the political realm, COSEF and other coalitions helped advocate for the parité law, which mandates equal representation of men and women in all elected positions through an electoral candidate quota system. The system was written into law and requires all political parties to nominate a minimum number of female candidates to their party lists (Rosen 2017). The law was said to have gained support from President Wade in order to garner votes from female voters, and it led to a parliament with 42.7 percent women members in 2012 (Tøraasen 2019). This new era of women in elected positions formalized women's participation in national politics, and it started with the leadership that grew from women's associations.

In the next part of this chapter, I explore the history of women's political participation in Senegal and the lead-up to the parité movement.

Parité and Women's Historical Participation in Senegalese Politics

Parité was the slogan of the French movement though it actually came from the German Green Party (Scott 2005). It is, of course, one part of a long history of women's participation in Senegalese politics that has been at times heroic and filled with stories of courageous queens and antislavery struggle against the Moors of Mauritania, and at other times marked by their absence in official archival documents or later on as elected representatives. "Power was transmitted through African women," said historian Penda Mbow in a newspaper article spotlighting women in history. "In Waalo, the Lingéer (a queen or princess), sister or mother of the king and the first wife of the king (aawo Lingéer) possessed

"The Tuesday of Ndeer," depicting the women of Ndeer in the antislavery struggle of 1989. Samba Fall, *Le Soleil*, date unknown.

significant authority. Their political role was even more significant because power could only be passed on to one of the three matrilineal princes" (Jean-Bart 1990).

In fact, women's marginality in terms of decision-making aspects of politics in the postcolonial era is what Aminata Diaw (2004) calls the présence-absence paradox, meaning that women have always played essential roles as a "hidden public" (Beck 2003) mediators of political campaigns, party organizers, and candidate promoters while men are the primary benefactors of this labor. And similarly, as archival records have shown, women were also crucial to economic stability yet absent from the decision-making that affected macroeconomic policies and those that affected their own access to development. Women's mobilizing power is not contested, but their ability to participate in politics in meaningful ways as elected officials is; still, men's political successes are intrinsically linked to women's silent work for the campaigns of their male family members or for a beloved male candidate. The queens and princesses of the various kingdoms in the Senegambian region were defined more by their access to power than their economic weight (Diaw 1998). In the struggle for women's equal participation in elected positions, the two narratives go hand in hand: the heroic stories of queens and revolutionary women serve to demonstrate that in fact women have always been political in meaningful ways, but in reality the day-to-day organizing by ordinary women has made the biggest impact, even if it hasn't directly benefited them.

Senegalese History's Powerful Women

Penda Mbow has been one of the most engaged scholars of women's history and theorists of gender in Senegalese academia: "the point in which we have always destined women to second rank, always thinking that they needed to be more implicated in economic and social development, we now must reflect on their situation over the *longue durée*" (2008). The longue durée of women in politics includes the heroic stories of the women of Ndeer, who courageously preferred to burn themselves alive rather than be captured and enslaved by the Maures, or Djëmbët Mbóoj, the queen of Waalo in northern Senegal, and her sister Ndaté Yàlla Mbóoj, who succeeded her; these women are known for their powerful influence in regional politics. Their influence came as guardians of the family wealth, among other strategies. Djëmbët Mbóoj, for example, decided to marry the king of Trarza, from across the Senegal River in what is now Mauritania, in order to secure alliances for the two kingdoms in solidarity against potential attacks from the Maures and Tukulóor (Sarr 1998, 56). Ndaté Yalla's mother, Fatim Yamar Khouriaye, was an expert strategist and controlled much of the kingdom from 1795 to 1816, when she named her husband, Amar Fatim Borso, as king of Waalo. She was also among the women of Ndeer who are regarded as antislavery heroes (Sarr 2011). Other women such as Yacine Boubou, princess of Kajoor (Sylla 2001), the region and kingdom just south of Waalo that follows the west coastline and includes present-day Dakar, were also influential in regional politics in the mid-eighteenth century. Yacine Boubou was a Lingéer who sacrificed herself in order for her husband, Madior Salla Bigué, to assume his position on the throne of Kajoor (Allou 1966). While some women were crucial to anticolonial struggles, the elite signare women of Saint Louis, the first colonial capital of French West Africa, intermarried with European men and thus helped facilitate the trade and diplomacy that led to colonial rule (Jones 2020). Signares (from *senhora* in Portuguese), "more than any other group, played a crucial role in fostering economic opportunities— and by extension, political possibilities—in early modern Senegambia" (Ralph 2015, 22). During the colonial period, Soukeyna Konaré, the cousin of Lamine Gueye, the first leader of the Senegalese federation, not only was instrumental in helping to elect Lamine Gueye but was equally involved with mobilizing the women's electorate through her self-named association to fight for women's right to vote in 1945, after being denied the same rights their French counterparts in the metropole had been granted in 1944. Senegalese living in the *quatres communes* (four districts) of Dakar, Rufisque, Gorée, and Saint Louis were considered French citizens. However, when French women were given the right to vote in 1944, Senegalese women of the communes were denied the same right. They organized, held marches, and relied on Lamine Gueye to pressure the French colonial administration. In a letter to the general governor of the AOF (Afrique-occidentale française—French West Africa), Gueye assured them they were "slapping the Senegalese with an unjustified humiliation."[14] Gueye was not the only ally in the AOF; Khalilou Kà, president of the Union Républicaine, wrote a telegram to the colonial administration on March 9, 1945, protesting the decision, saying it was "particularly anti-democratic" to refuse the right to vote to Senegalese (female) citizens "whose children and brothers have fought for France."[15] Following a public town hall on March 5, 1945, a correspondence from a colonial official recounted the event and mentioned several "indigenous women" were present, including a woman by the name of Gnagna Sene, who called the injustices of denying women the right to vote "inadmissible."[16] Konaré is said to have been the first woman politician in Senegal and was quoted as saying to her cousin, "Si tu es le digne descendent de Bacre Waly Gueye, tu ne devrais pas avoir peur . . . si tu recules, donne-moi ta place et tu verras comment une femme se conduit [If you are the dignified descendant of Bacre Waly Gueye, you should not be afraid. If you retreat, let me take over and you will see how a woman leads]" (unknown 2020). Gueye, who led the Bloc Démocratique Sénégalais, understood early on the importance of women's voting and advocacy power, and with women's newly gained voting rights, he won a resounding victory to become the first Black mayor of Saint Louis (Sylla 2001, 58). Although initially engaged with the women's movement, Gueye and other established politicians did not return the favor by investing in women's integration into political positions, meaning that women's main influence remained as voters and protagonists for men's campaigns (62). It wasn't until 1963 that the Union Progressiste Sénégalaise (UPS), parent party to the Parti Socialiste, established a quota of 25 percent women, which saw Caroline Faye Diop elected as the first woman to Lamine Gueye's parliament. Only in 1973, in the fourth legislature, was another woman elected to a similar position (Sarr 2013, 16). Faye was also included in Diouf's cabinet of ministers in 1978.

Penda Seck talks about her mother's generation of women, who stayed at home and yet gave way to a new generation of women in politics.

Before, women were confined to a supporting role. They just accompanied and applauded men. Before, women had no role. They were not elected but the ones who got men elected. Before, they didn't have anything to do with politics. They stayed home, took care of the children and their husbands. Then people started going to school, and women began going out and getting involved in politics. Currently, we are third in Africa regarding parité and eighth globally. In this moment that I'm speaking to you, practically every Senegalese woman is involved in politics or interested in politics.[17]

Mame Mbayame Gueye Dione Ba, another parliamentarian whom I interviewed regarding her thoughts on women in politics, made a similar point.

In Senegal, if you look closely, we don't have a problem with women doing politics. Ever since the time of Senghor, or even before, people gave a lot of importance to women in politics but as organizers, everything that had to do with organization. When it came to a meeting women, would gather people, lay out chairs. For a long time it was women who were in charge of *animation*, or the entertainment. Even before independence women were involved in politics. Women in politics hasn't been too much of an issue, but to give women a voice depends on the society. For example, societies that we call matriarchal like the Lébu, or if you go to Waalo, women were queens. . . . So among the Lébu they give women more rights to commerce. In terms of authority there were Lingéer [queens], like Ndaté Yàlla, women were royals. So generally speaking, women have been a part of decision-making power in Africa. But when you get into the thick of it, after gaining independence, modernity sets in, and women come and stand up, and have an important role to play, a significant presence, but once women wished to have decision-making opportunities, they don't give them the space they deserve. People want to confine them to the house and make them believe that their religion says so.[18]

Mame Mbayame Gueye Dione Ba was one of the few women in politics who wore a hijab during her everyday activities. In chapter 5, I further discuss the question of women's positionality and feminism within Islam. Her party, Mouvement de la Réforme pour le Développement Social (Movement for Reform and Social Development, MRDS), was a religious reformist party focused on ethics as part of its founding doctrine. When I met her in 2017, Mame Mbayame had joined a new coalition called Ndawi Askan wi (Youth of the Nation), which was led by Ousmane Sonko, who would become the main opposition leader to Macky Sall in the 2019 presidential election and the prime minister in 2024. Her comments, along with those of Penda Seck, demonstrate an awareness of the historical implications of women and authority in Senegal and Africa more broadly.

Much of the action of women in politics began in the 1970s with university and intellectual women's groups such as the association of women pharmacists and the female lawyers' association, Association des Juristes Sénégalaises

(AJS). In 1977, at the Ministry-sponsored event Quinzaine de la Femme, an annual commemoration of International Women's Day, the FAFS was launched to support such associations. Toward the end of the 1970s the Association des Femmes Africaines pour la Recherche et le Développement (AFARD) was conceived as a feminist organization of intellectuals who argued for a "decolonization of research" (Ellerson 1991) long before decolonization of knowledge became a buzzword in the Western academy. It was thus African feminists who argued against the "intellectual colonialism of the West" and for the production of knowledge about African women by African women. In 1977, a group of leftists led by Marie-Angélique Savané, the president of Kiné's desired, fictive female government, created the women's political association Yewwu-Yewwi (For Women's Liberation), a partner organization to her husband Landing Savané's communist party Ànd-Jëf (Mutual Action) (Kane and Kane 2018). Designed as a feminist think tank, the association awarded prizes to leaders such as Thomas Sankara, president of Burkina Faso, for the promotion of women (24) and for speeches such as the one he gave to a crowd of women to celebrate International Women's Day on March 8, 1987 (Sankara 2007). The speech was just a few months before his assassination, and he called for extending to women the gains of the Burkinabé revolution. Through a regularly published magazine, Yewwu-Yewwi's goal was to publicize the struggles of women in order to lobby the Senegalese government and public to acknowledge and honor their contributions.

Elite women weren't the only ones important to the conversation for independence and postcolonial politics. In fact, many of the first women in parliament were considered illiterate, meaning they had not attended French school, although linking literacy rates to French education has now been debunked (Ngom 2016; Hill 2011). Two of them, Arame Diène and Thioumbé Samb, were children of the Lébu population in Dakar that discouraged girls from attending French school because it would corrupt their sacred native culture and traditions (Fall 2005). Arame Diène was what Babacar Fall (238) calls "a militant, first in pre-colonial Senegal, then in neo-colonial reform" and was part of the Senegalese Democratic Bloc, which then became the Senegalese Progressive Union and then joined with the Socialist Party in 1976. She was said to be a political force in her neighborhood of Medina. Diène was named by Abdou Diouf as a representative to parliament in 1983. Thioumbé Samb had a very different political trajectory. She was a radical nationalist and anticolonialist with the Union Démocratique Sénégalaise (UDS) and vice president of the women's movement within the party (235). She was also a leader of the African Party for Independence (PAI), a Marxist anticolonial party. When she switched to the

Socialist Party in 1983, she was mostly rejected by suspicious party members because she had been against the party since 1945, and this effectively ended her political career without her being given any significant position in Diouf's administration.

Despite women's sustained engagement in politics, the number of women serving in elected positions remained consistently low. For example, when the Union Progressiste Sénégalaise, Senghor's party, became the Parti Socialiste in 1974, the number of women representatives went from 4 out of 80 to 8 out of 100. Only 13 women were elected to the 1983 parliament. By 1988, 18 of the 120 representatives were women. And yet in the 1993 legislature the numbers dropped from 18 to 14 (Ndiaye 1998). As noted in the introductory chapter, the representative from Keur Massar, Aysatu Daouda Dia, made an important distinction that "you can't do development without politics, and you can't do politics without development." In this context, the efforts of civil society shifted from mostly economic development to women's political representation in order to facilitate decisions about development policies.

Parité Law

The parité law was historic. It meant Senegal was joining the ranks of a growing number of African countries mandating gender quotas. There were earlier signs of parité-like initiatives as a result of the COSEF studies such as men-controlled parties adopting quotas within their party structures. Professor Iba Der Thiam, of the Convention of Democrats and Patriots/*Garab gi* (medicine/tree), opted for a 40 percent quota, and professor Madior Diouf, president of the Rassemblement National Démocratique (RND), and Landing Savané, founder of the African Independence Party (PAI), set a minimum quota of 33 percent. President Abdou Diouf named the law professor and first female presidential candidate Amsatou Sow Sidibé as the first female member of the National Elections Observatory in 1998. This action prompted Abdou Diouf to promise at least one female member in each departmental and regional observatory. Despite these efforts, the actual number of women voted into parliament in 1998 did not reflect the promises made by party leaders.

It was in this context that COSEF was founded in 1995, with the mission to pass legislation for equal representation of men and women in elected positions, parité. They did so by conducting diagnostic surveys and working with community members and party leaders. The next section will look at COSEF and other participants in the parité movement. In 2001, there were only 19 women out of 140 representatives, despite being the majority of the electorate at 50.5 percent (Sylla 2001). In the legislature of 2007–12, before parité took effect, the

Samba Fall cartoon, "Women and Politics," and a sign guiding the woman to the political arena. Appeared in *Le Soleil* newspaper, August 5, 1998.

number of women in parliament was a mere 22 percent. By the time it took effect in 2012, a newly elected parliament ushered in 64 female representatives out of 150, bringing the percentage of women in parliament to 42.67 (Sarr 2013). In the legislative elections of 2017, the number of female representatives rose to 70, but the total number of representatives also rose from 150 to 165, meaning the number of women in parliament remained at about 42 percent. Between 2012 and 2017, "Senegal had the second highest percentage of female parliamentarians in Africa" (Telingator and Weeks 2019, 227). As a country that had never experienced significant violence, Senegal had been considered an outlier in the trend of postconflict countries, such as Rwanda, Liberia, and Uganda, that saw women's participation skyrocket following years of war or episodes of significant violence (Tripp et al. 2009). Organizations from Spain and from other African countries began contacting COSEF to share their experiences with parité. COSEF spent years engaged in awareness-raising campaigns among local populations and religious and political leaders.

COSEF, Parité, and Other Movements

Rokhyatou Gassama was initially a private consultant for COSEF, and in 2019, she was named president. I first met her in 2011 during a training she held with COSEF and Siggil Jigéen regarding women's involvement in local political

office. In between trips to the rural areas of the country during the 2017 election campaign, I was back in Dakar for a few days, and I caught up with her
and sat down for an interview. We sat at a children's table in tiny chairs at a
school where she volunteered. I began by asking her about the movement and
how parité came about. She insisted that parité was simply one part of a long
history of women's rich political engagement in West Africa in general and
Senegal in particular.

> I work as a consultant and trainer on themes of gender and leadership, gender
> and development. I also work in education, as I have a diploma in educational
> science from the University of Paris 8. I am a member of several organiza-
> tions, most notably COSEF, but also the National Counsel for Governance.
> What we noticed is that all of these civil society and women's organizations
> that were created around 1994–95, our objective was to promote women's
> leadership. Parité was a process that started out with something that wasn't
> called parité. But the work for me, it was work that our elders have been
> doing for a long time. It wasn't called parité but simply implicated women,
> quote-unquote liberated women, to be able to occupy decision-making jobs
> and to participate in the life of the nation. That's what it was at first. It was that
> Senegalese women wanted us to do a sort of diagnosis of women's participa-
> tion in decision-making positions. We found that there was a significant
> deficit of women in these positions.[19]

COSEF was, of course, not alone in its efforts. Part of a self-named Group of
Five, they were joined by Réseau Siggil Jigéen (Women Stand Up Network),
the Association des Professionnelles de la Communication (APAC), the Association des Juristes Sénégalaises (AJS), and the Forum Civil. In 2001, they
held a joint conference under the slogan "Électrices c'est bien, élues c'est mieux!
[Women voters, that's good, women elected representatives, even better!]"
(Sylla 2001) to denounce gender discrimination in Parliament. Rokhyatou and
her colleagues realized that in order to advocate for gender equality in politics,
they needed to understand the source of the issue. One source, as Fatou Sarr
argues, was "during the process of political parité, we first had to identify our
adversary. Once it was clear that it was men politicians holding on to their
unwarranted privileges" (Fassa and Escoda 2016, 96). Rokhyatou is a bit more
diplomatic: "Around 1996/97 COSEF did a survey and created a counsel to provide recommendations to promote women's participation in decision-making
positions. Especially at the level of the government, institutions, but also local
collectives. So after this diagnostic work we needed to go around and talk to
leaders of parties, religious and cultural leaders, and see what their perceptions

were of women in decision-making positions. We first started with the party leaders, because at the time there were only really the big parties."[20] The surveys and awareness-raising campaigns conducted by COSEF took them across the country as they worked with local administrative officials and women's associations. As a *Le Soleil* article entitled "Elected Officials and Local Advisors: The Future of Women in Question" in 1999 states, "The objective is to present opportunities for women who are the important link for economic and social development in this country" (Ndiaye 1999); women represent the economic and social development link to politics. In other words, COSEF's mission was to study and propose legislation to integrate women into positions of power as part of their economic and social development strategies.

Legal Structures of Parité

The first law of parité, elaborated in 2007, was rejected on the basis that the constitution already stipulated that men and women are equal. After several years and revisions with constitutional experts, the law passed in the Senegalese parliament and was signed by President Wade on May 28, 2010. The law was important in mandating that all parties include women as viable candidates. The first article of the law mandates absolute parity of men and women—equal parts—in all elected and semielected institutions. The second article requires all party candidate lists to be composed of alternating sexes; otherwise, it will be rejected by the commission of elections. This second article was crucial, given the nature of party composition and electoral rules. For parliamentary elections, there are two types of representatives: those who represent a local district and those who represent national interests generally. The national list requires sixty candidates from each party; the departmental lists depend on population size. Regardless, all lists are mandated to respect the parité law requiring alternating male and female candidates. If a man is head of the list, the second in line must be a woman, continuing to alternate down the list in a similar fashion, an important requirement since previously parties with gender quotas could simply put all the women candidates toward the bottom, giving them almost no chance of election. Each party has a sheet with the names of each candidate according to the number of districts and national representative spots, in hopes that if the party wins enough votes, the majority of their members, proportional to the votes, take seats. Priority is given to the first name, the head of the list, and then others follow based on importance. The ballot displays a profile of the party leader and party colors for easy recognition. At the polling place, voters are asked to choose the campaign flyers of each party from which they will cast one ballot. Therefore, voters choose representatives by party and leader, not by individuals within a party. For each ten thousand votes, a party wins an individual seat in parliament. This factor means that parties construct their lists, and lists that technically respect the parité law can still end up favoring male candidates, depending on who is at the head of the list. The 2017 parliamentary elections, for example, had a record number of forty-seven registered parties and coalitions; of these, only four were led by women, with a male candidate in second position. Because there were so many parties, several had only the head of the list elected, and these were overwhelmingly men. In the case of a district with only three representatives, parité was impossible and usually also favored men.

Despite these shortcomings, parité was a historic event in Senegalese political history and marked the advocacy achievements of COSEF and other organizations for women's and human rights, as well as the achievements of influential women who held considerable positions in small and large political parties. It also proved the weight of women's voting power. In the early 2000s, in an article entitled "Local Administration Rebels against Feminism," Macky Sall—minister of energy at the time—said, "I do not believe in parité. It is not realistic" (Sow Ba n.d.). But by the time he became president in 2012 and it was up to him to ensure that parité was applied, he had changed his tune. "Pour man, parité, opportunité la pour jigéen ñi [For me, parity is an opportunity for women]," Mame Mbayame told me.

> Before they just used women for when they needed them to come out so they could say that they had a crowd of supporters. But when it came to making decisions, they took the women and put them in the back. My husband, Mouhamet Seydou Bâ, was one of the founders of MRDS. So when they had their meetings they would come to our house. In 2001 or 2002, they asked me to be the leader of the National Women's Section [of MRDS]. Imam Mbaye Niang was the president of the party, and I was the leader for the women's section for fourteen years.[21]

Mame Mbayame was introduced and incorporated into party politics through her husband. Mame Mbayame was a doctor and nutritionist trained at the Université Cheikh Anta Diop of Dakar, was part of the first generation of doctors to graduate nationally, and worked for the Hôpital Gaspard Kamara in Dakar and consulted with USAID's nutrition program. As she said, her involvement in politics came naturally because "I was around during their meetings and found I had things to add. After some time, they started listening" (Bâ 2017). Other parties long had women's sections led by women—such as Penda Seck's work with the Women of Bennoo Bokk Yaakaar—and a smaller group of parties had instituted their own internal gender quotas.

Similar to Mame Mbayame's husband, Penda speaks of the support her husband provides regarding her political pursuits:

"There are some husbands who forbid their wives from getting into politics or to stay at late-night meetings. Then there are husbands who accept it. In my case, as I tend to say, I had to negotiate about this from the beginning of our marriage."[22]

"Donc ça a été dans le contrat de mariage que tu puisses faire de la politique? [So it was in the marriage contract that you are able to be in politics?]" I asked half jokingly.

"Exactement. C'était dans le contrat! [Exactly. It was in the contract!]"

We both laughed.

"Heureusement, j'ai un mari vraiment qui me comprend. Je voyage quand il le faut et vraiment j'ai pas de problème. Il me fait confiance. Si le mari et la femme se font confiance mutuellement, les problèmes ne se posent pas [Luckily, I have a husband who understands me. I travel when I want and don't have problems. He trusts me. If the husband and wife mutually trust one another they don't have problems]."

Penda Seck and Mame Mbayame's cases demonstrate there are men who are understanding and welcoming of their wives' involvement in politics. However, as Rokhyatou notes, that part of the mission of COSEF and their partners was to include men in their trainings in order to reinforce the idea that women's successes are for the benefit of the entire family. She notes:

We made a lot of progress. Even before the law was passed, we made important strides. That means women are leaving the homes where they have been confined to go out and work, in politics. Parité helped solidify that. But still there are a lot of homes where it is very difficult for women to go out and work or participate in politics. In rural areas men really tend to say that the place for women is in the home. She has to take care of meals, children, and their education. Now we have trainings even to get men to understand that beyond the home women can also bring a lot to public spaces. And if she brings something positive, it is not only for herself but for her family. If it is a household that doesn't have a lot of resources, and she is able to earn something, she has contributed.[23]

Parité: Its Supporters and Opponents

The strong opposition to parité seemed to run along three main axes: in a Muslim majority country such as Senegal, women's work was not in politics, and

Samba Fall cartoon, "Regional Elections for Council President." Appeared in *Le Soleil* newspaper, December 2, 1998.

their quest for equality was against local beliefs. Second, men argued they were not actually against parité; they were simply interested in assuring the quality and experience of candidates. And last, many argued that there was a lack of candidates due to women being uninterested in running for office.

Parité Threatens National Harmony and Religious Convictions

On Wednesday, November 4, 2009, just a few months before parliament voted to establish the parité law, *Le Soleil* published a debate with the title "Grave Consequences of the Fight for Equality of the Sexes and Parity for Western Society" (Daour 2009). The author makes numerous connections between the wish for equality and parity and feminism, which has "constructed itself against men, against the patriarch, against established order, but also against femininity and against the profound identity of the woman by wishing to place her at the same level as men" (Daour 2009). The author cites the fiftieth anniversary of the French parité movement, despite it having been passed on June 6, 2000 (Scott 2005, 2), less than a decade before, during which many members lamented the issues and regrets they had about unforeseen consequences of their own liberation. These examples reflected a fear that laws such as parité were aiming to turn Senegalese women into Western women and Senegalese society into Western democracies. Another article questioned whether imposing quotas would "twist the neck of democracy" (Sow 1998). Yet another article in August 2010 documenting a conference on "Islam and Parité in General" called for "women to avoid all copying of western practices of parité between men and women" and reminded the women in attendance that "men remain the head of the household" (Agence de Presse Sénégalaise 2010). Men's general fear that parité would mean much more than equal opportunity within government was something I heard often. A popular trend of women claiming parité as equality within their marriages and in society paralleled many men's apprehension that women suddenly wanted to be seen as equal to them. During the conference, a certain religious leader Serigne Ameth Sarr addressed a room of mostly women and called on women to "avoid falling into the trap of parité, which would feed the temptation to practice it within the home" (Agence de Presse Sénégalaise 2010). Another panelist under the theme of "Islam and parité" mentioned it was "God who asked that the learned woman be privileged in regard to a man with the same intellectual level when considering a position of responsibility is the first defender of parité for elected positions" but went on to remind them that "the head of the house is and will remain the husband" (2010). According to Mame Mbayame, this anxiety is not based on a correct interpretation of the Qur'an or the life of the Prophet Muhammad.

> If you don't study your religion or someone has taught you it, you as a woman will think you know what religion says. But that isn't the case. Because when you look at the history of Islam and the importance our mother Khadija had, the first wife of Prophet Muhammad, she was a woman, a trader who had a lot of money. Then we have another example of our mother Aicha, the Prophet Muhammad's youngest wife. Maashaallah, she was blessed with a great deal of knowledge. The Prophet said that half of your knowledge comes from Aicha because everything he did, our mother Aicha taught him. When they tell you that religion says that women should stay at home, he says no because the wives of the Prophet, may peace be upon him, were involved in trade, [and] others studied like men were studying. Women should be able to benefit from society. If you don't have access to resources or a way to learn, they refuse to teach you and then they dominate you forever. They tell you lies about your religion.[24]

As Mame Mbayame notes, the opposition to women in politics or parité was often framed within conservative religious ideas about gender roles. It was also about equality of the sexes, or rather a debate about whether parité meant égalité of the sexes. Her reference to independence and modernity as a hopeful transition for women to participate more fully in national politics meant instead superficial, if any, changes. Instead, she understood modernity as another form in which women's participation in public life is limited, and their disenfranchisement is explained by way of purposeful misinterpretations of religious texts. Not only mentions of the Prophet Muhammad's wives and daughters were common references for women when it came to debating about equality, but they were also used as an argument for women's place outside of the home.[25]

Other Arguments against Parité

Other arguments against parité claimed it was in contradiction to finding competent and qualified women and men. Mandating parité meant dumbing down elected positions. This was partly to discredit women as being unqualified, and to mask the reality that men-dominated parties felt threatened by women's presence.

> In general, it is a bunch of jealous types. Many men think that it is women who block them. That women prevent them from turning around and around. They have no real reason to be against parité. There are people who say that women are not capable. There are women who are not capable, but there are also men who are not capable, and they hide their inabilities and attack those of women. It's true that what women lack the most is training, but even now we have fought for women to receive trainings. There are men who just can't swallow parité, who fight against it.[26]

In addition to Penda Seck's comments above, feminist scholar Fatou Sow mentioned to me in an interview, "They don't want capable, intelligent women so that they can manipulate us" (Sow 2017). I heard this line of thinking many times as women struggled to shake off critiques of the parité law. Instead of changing the hearts and minds of Senegalese citizens by proving the substance of the women recently elected to parliament, women were talked about by men in terms of being ineffectual, immature, and unprofessional, as well as lacking serious capacity for the job. The majority of men I spoke with during the 2017 election were under the impression that women could not be taken seriously in government because they were unprofessional in their approach to politics, hinting at women's conduct of family ceremonies. Their fear was that these practices would infiltrate politics, forgetting that women had been instrumental in men's campaigns that employed similar tactics. One of the most outspoken critics of the law, representative El Hadj Diouf, argued that one's nomination should be based on "competency and merit, not a juxtaposition between men and women" that was created by "feminists who wanted to take this country hostage" (Xalima News 2012). He made these comments in the context of his proposal years later to annul parité. At some point during the twelfth legislature, which began in 2012, newspapers, popular discourse, and even representatives themselves began referring to the legislature as *le plus nul*, or the most incompetent since the first national assembly in 1963. No real measure or evidence can back this claim; however, the statement mostly reflects the opposition to more women in parliament. Many lamented the irony of needing to be effective and have the necessary experience if men excluded women from critical cabinet positions with real decision-making impact. Speaking about Senegalese women in parliament, Telingator and Weeks (2019) argue that women parliamentarians have had to be creative in order to fight the barriers placed by men's domination of political institutions such as the "lack of training and language skills" and that those women who "had limited capacity to address relevant issues that were debated and voted upon in the legislature turned to external resources."

It was the help of civil society organizations such as COSEF and the other activist organizations of the "Group of Five" that have accompanied women parliamentarians in their work. In fact, a state-sponsored *parité* watchdog, the *Observatoire Nationale de la Parité* (ONP) created in 2011, is in charge of ensuring parité in all public political positions (Diedhiou 2014) and has the task of verifying all party lists submitted before major elections. If a list is not equal and does not follow the alternating gender scheme, the ONP can recommend the list be rejected. This has been complicated in the past, for example, by cases of party lists within districts of the Murīd city of Tuubaa that have failed to respect *parité* yet have been allowed to stand. This is due of course to the historically complex relationship between the state and the Murids, as marabouts have been "grands électeurs" or "brokers" who mobilize large blocks of votes, particularly among the Wolof, which has created an "interdependence based on the mutual benefits derived from their collaborations and thus the relative autonomy of these brokers in social and economic terms" (Beck 2008, 72). This same interdependence has allowed for nonequal party lists among communities in Tuubaa to proceed. Despite these institutional limitations women's organizations continue to fight for the vigor of the parité law and access to trainings and support.

And yet, the opposition to parité or women in politics was expressed not only by men. Jealousy among women was also common. Caroline Faye, the first woman elected to parliament in 1963, reflected on her time in politics thus: "I fought a whole life of forty-five years without rest, without vacation, without happiness. It's difficult because certain jealousies from women slowed me down a great deal. Every time a woman should succeed, we tear them down by their feet to ruin them. Up until now [speaking somewhere around 1968] in Senegal, after forty-five, fifty, or sixty years, we can't point out a woman who has succeeded in politics." During my fieldwork I also heard women lament that it was their female peers who sought to undermine them, what they interpreted as jealousy. However, as Fatou Sow Sarr observed previously, men would do anything to assert dominance, including sowing divisions between women.

Women Are Not Interested in Politics

In 2017, I was present for the prelegislative election press conference of Ndawi Askan wi, Mame Mbayame's coalition with Ousmane Sonko, held in a beautiful hotel in downtown Dakar. The hotel was popular for conferences and events; in fact, there were posters left over from an election party for French president Emmanuel Macron. Acting alongside journalists, I asked Mr. Sonko a question about his views on parité. He took my question and said, "I think I'll let Mame Mbayame Gueye handle this question as she knows much more about women." He handed her the microphone as she was sitting behind him and she responded, "Yes, Emily, I think it is time for women to do more than just organizing people within the party. Often women are there for the social activities and folklore, but women are ready to engage within their parties and within parliament."[27] I pressed a bit further and asked Mr. Sonko what he or other men thought about parité.

> Well, we know that equality between men and women does not exist here. Which is why we have had a lot of problems with parité. For me, the most important thing is to put the right people. Women who have all the qualifications, and God knows they exist. The problem we have is to get them to engage. Sometimes, it's under the pretext that a woman has her domestic duties or work. So, to find two or three women who can engage with a political office, it's really difficult. So I think the question of gender is just like that of ethnicity, religion, etc. They shouldn't divide us. We just need the right Senegalese men and women for the job. We know that women when given a task, they see it through.

When Mame Mbayame and I sat down for an interview shortly after this press conference, she reiterated the issue of women as political organizers versus political decision-makers. Ousmane Sonko's response was like many arguments against affirmative action or positive discrimination: it shouldn't be about gender or race but about who is best qualified. However, as Penda pointed out to me, "There are a great deal of men who are not qualified and yet continue to be given opportunities over women who are qualified." More importantly, Sonko's assertion that women are not engaged also seemed misguided, given the quote from Mame Mbayame above and since I was constantly told by women that there were a number of women rejected as candidates despite the tireless work they put in as organizers for their male counterparts. Examples were given that as soon as women needed to return home to cook dinner for their families, men would vote on crucial measures or elect candidates in their absence.

Parité in France and Senegal

Opposition to women in politics is certainly not unique to Senegal. Nor is the question of parité. In fact, France had its own parité movement that began during the last decade of the twentieth century and became law in 2005. And the different expressions of opposition to parité and to women's representation in politics in France and Senegal reflected drastically different ideas of what it means to be a citizen and, therefore, the political representation of those citizens in each environment. In the French context, those who resisted parité argued that it challenged universalist ideas of representation that supposedly paid no attention to sex or gender (Scott 2005) let alone the personalities of those representatives. Parité complicated the fundamental ideas in France that saw citizenship as an abstract collective instead of individuals with characteristics such as gender, religion, and ethnicity. In stark contrast to the French Republican philosophy that politicians were not recognized for personal accolades but for their commitment to upholding the principles of the republic, Senegalese culture and politics is very much about the individual politician's qualities, their genealogy, and the personal reproduction of specific cultural values. In the French case, feminist groups' argument for parité was based on highlighting differences such as gender and sex rather than muting them and thus disturbing the abstract individual as citizen that Rousseau argues in *The Social Contract* (Diaw 2010).

In Rousseau's understanding of civic identity, the citizen is an abstraction of the public, which, because it is public, is therefore naturally male. The *paritaristes* of France adopted a strategy of challenging the arbitrary idea of the public being categorically male. As Scott (2005) says, "In an echoing of the traditional arguments used to exclude women—that their sex distorts their ability to be abstract individuals—the paritaristes insisted that the male monopoly of political office also distorted; but this time it was the political body of the nation, not the individual, that was at issue" (52).

In the Senegalese case, the hostility toward parité—and women's continued presence in state politics—has had more to do with *what* Senegalese women represent, rather than *whom*. That is to say, it is not so much the sex of the representative but the social constructions of what gender represents in the modern political realm. This means men being opposed to women because they represent frivolity and folklore—even if the folklore entails applauding and creating the lively environments necessary for the success of men's campaigns, just as long as they remained in this supporting role. While Senegalese women are praised for their generosity and economic savviness within family ceremonies and development projects, these tactics are seen as irresponsible, unprofessional, and antiquated, especially as political strategy. Women are joining the ranks of state politics or somehow symbolizing the domestic space is not the cause of public objection to them—although in reality that is part of it: their form of "doing politics" that threatens the modern model of an aspiring Senegalese Republic. As Diaw (2010) points out, the very notion of modern citizenship has been built around the exclusion of women in the public political space (37). The particularity of the Senegalese parité movement and its oppositions have had everything to do with the postcolonial and neoliberal realities that this chapter has highlighted. The question of women disrupting a public politic that is assumed to be male is embedded in the historical changes to the relationship between labor and gender, the gendered norms of social and economic transfer and the political strategies that have arisen both in spite of and as its beneficiaries. That is, women's central role in creating the link between state salaries and family social obligations became both economic lifeboats following structural adjustments to state budgets and fodder for debates about the excesses of teraanga and family ceremonies, and women blurring the lines of private and public space and conduct. Therefore, organizations like COSEF and strategies among female leaders of women's sections of male-dominated parties or leaders of development associations focused on a gendered identity that has been intimately linked to their contributions to society by way of development organizations, religious associations, and now political aspirations. And although gender had not always been the principal factor regarding women's access to authority, it has certainly become such. Therefore, the focus on gender as political strategy was in many ways an effort to recapture women's due on behalf of their long-term commitment to national development as much as it was about representativity.

Conclusion

Senegalese women's economic and political history has been about struggle and constant negotiations of identity and representation. They represent the discontents of the neoliberal reality as well as its opportunities. The stories of reputable queens and heroic women fighting against foreign invaders serve as a historical imaginary of women with significant authority. As the historian Penda Mbow points out, "Women have never been revolutionary. They have preferred daily action over fiery discourse. What is in fact revolutionary is the emergence of women onto the historical stage" (Jean-Bart 1990). However, since Mbow made these comments in 1990, I would argue that women have done some significantly revolutionary things. Nevertheless, her sentiment symbolizes the continuous ways in which Senegalese women forge ahead in the face of limitations and fashion opportunities out of marginalization through their daily work and daily interactions. Despite being up against the impossible standards of representing the modern, pious, and progressive subject, they have leaned into these challenges.

This chapter has served as a road map of sorts to demonstrate the rich history of Senegalese women in politics and, more recently, the pathway toward the parité movement. I have discussed the intensity with which women were tasked with keeping families afloat during the austerity of structural adjustment and its consequences. In the same article quoted above, Penda Mbow notes that "at the very moment that we push women aside is when we realize the necessity to include them in development" (Jean-Bart 1990). In addition, I have argued throughout this chapter that even as the Senegalese state and international organizations have invested in women's associations for the purposes of national economic development and recovery, in many ways they perpetuated women's marginalization in the Senegalese political economy by creating specific parameters in which they could participate economically. Nevertheless, as on so many occasions, women found ways of making the best of a difficult situation. I have argued that as a result of confining women to a micropolitical economy based on small private market enterprises—effectively technocratizing and commoditizing ideas of solidarity and teraanga—they were in fact able to develop sophisticated networks of leaders and eventually state politicians. In other words, the organizing born out of development projects gave way to the parité movement in part because it developed the leadership skills of women who directed associations and identified the necessity of having a say in how these projects were run.

In the next chapter, I demonstrate the personal side of the relationship between women's associations and the development of political careers. I also
discuss new forms of patronage networks driven by these very relationships
and those between women patrons and women clients. Before moving onto
the next chapter, I present the biographies of Ayda Mbóoj, Mously Diakhaté,
Aysata Tall Sall, and Aminata Touré.

Biographies of the Women of the Teraanga Republic

Excerpts from interview with Ayda Mbóoj, December 18, 2013, Dakar, Senegal

My name is Aysatu Mbóoj. Most people know me as Ayda—that is what it says on my birth certificate. I was born into a large home, and I was born into a political environment because my mother was a one-of-a-kind woman who was involved in politics. She was born in 1928. When it comes to my father, I was born when he was in the Progressive Union of Senegal (UPS). My father is Alaaji Amadu Mbóoj, and he was born in 1891. I am one of his youngest children. He and my mother are both Waalo-Waalo; they are cousins. Those who are named Mbóoj come from Waalo in the north of Senegal. A royal family, meaning they are kings. When his family left, he was a boy. They came to Tuubaa at that time and sent the oldest children of the family to a school for the sons of chiefs.[1]

From Saint Louis, Ayda's father was sent to Tivaouane, where he became good friends with the Sy religious family of the Tijani Sufi community. He made it to Bambey, where Ayda was born, and worked as an economic control inspector for the French-controlled peanut industry.

You know, women aren't supposed to say their age, but since I know you might need it to understand my generation, I was born on March 20, 1957, in Bambey. My mother got involved in politics very early; in 1945 when Senghor was touring the whole country, my mother welcomed him. Even though she couldn't write, she was a leader. Even my father was in politics, supporting Lamine [Gueye] when he and Senghor were campaigning together. My

Aysatu Mbóoj official campaign poster, National Alliance for Democracy, Work and Grow Together.

mother supported Senghor. Bambey was an important place, and Pierre Senghor, his brother, was the first mayor of Bambey.[2]

Years later, Ayda would become the first female mayor of Bambey, holding that position for many years. Her political story is also her family's political story. She grew up in the Socialist Party with her parents, but as an adult, she turned to Abdoulaye Wade's opposition party Parti Démocratique Sénégalais (PDS) in 2000. She quickly became the darling of Abdoulaye Wade and was named minister of women, the family, and social development in 2004, and in 2006 (when the name changed) minister of women, the family, social development and female entrepreneurship. This last addition to the ministry was a crucial aspect not only of Ayda's responsibilities as minister but of the government's engagement with funding women-led associations. She returned to that position in 2011.

Ayda served as a representative of Bambey in parliament from 2004 to 2012, during the Wade years, and again in 2012 as part of the opposition to Macky Sall's new government. Many say this is a testament to her popularity despite being in the opposition. "My mother's generation was happy to have their man [politician]. It was unthinkable that you as a woman would do politics alone. You had your man. You would involve yourself with your women's group and be a leader amongst them, but you wouldn't be mayor or head up the list for your department in the legislative elections, not like I did in 2007 when I was the head of the list and a man followed behind me.[3]" She explained that this was the result of her being more representative of or popular in Bambey; as Fatou Sarr writes (2013), "She is gifted, with a remarkable ability to mobilize better than anyone." I will focus on this sense of mobilization throughout the next sections of the book, as it has served her well throughout her political career. Even after the PDS lost power in 2012, she remained active within the party and loyal to Abdoulaye Wade. Despite being one of the party's most important members, she was not granted a major role in leading the party. In 2016 and 2017, ahead of the legislative elections, Ayda broke off from the PDS to form her own movement called Alliance Nationale de la Démocratie (AND), or the Wolof version Ànd, Saxal Liggéey (Work and Grow Together). One can really only speculate why she left the party, whether it was personal ambition or issues with new leadership, but she has remained clear about her allegiance to Wade. With her new movement, which she led as the head of the list, she won a seat in parliament. As mentioned above, she also ran a campaign for president in 2018–19 and again in 2024, but had to resign as her campaign was invalidated.

Ayda is well known across the Senegalese political landscape. She is liked by those in the opposition because she embodies a strong and confident leader.

> There are women who are just born leaders and women who do develop-ment politics, meaning they mobilize people, organize them, and show them the way. For me, that is politics. We are doing development politics. We are representatives for health prevention, for education, and to encourage people to put their kids in school, especially girls. For me, that is politics. But we also have to get involved in political parties. Most people don't even know if they are with the socialist or liberal party. Senegalese don't understand that. They get into politics because they say Suleyman is my younger brother and we go back a long time. Suleyman, I am the honorary sister of his wife, or my mother is his mother. So Suleyman is doing politics, and that is what he knows, and that is what he should do. This goes especially for women. But for a woman to dare and face a man like I do, they will tear you down. Not all women can do that. It's tough.[4]

Excerpts from interview with Moukhsinatou (Mously) Diakhaté, May 5, 2017, Dakar, Senegal

Mously is among many women in Senegal who either never attended formal French schooling or were educated in Qur'anic schools called *daara*. Even though some have criticized her for not speaking French, she is proud of being self-taught in French.

> I think what is important is to study, to gain knowledge. I studied Arabic also. But since in Senegal the official language we use for work is French, I got my certificate. When I was younger, my elders came, and I got married. But when I came back and started in politics by the grace of God, I was a leader in the party Jëf-Jël as national president of the women's movement of Jëf-Jël, the party of Talla Sylla, where I was a supporter. In 2002, I became a municipal adviser of Hann Bel-Air; in 2007, I became a representative in parliament. In 2009, I was an adviser to the mayor, and in 2012, people reaffirmed their confidence in me and reelected me.[5]

Mously was first married to Sëriñ Sidy, a grand son of Sëriñ Tuubaa, founder of the Murīd Sufi community, but divorced after not being able to have children with him. "That was just what God had planned," she said when reflecting on her marriage and continued friendship with and devotion to him. She married again in Hann Bel-Air, a neighborhood of Dakar, and had two daughters.

Mously Diakhaté poster for her association of women,
"Unity, Solidarity, and Peace," supporting Macky Sall's
reelection in 2017. The title reads "Support Macky Sall's
reelection."

Her grandfather was also an important businessman and owned one of the first
large cargo trucks in the Kébémer area, in northern Senegal.

My grandfather was involved with Léopold Sédar Senghor. He was a leader,
even an icon. Amadu Gaye Ndickou. He had charisma. He was the *chef de
village* [town leader]. But even my grandmother on my mother's side was
mayor, mayor of the women and leader of their association. And she would

help her husband with his political activities. That's what women did, helped [*jàppale* in Wolof]. People said I'm helping my friend or my husband . . . but my grandfather was an important person. Not only was he a politician, he was the town leader of Diakhao Gaye, which is near Ndande. Between Diakhao, Kabu, Tallene, Ndiakane, he was what they call *boroom dëkk bi* [village chief].[6]

She recounted an anecdote of when Senghor came to visit their home and work with her grandfather: "Bi nu màggee, dañu fekk benn taabal bu mag ci kër gi, ñeenti nit ñoo ko jàppo mais comme Senghor taille moyenne lawoon, bi mu mëse ñëw te nit ñe bare, taabal bi lañu ko doon servir comme podium mu taxaw ba nit ñi mën ko seen [I remember as a kid we had this huge table in the house. It took five people to move it . . . but because Senghor was short, and when he would come by and there were a lot of people, we used the table as a podium, he would stand up there so people could see him]."

One important lesson she learned from her grandfather was that people will follow you if you are sincere: "Nit ku amoon fula, ku amoon mboolo mu topp ci ginaawam la. Bu daan wax nit ñi déglu ko. Te xam nga bu kennen di wax ak yaw dangay indi wax bu ñu mëna gëm moo leen di jëriñ. Aussi li ñu wax, wax ju genne ci xol ci xol lay duggu [He was someone who was serious and had a lot of followers. People would listen to him and take his advice because you know, when you talk to someone you tell them what you believe and what will be useful for them. As we say, speech that comes from the heart, to the heart it will go]." Mously's path toward politics was through her relationships with people and neighborhood women's associations.

> It's not everyone that God gives a chance to be part of women's associations as I have. I created several associations and saw them grow until they could function on their own, and I let them be managed by others. The first one I created was the Women's Association of Sicap-Urbam [Mously's neighborhood] in 1993. That was before my eldest was born in 1994. I started another one called Kaay Baax [Come and Do Good] and then went off to work on the A3J movement Be One, Support, Act in Peace.[7]

A3J was mainly a movement of women who supported Macky Sall's party, which Mously joined years after the Jëf-Jël party was dissolved. When I first met Mously, she and her fellow members of A3J were hosting a major conference for the upcoming legislative elections. Mously was up for her third "and final" term in parliament. She said she had plans beyond political service, such as continuing with the development work of her associations.

Aminata Touré campaign sign that reads, "With Mimi, Senegal Opts for the Essentials."
Photo by author.

Excerpts from interview with Aminata (Mimi)
Touré, January 14, 2021, by telephone

My grandfather, my mom's dad, was very involved in politics in Kaolack.
And at some point, he wasn't the mayor, but the mayor got into trouble,
and he was sort of appointed to replace him. But very much involved in
politics. When I was young, I would see him organizing meetings in his
house. He was also sort of a businessman. So, he was quite well off. And
yes, my dad, who was a pediatrician at some point, was the head of the
medical doctor's union, and he was in his younger age a member of PAI,
African Independent Party. He worked with Mamadou Dia when he was
retired because Mamadou Dia had a foundation. And he was a member of
that foundation.[8]

Mamadou Dia was the first prime minister of Senegal and espoused socialist
rural revival ambitions for Senegal.

My dad was also involved, but he was more active in his profession, I would say.
But he was politically involved. And I have my bigger brother, who was part of
the Leftist movement—I could even say the far left movement. And I was curious to read his books; that's how I got more interested in politics. But one of
my teachers who was teaching us history and geography was the one who sort
of really got me interested in social justice. So there were some certain circumstances that led to my involvement in politics at quite an early age, I must say.

Aminata grew up between the towns of Kaolack and Tambacounda and did most of her secondary schooling in Dakar.

> I did my primary school in Tambacounda, which is in the east part of the country. At that time there was not much to do. My dad was the only medical doctor for the whole region . . . and we moved around quite a lot. When we were in Tambacounda, there was no high school. So, I studied high school in Kaolack, where my grandfather had a big house. But I just spent a year because my dad was appointed as the director of the hygiene service. And then I did most of my high school in Dakar, and from there I went to France for college and university studies.

While finishing her doctoral studies in France, Aminata accepted a position as program coordinator for the United Nations Population Fund Gender and HIV section. She also lived throughout parts of West Africa working on reproductive health, in Côte d'Ivoire, Burkina Faso, and Senegal. She returned to Senegal to join Macky Sall's budding political party for the 2012 presidential election. She was appointed as Sall's minister of justice at a pivotal and tense moment following former president Abdoulaye Wade's attempt to run for a third term against constitutional rules. The Senegalese had taken to the streets to protest his move and to express general misgivings regarding the governance of the Wade administration. Clashes produced rare violence in Dakar, and Aminata began as minister with a mandate to investigate corruption among Wade's inner circles. The now infamous Cour de Répression de l'Enrichissement Illicite (CREI), which aimed to track down cases of corruption starting with the former administration, was headed up by Aminata. It was a controversial process, and Aminata came out of it with nicknames such as Dame de Fer (Iron Lady), after her English colleague Margaret Thatcher, and, more affectionately, Mimi.

During her time as minister of justice, she spared no one, including police officers, the controversial religious leader Cheikh Béthio Thioune, and Karim Wade, former minister and son of President Abdoulaye Wade. She also oversaw the historic trial of Hissène Habré, the former leader of Chad who was accused of crimes against humanity, who had lived in Senegal in exile after being chased from power in 1990. His trial in 2012 was hailed as the first trial of this scale conducted on the African continent by African judges. Aminata was an essential part of lobbying for the trial to take place in Dakar. However, not everyone was happy about it. Habré had lived in the Dakar neighborhood of Ouakam for two decades and was known to many there. Many neighbors had gotten to know him at the mosque or via secondhand stories, and they were outraged with Aminata and the whole trial. This did not represent the Hissène they had gotten to know as a neighbor, nor was it an example of teraanga (or rather an example of *maaslu/baalu*, forgiveness of which most Senegalese were more used to in terms of seeking justice).

Due to her work in the Justice Department, Macky Sall named her prime minister in 2013 and fired her in 2014 after she lost a mayoral election in her neighborhood of Grand Yoff to the powerful mayor of Dakar, Khalifa Sall. Since then, she has fulfilled several other roles under the Sall administration, including as a special envoy of the president in 2015, and in 2019, she served for one year as the president for the Economic, Social, and Environmental Council. In 2020, she was replaced by another former prime minister under the Wade administration, Idrissa Seck. When I spoke to her in January 2021, she was considering a run for mayor of Kaolack, where her grandfather had also been mayor. In 2023, despite serving as a representative for Bennoo Bokk Yakaar in parliament—and rumors she would be appointed as the first woman president to preside over parliament—she was ousted by Macky Sall. She consequently joined the opposition and was named High Representative to the President of the Republic in 2024 (APA News 2024).

Excerpts from interview with Aysata Tall Sall, August 7, 2017, Dakar, Senegal

Beginning with her quote I cited in the introduction, Aysata frames her identity as a woman in politics thus:

> There are women in politics, there are African women in politics, and then there are Senegalese women in politics. Regarding all three, I think we have a lot to say. My professional life doesn't start with politics; it starts with my role as a lawyer. I was born to a marabout family, which is why I say it is important to talk about Senegalese women in politics. I come from a very conservative family where even men don't go to school.[9] They go to Qur'anic school. They are marabouts. So if girls go to school it is really an exception. We were lucky to have a father who said we would go to school. We are eleven children in our family, nine girls and two boys. My father understood very early on that boys and are girls are the same and that we shouldn't differentiate the girls and the boys, which in Senegal is quite exceptional. Not all fathers are like this. So I went to school with this in mind. In Podor, which is a very conservative society. A woman has her place, and she stays there. It is up to others [men] to run society. I remember that even for presenting condolences I had to go at

Aysata Tall Sall official campaign poster. It reads, "Dare the Future. A Strong Woman for Senegal."

night accompanied by a young boy because women weren't even supposed to walk around outside during the day to work, let alone participate in politics. So that is where I'm from, and under these conditions, I went to school.[10]

Aysata, a Pulaar girl, grew up in this environment and as an adult has come to be mayor of that same town, Podor, the capital of the Fuutaa region in northeastern Senegal.

My grandfather, who was the marabout, always told my dad, "You must take us girls out of school," but my dad said, "No, no, no, they are brilliant. They get good grades. They must continue." And we continued until the BAC [end of high school exam] and our grandfather said, "These girls are ruined. They won't get married. They should be nuns sent to a convent." Well, it was my grandfather's way of talking. Then came university, and I told my father I wanted to study law. That is when I got some pushback from my father. He didn't want me to study law; he wanted me to study literature. After that, I would become a professor. It would be easier. And after that, I would get married and have kids, three months of vacation—that would be more manageable. I didn't see things that way and felt I was destined to practice law. So, if I had insisted, that would have been the end of discussion. We compromised, and I said I would do local administration, working as a regional governor.

But then my dad understood that I would be a lawyer, because I knew how to put things in order. People say that even when I was a little girl, I was maybe three years old, if someone said something I responded right away. I had a natural talent for that [argumentation]. I've been a lawyer for thirty years, and every time I win, even if it's just a little case, I am happy, I jump with joy like a little girl who just got a lollipop. I love being able to persuade someone, and winning for me is extraordinary.[11]

Aysata likes to win. Whether winning a case as a lawyer, or as a politician, she is competitive. She is assertive and strikingly beautiful. A fair-skinned Pulaar from northern Senegal, Aysata comes from a religious family that shares a genealogy with the Tijāniyya religious leader Thierno Seydou Nourou Tall and with the grandson of the nineteenth-century jihadist leader Umar Tall (Seesemann and Soares 2009). Growing up in a conservative religious family, she was lucky to have a grandfather and father who believed in the education of girls. Her professional career took off after she earned her law degree at the Université de Cheikh Anta Diop in Dakar, and she began practicing law in 1982. She even played a lawyer in Abderrahmane Sissako's 2006 film *Bamako* and proudly showed me a painting made of her character. She said her political career found her. She told me the story of how this happened and seemed to take great pleasure from it.

> What happened for me was that one day I finished a really difficult case and won, but the minister of justice wanted to talk to the prosecutor to undo my judgment. I revolted because they wanted to take my victory, and I can't accept that. I sent President Abdou Diouf a very severe letter denouncing that. I threatened that if he supported that, I would denounce it wherever I could. The president received the letter where I asked to have a meeting with him to tell him what happened, because I'm sure his minister didn't explain it to him. He asked one of his advisers to talk to me. I refused because the president had spoken to the other party and should then respect me and also speak with me. The president didn't like that someone refused what he asked for. Then later he understood why I had refused and happened to meet with a cousin. He asked if we were related, and she said yes. Then three months later, they were reconfiguring their ministers, and so he called me, and he just said, "I want to make you my minister of communication and the spokesperson of my government. I remember that you speak and write French well. I need a new face, especially a woman." He gave all his reasons. I thought about it and spoke to my father. I accepted and was appointed eighteen months before the presidential election. That was in 1998.[12]

Undoubtedly, her insistence made a good impression on President Diouf and others in the Parti Socialiste. That insistence has been her modus operandi: elegantly assertive, courageous, and competitive. The combination most likely comes from her parents. According to Aysata, her mother was "a traditional African mom who stayed at home. She didn't really have an education. But she understood the political game and was my biggest supporter." Her father, on the other hand, was a close adviser to Senghor who was close friends with Seydou Nourou Tall. Her father originally had not wanted her to be a lawyer but gave in once he discovered she was good at it and wasn't going to give up. The same happened in politics. She had attempted to take over as the party's general secretary but was blocked by procedural means, losing out to Ousmane Tanor Dieng in 2014. For reasons of personal deception and disagreement as to the direction of the party, Aysata stepped back from her role within the party. Tanor Dieng and his supporters wished to join Macky Sall's coalition, whereas Aysata and Khalifa Sall opposed this move. In our interview in 2017, she blamed Abdou Diouf's loss in 2000 on switching sides (*transhumer*) by Tanor Dieng and others who left the PS and went with Abdoulaye Wade and the PDS. She said, "J'ai pensé, mais ça ne peut pas être la démocratie . . . il faut que les gens comprennent que la politique a sa part de noblesse. Que le courage fait partie de ça. Ce sont les convictions et des valeurs qui font partie de cela [I thought, that can't be what democracy is about. People have to understand that there is a part of politics that is about nobility and courage. Conviction and values are part of it]." Ironically, Aysata switched sides during the 2019 presidential election to support Macky Sall once her own party was disqualified. The issue is not so much that Aysata switched sides, as many before her had done, despite her indignation to it; rather, it is the fiery reaction she received, packed with tropes about gender and capabilities, directly questioning her sincerity and commitment to women's struggle. She had, after all, made her whole campaign about that.

Therefore, her idea of democracy is not simply about one person one vote (that is certainly part of it), but it is also about considering what one is due. What one has spent their life working toward. When she says "politics is also about nobility," she is concerned with party leaders recognizing the reciprocal aspirations of the party. In her letter to the Socialist Party, following the deception of being pushed out, she repeats the sentiment several times that politics must be a noble cause, and that comes with respecting what members have sacrificed for the party.

"La société le rend difficile pour les femmes de parler [Society makes it hard for women to speak up]," Aysata said in response to my question about being a woman in politics. "Already it's difficult to be a woman in politics. Even in the West. Mrs. Clinton, everyone said she was the perfect candidate, that for sure she was going to win, but then when you ask men why they didn't vote for her they said, 'She was too strong a woman.' She lost because she went beyond a woman's role. She represents too strong of things and was a victim of what it means to be a strong woman."[13] In the context of her failed bid as general secretary of the Parti Socialiste, Aysata said people always commented that "elle est trop ambitieuse; elle va casser le parti [she is too ambitious; she is going to break the party]." And of the successful passing of the parité law, she said, "C'est bien, mais il y'a un danger. Le danger, c'est quoi ? Ce sont les hommes qui proposent les femmes pour la parité [It is good but dangerous. What's the danger? It is men who propose women for parité]." The danger comes when men run parties and coalitions and seek to collaborate with women who are not a threat: "Un homme ne va jamais, pardons l'expression, une emmerdeuse comme Aysata Tall Sall qui va aller à l'assemblé. Il va proposer une femme qui applaudit, qui met son tissue et qui dit 'tu es mon Président' [A man is never going to, excuse the expression, let a pain in the ass like Aysata Tall go to parliament. He is going to propose a woman who applauds and wears her outfit and who says 'you are my president'].'' The reference to "particular outfits" has to do with women being supporters of men's parties in a visual sign of alliance. These women, often referred to as *sama jigéen* (my woman) by men politicians, were silent organizers, cooks, or entertainers for political rallies. They were certainly not the disruptors who sought authority within the party, as Aysata has: "Si on avait la parité de competence, ça aurait été formidable. On dit okay, on va envoyer les femmes selon les compétences, selon leur profile mais comme ça n'a pas été fait. La parité a même desservi la cause des femmes. On a même pensé que ça a saboté la parité. Donc, voilà ce que les femmes rencontrent dans la politique en générale et au Sénégal en particulier [If we'd had parité based on competence, that would have been amazing. We say OK, we will send these women based on their competence, but since that is not what happened, (parité) has actually been a disservice to our women's cause. So those are some of the things that women in politics in Senegal particularly have to deal with]."

4

Patronas and Hustlers

Women's Associations and Patrona-Client Networks

This chapter is based on my time with Mously Diakhaté and Awa Ka during the summers of 2017 and 2018. In 2017, I accompanied both Mously and Awa during their associational meetings as well as on the campaign trail for the legislative elections. Awa Ka was a local associational leader and political hopeful. I visited many homes in Cambérène and the Yarax Han Belair-Maristes neighborhoods of Dakar and saw firsthand the personal relationships they had with members of their associations and, by extension, the members' families and neighbors. Beyond in-person meetings, Mously and Awa were constantly in communication with their members via phone calls or WhatsApp voice notes to organize events or simply to listen to their grievances and see how they could help. Upon my return to Dakar in 2018, I was able to spend more time with the members as well as take a trip with Mously to the holy city of Tuubaa, in central Senegal. By way of observations, interviews, and primary sources, I demonstrate how associations have become increasingly prominent spaces for women's political participation that is driven by intricate social relationships on many levels.

Mously and Awa both represented the same party, Bennoo Bokk Yaakaar, headed by the president, Macky Sall. They had two general things in common. First, both were vying for a coveted position in parliament. Mously was fighting to hold onto her seat in parliament, and Awa was looking to cash in her social capital for a spot on the presidential party's roster. Second, they saw women's associations and social relationships as the gateway to make this happen: politics as a resource for their social and economic development.

Their investments, in the form of monetary contributions to kick-start projects or provide encouragement for said projects with association members, create what Buggenhagen states "is intended to bestow the rights and obligations due to kin onto non-kin in order to expand one's circuit of exchange" (2012, 34). To some extent, this also what Vincent Foucher calls "performing munifi-cence" (2007, 115)—a political strategy of generosity and patronage historically between a male politician and his female or male supporters. In this chapter, I argue that in the era of women's increasing formal participation in and ac-cess to state politics, it is women who form their own female-driven patronage networks in the form of associations. Their performances of munificence, or teraanga, cultivate horizontal and vertical relations of hierarchy and depen-dence (Creevey 2004) that utilize the arena of politics to advance personal am-bitions as well as collective opportunities to intervene in the allocation of state resources and policymaking. Furthermore, their patronage networks allow for women to emerge from the "hidden public" (Beck 2003) of male-dominated networks and, as Bayart (1989, 87) argues, potentially complicate the nature of the African state as a space of engendered inequality.

Two commentaries I had from friends who are imposing figures in the femi-nist activist spaces of Senegal demonstrate the growing authority of women in politics. The first was an online interview of sociologist and journalist Mame Fanta Diallo with WATHI (West African Think Tank) where she made the following statement: "Women like Mously Diakhaté are much more pertinent than any man in parliament. Even at local governing levels, women are the majority. Beyond Navetanes[1] (football tournaments during school vacation), men do not have any associations that have gathered them together. While women, they are in tontines, calebasses, and many other ways of gathering. So they have the support."

Although this interview with Fanta Diallo was done with the WATHI asso-ciation, which I found via Twitter, I met Fanta during my 2017 research stay in Senegal during the legislative elections. She was part of a digital activist group called Africtivistes, which started small with a few journalists, bloggers, and students but has made a significant name for itself, notably protecting Gambian journalists following the political crisis that ousted Yaya Jammeh from power that same year. Fanta Diallo's statement about women being more relevant than men in the political realm resonates with the experiences I encountered while following women's campaigns, watching their dynamism in action and hearing passing comments about their character and leadership skills.

The second example is from a conversation I had with a friend and activist entrepreneur, Maïmouna Dembelé. In fact, I followed the activities of Maï-mouna and her fellow coalition members during the 2017 legislative election. Their coalition, Ndawi Askan wi, chose budding and little-known politician Ousmane Sonko to be at the head of their list. Maïmouna, a Muslim woman, spoke about women's power and significance in reference to Islam, saying, "When we talk about economic power and women in Islam, the first wife of prophet Muhammad, peace be upon him, Khadija, was a successful and rich businesswoman. Not only was she older than him, but she was also his *patrona*, or boss."[2]

Thinking of women as patrons has not been part of the historiography of patron-client networks. At best, they have been described as clients to powerful male politicians but rarely considered bosses in their own right. The word *patron* is the Spanish word for boss, and in this spirit, I use the feminine version, *patrona*—as does Maïmouna in French—to signify a female boss. I argue that the results of the *parité* movement along with the development of women's associations as political hotbeds have created new clientele relationships with women as the patronas as well as the clients. I think of this dynamic as the glamour and hustle of politics—that is, a different kind of power dynamic between women who are the politicians and those who work tirelessly for them, as they have done for men's campaigns. These hustlers are those who work for the campaigns and associations run by politicians in hopes that their efforts will mean their own political successes or at least the means to contribute more substantially to the development of their community circles.

Associations: Cornerstones of Social and Political Life

Women's associations in Senegal have long been a source of support and financial stability and a reliable heartbeat to gauge the wellness of communities. As Ferguson (2015) points out in the case of South Africa, in colonial settings in which large portions of the population were both impoverished and outside the wage economy, informal social security such as an "African extended family" (15), or *mbokk*, as I mentioned earlier, was the only solution that could be imagined, such as the women's associations in Dakar I describe here. Since precolonial times, associations have been how women assert power in their communities as well (Creevey 2004). They range from small groups of friends within a neighborhood that *nàtt*, or share a stretched-out mat designed for socializing and pooling resources, to more robust associations—*mbootaay* in Wolof—with large numbers of members unified by age or profession or as friends or neighbors. In Dakar, the capital, it seems as though one could map the city neighborhoods based on the reach of associations and their members' residency. Mbootaay commonly bear the names of their neighborhoods or, more often, the names of their founders.

Women-led associations continue to be spaces where development projects and agencies such as those mentioned in chapter 3 focus their efforts. For-profit outfits remain a source of funds for women and their projects of financial need; however, given the high interest rates of these loans and a tough economic climate for microenterprises, women are "pioneering new modes of livelihood and making new kinds of political demands" (Ferguson 2015, 15). In this chapter, I argue that since the installment of parité, and with the historic number of women elected to state politics, women's associations have become both the source and the beneficiaries of female leadership. That is, women's quest to align themselves with women politicians and their wealth is the new political demand for distribution to which Ferguson refers.

It became strikingly clear to me during the legislative elections in 2017 that a major shift in associational strategies had occurred as women talked about seeking partnerships with women politicians and helping them with their campaigns in exchange for financial aid for their associations and participated in politics in new ways. I rely on ethnographic examples and a semibiographical look at Mously and Awa in leadership roles. The relationships among politicians and their associations and networks are established and maintained by formal and everyday displays of teraanga such as personal investment in the well-being of associational members via cash and material gifts as well as professional support such as investing in the moneymaking actions of the association. Women recognize the opportunities these relationships bear as benefiting from female support, which is different from state institutional aid that comes with greater financial risk. In a similar study of members of several Ghanaian women's associations, many argued that "only women can represent women" (Fallon 2004, 82) and that organizations should use women's established informal networks to mobilize women for formal political participation (2004, 84). The women I spoke with also felt that an increase in women holding political offices would directly result in long overdue attention paid to women's issues that male politicians had historically ignored and that associations were the natural place to find future female leaders. Based on the archival data from the previous chapter, associations have indeed been spaces where women have been primed for leadership roles.

This chapter also considers the politicians' relationships with the hustlers that make their associations and campaigns run and turn development opportunities into political advantages. Beyond associations, family members are also central to their election strategies. These relationships are the gateways to election and reelection—politics as a resource for their individual, social, and economic development. The types of associations such as *mbootaay/*

tontine and *leket/calebasse*[3] have historically been the most visible ways to rely on social debt to pool resources for further forms of exchange such as family ceremonies, including those defined by marriage, or to fund other projects. These organizations have now been heavily supported by formal microcredit loan institutions—a situation that proved unsustainable in more than one case. Thus, many associations have turned back to the social debt systems that women politicians can offer.

I demonstrate that as a result, these spaces, injected with development funds—and politicians' personal contributions—established parallel economic activities that necessitated female leadership, thus priming women for state political positions. Newly armed with access to state funds, women politicians (local and national) reinvested in these associations or created new ones. For Mously, on the one hand, the benefit of investing in these associations is having her peers active in ways that spur political support by helping her campaign. For members of these associations, they have access to funds to pay off debts and to create more income. Awa Ka, on the other hand, is the leader of a neighborhood women's association that seeks to benefit from the political capital she has with members of the party. Alternatively, Awa Ka, with the help of her members (oftentimes family), aligns herself with the party in order to launch her own political career. An ancillary benefit is that affiliation with the party helps provide support for the various projects that her members wish to finance. As Kelly points out, Senegalese parties "are often the expression of the ambition of a single politician, whose organization consists of the politician's family, friends, and neighbors who are socially and materially invested in his success . . . and consistently an expedient way to access state resources" (2019, 8). These relationships are sustained by daily demonstrations of teraanga from a leader such as Awa in the form of gifting, sociality, and the generosity of a woman in Mously's position who has access to these funds.

I begin with Mously, using excerpts from her autobiography, my observations of her campaign, and anecdotes from our conversations to analyze the dynamic of her relationships with her associations and their members as well as her political process.

Mously Diakhaté

In her autobiography, *Du Daara à l'Hémicycle* (*From Quranic School to Parliament*), Moukhsinatou (Mously) Diakhaté tells the story of her childhood, her religious upbringing within the Murīd community, and her political career. The Murīdiyya, or Murīds, were founded by Shaykh Ahmadu Bamba Mbakke in the regions of Bawol and Kajoor in 1883 when he first called on his community. Although not commonly considered the largest order in Senegal—which is now debated—the Murīds arguably have the fastest growing youth population and global visibility. This is due to decades of extensive trade networks established throughout Europe and the United States (Ngom 2016; Babou 2007). The second half of the book is reserved for testimonies from her family, friends, and colleagues who share their connections with Mously and observations of her life. Because she grew up with ties to the religious family Mbakke, descendants of Sëriñ Ahmadu Mbakke, she was educated in a Qur'anic school (*daara*). It was not until her adult years that she decided to learn French. Her father was a fervent follower of Sëriñ Abdu Lahad Mbakke, son of Sëriñ Tuubaa (Shaykh Ahmadu Bamba) and third khalif of the Murīds. During a recent visit with Mously to Tuubaa, the holy city of the Murīds, I came to realize just how important Sëriñ Abdu Lahad was to her as well. As her relative Sëriñ Mahmadane Mbakke notes, "Moukhsinatou Diakhaté cannot represent anything but the heritage of a child of religious education. When she was born, it was Sëriñ Abdu Lahad Mbakke who baptized her, giving her the name of Moukhsinatou Mbakke, his own daughter. It is also Sëriñ Abdu Lahad Mbakke who gave her away in marriage to his son Sëriñ Sidy" (Diakhaté 2011).

In addition to being raised within a religious family, Mously also had plenty of mentors in the political realm. Her father was a local politician in Tambacounda, where she was born. "I was born in Tambacounda in 1965 then went to Ndande[4] at my grandparents' house, my grandparents who gave birth to my mother were in politics. From there I went to Tuubaa to attend Quranic school and then back to Ndande. Eventually, I went and joined my mother in Géejawaay, where I would take French classes during my vacation."[5]

Tambacounda is situated "467 km from Dakar . . . a climate of the Sahel with a heat that is often unbearable, it is a melting-pot of ethnic groups . . . as the town served as a point of commercial transit between Dakar and Niger, Dakar and Kayes in Mali by way of the railroad" (Diakhaté 2011, 30). Mously sourced her knowledge of local politics from the guidance of her grandmother, Fatou Njaay, who managed a number of neighborhood associations and "was a reference for the women of her neighborhood of Darou Diène (in Tambacounda), where no one made decisions without speaking with her first. She was their *meeru mbootaay* (mother of the association) and their political leader. She managed money-pooling groups (*leket*) of women even before I was born" (Diakhaté 2011, 36). Mously stayed with her grandmother until she was eighteen, when she went to live with her mother in the Dakar suburb of Géejawaay. "Women of [her mother's] generation were active in these local politics, but they also

Mously Diakhaté campaigning with party members in her district of Hann Bel-Air, Dakar. Photo by author.

helped (*jàppale*) their husbands or other family members who might be campaigning. These women were often referred to by male politicians as *sama jigéen* (my woman), who were essential to the public relations of campaigns but had no real stake in decision-making for the party."

Mously, like her grandmother, worked as a member and leader of several neighborhood associations in the Dakar suburb of Géejawaay. "J'ai crée beaucoup d'associations de femmes [I created a lot of women's associations]," Mously explained during our interview; "Dama leen di tàmbali ba ñu dox, ma dem ci leneen. Le premier tudde naa ko Associations des Femmes de Sicap-Urbam que j'ai crée balaa sama taaw bi juddo [I start them and work with them until they can drive themselves, and then I move on to others. The first was called Women's Association of Sicap-Urbam, which I started in 1993 before my first child was born. This local leadership was the beginning of her path to becoming one of the most influential women to hold office in modern Senegal. Due in part to the increasing size of her associations, she was recognized as having significant influence in her Dakar communities of Hann Bel-Air and Sicap-Urbam. This led her to accept positions as a municipal adviser and then as an assistant to the mayor. She was president of the Women's Alliance for the political party Jëf-Jël, created by Talla Sylla, an important opposition leader to Abdulaye Wade's administration. "Nekkunuwoon opposition bu mag waaye danu amoon nit ñu amoon solo, ñu amoon kàddu [We were not a large

opposition party, but we had people of importance who had weighted words]."
Her parliamentary run began in 2007 due to her leadership among the women's
group of Sylla's party. Mously has since been reelected twice, with Macky Sall's
coalition Bennoo Bokk Yaakaar (BBY). She was also involved in the parité
movement as an advocate and then as a member of parliament who voted for it.
"Yombul nekk ci ñi bokkoon mouvement bi, xeex-a-xeex ba dara sotti te bokk
ci ñi ko daan voter te appliquer ko. Du ñeppa ko am [You know, it's not easy to
be part of a movement, to fight and fight until something comes out of it and
be part of those who vote for it and those who apply it. That is not granted to
everyone]," she said, referring to her fortuitous role as an advocate for parité,
and during her first term as representative in 2010, she voted to pass parité and
was reelected to parliament when parité was finally applied in 2012.

Association Building

"There are those destined to be leaders like women who create things in their
neighborhoods, like the associations that make the mats for ceremonies they
participate in. They are women leaders. Those in politics seek out women like
them. They want women like that to be responsible for women's promotional
groups (GPF) and get into politics."[6]

As Ayda Mbóoj's testimony notes—and as the archives indicated in the
previous chapter—women's associations are both where many women get their
start in politics and spaces that become important for the reproduction of a
kind of female leadership. She also emphasizes the connection between politics and development. When I asked Mously a similar question about what her
idea of politics was, she responded in a sort of Foucauldian way, saying, "La
politique, c'est le développement, c'est l'art de développer la cité [Politics is
development. It is the art of developing the city/nation]." She and many of the
women politicians I spoke with frame politics as simply finding ways to get
people what they need, a constant process mentioned in previous chapters as
lijjanti, or the persistent hustle and solicitation for solutions to economic and
social problems. Having certain social networks helps facilitate the constant
need for cash. In Mously's case, the associations she created began as a way
for newly married women like her, who were yet to have children, to get to
know one another. Much like sister associations across the city, the women
gathered to pool resources from an initial investment or leket from a woman
of resources such as Mously. Leket, hollowed-out gourds, serve as receptors
and hold a symbolic role in life cycles, used to catch the baby's shaven hair in
preparation for their naming ceremony, collect the contributions for a grieving
family at a funeral, or hold the *soow* (milk) shared by newlyweds in their new

home. The structure of the associations varies from a twelve-month calendar cycle in which one woman takes the whole pot to use toward whatever expenses she might have to a system in which the total is evenly divided among the members. Some leket begin with an invested amount from an external or internal donation that members add to or divide among themselves with the expectation of repayment with a small amount of interest (depending on the loaning party). Daba Codou, the coordinator of thirteen leket groups in Yarax established by Mously for Ànd, Jàppoo Jëf ci Jàmm (solidarity, mutual support, and peace; A3J), was chosen by a male colleague to be introduced to his "*jigéen*" Mously. They have been collaborating ever since. "Bi ma duggee ci Mously ba tey, regrettewuma benn yoon [Ever since I started committing myself to work with Mously, I have never regretted it]," she said.

Associations have long been a reality for many women as part of their social networks among family, friends, neighbors, and members from other associations, often religious ones. For example, Daba and her friends in A3J often organized religious conferences and named Mously as the honoree. Mously attended and reinforced her solidarity by giving gifts of money and encouragement. Looking for investment from individuals within parties rather than from lending institutions after previously relying on mostly small member contributions is arguably a newer phenomenon, but it is no wonder that they would be a source for politicians to garner supporters by either founding the associations themselves or tapping into an already influential one. While such associations are nothing new, they have become even more relevant as a way for women and their households to cope after structural adjustment, which has shifted much economic activity to the informal sector (Hannaford and Foley 2015). In addition to providing everyday support, many mbootaay ease financial burdens by paying for obligatory family expenses such as funerals, weddings, and naming ceremonies. Such support is necessary, considering that these social events have only increased in fervor and price.

Political Gateways

On the eve of the 2017 parliamentary elections, I shadowed Mously and her campaign team for several weeks as they visited every small crevice of the tightly packed homes nestled along the seaside neighborhoods of Hann Bel-Air and Yarax. I felt simultaneously squeezed by the walls but then emerged to see the ocean only a few steps away, the beach lined with colorful fishing boats called *gaal yi*. Mously preferred to campaign within her district alone instead of scouring the Senegalese countryside with other party members. Even with all her political ambitions, I could tell she was a homebody at heart—she said she liked being alone so she could have time to think, away from the chaos of campaigning and daily life. With official aides and family members doubling as assistants in tow, we walked and greeted residents, stopping briefly in the homes of her A3J members to receive prayers and well wishes. In some cases, the houses were so close together that a short visit would cause a traffic jam since everyone who fit into the house or courtyard had to backtrack in unison to exit.

On one occasion, we gathered on the rooftop of a newly constructed building that looked toward the Port of Dakar with a group of women who sat in a semicircle of chairs listening intently as their peers gave testimony to the support they received from their leader and representative in parliament, Mously. She sat among them wearing a striking pink dress with a black shawl for public discretion or for use to cover her head during prayer. A3J, was initiated by Mously to invest in income-generating activities of women in her districts of Yarax and Hann Bel-Air. As Marieme Lo notes, associations have often used references to cultural value systems such as jàppoo or others like "commitment, dignity, and hope" (2011, 170). The A3J group was like other groups focused on development but also served as political support groups that were her base in political campaigns. One member stood up in front of the group and gave an emotional testimony of Mously's influence, saying, "Mously, mës na ma teral, mës na ma bëgg [Mously, she has always honored me, she has always loved me]." Mously was behind her, gazing at her rings shyly, rotating them around her fingers. The rest of the group erupted in chanting, "Jom rekk, ku ko amul du dem [Dignity alone, those who don't have it, go nowhere]" while banging on metal bowls to keep rhythm. Later, during our interview, Mously referred to this moment, saying, "Danga fàtteliku li ñu waxoon ci réunion booba? Jom moo doon sunu xaalis. Soo amul jom, doo dem [You remember their words at that meeting? Courage is our currency. If you don't have courage, you won't make it]."

The woman's praise for Mously demonstrates an affinity for her as a source of inspiration and support and, as the women noted here, teraanga. The insistence on framing Mously's financial support for the association as a form of care suggests something moral as much as economic and illustrates the long-term investments made by women like Mously in the numerous associations throughout the city of Dakar.

The main purpose of the A3J meeting during the campaign was to inform newer members about what the association does and to update older members on any new developments. It was also an occasion for Mously to solicit their support for the election, although she and her associates were careful to make the distinction between the work they were doing with the associates and their political participation. Her A3J technical adviser, Fatima Njaay, stood in front of the group and gave a report-like speech about the type of funds they had and would continue to receive and their purpose. She began:

> Everything you are involved in you should know where it started and where it's going. A3J means, Solidarity, Aid, and Peace and is an association created by our Honorable Mously Diakhaté in 2011. She is a woman of courage who created FADES, Economic and Social Development Funds.
>
> A3J is involved in politics, but beyond that, it promotes sustainable community development. What does that mean? It means to promote self-sufficiency. When her party took over the government, she could have said, "What I have, I'm going to share it with my family," but she didn't do that. Currently, A3J groups together 250 associations within Senegal and internationally, right? FADES works on reinforcing personal ability such as teaching those who do not know how to write their own name or training them to learn how to plant urban gardens in members' homes.[7]

Fatima continued framing Mously's investment in A3J members as a sign of generosity and charity because she used her own funds and put her reputation on the line with international donors. "Du fonds politique. Dama bëgga mu leer, du fonds politique, dafa téye ay biens-am, dem banque di fa leb ngir jàppale jigéen yi. Kooku amul jom? [These are not political finances. I want that to be clear, these are not political finances. She uses her own means, goes to the bank, and borrows money to help women. That person doesn't have dignity?]." The women erupted in a chant and resumed banging on their metal pots "Jom rekk yombul, dooleem amul, jom rekk! [Pure dignity, it's not easy and she doesn't have much strength, just dignity!]" I heard this same chant at various A3J meetings or rallies during the campaign as it served as Mously's anthem.

Conveying Mously's dedication to the women's associations despite a lack of funds was a way to demonstrate her benevolence and goodwill. Her lack of strength referred more to her status as a woman having less political capital than actual motivation or money. However, women's political capital is quickly augmenting as their presence in political positions increases. Alassane Kitane argues that what was once a treasured safety net of a moral identity, *jom*, has become descriptive of the strategies that one employs in order to survive economic difficulty (2010). Many of the women in Mously's sphere see her and the political environment as one that can solve their economic problems. "Looy def, nu defko. Soo taxawee, nu taxaw. Lu nu bëggoon rekk mooy ku nu jàppale. Jigéen amuñu ku leen jàppale [Whatever you do, we do. If you stand up, we stand up. We only wanted someone who would help us. Women do not have those to help them]," one member said. When I sat down with Mously for an interview, she reflected on her role as the leader of A3J and the opportunities they offer her and her constituents. "My association, A3J, is mixed with men and women, but mostly dominated by women because I have empathy for them. Because we are tired of associations, money-pooling groups, with movements, with political parties, and revenues don't come easily. In addition, banks want to kill them because the interest rates for most financial institutions are expensive and the loans do not last long. Senegalese women have a lot of courage to take care of their families. Even those who have husbands, they are the ones taking care of their families about 80 percent of the time."[8]

Here Mously gives a strong testimony of just how much weight she gives her role as a politician to the successes of the women she organizes. Beyond herself, she sees women politicians' mediation of state resources as a more benevolent partner toward women's causes, saving women from unproductive debt that private financial institutions force upon them. Dr. Biaye argues that one result of the Wade era's emphasis on increased state control of development projects is what he calls the augmentation of "grignoter au de-là politique," or a strong dependence on the state that has co-opted women's associations as the focal point for state control (Biaye 2017). Because the state has in many ways usurped major aspects of civil society, development projects that had been overseen by NGOs not only were now offered by the state but more often were initiatives stemming from individual politicians. It then makes sense that Mously's long-term cultivation of relationships with the women concerns how the funds reach them. She sees this as a kind of personal charity stemming from a shared experience of being a woman. The testimonies of her associational members suggest they feel similarly. "Moo may encourager jël mairie bu Yarax, comme góor bu fa nekk deful dara [She has encouraged me to run for mayor of Yarax since the man who is there now doesn't do anything]," Daba mentioned (Codou 2019). My interview with Daba took place in the summer of 2019, and we reflected back to the 2017 campaign. She smiled and asked, "Danga fàtteliku bi nu ko waxee maarse bu Yarax aka tilimoon? [Do you remember when our members told her how dirty the Yarax market was?]" I remembered very clearly indeed that the women recounted having pled with the mayor to have the market cleaned, but to no avail. Upon hearing this, Mously marched down to the market, staged a made-for-TV interview with the women, and used it to publicly shame the mayor. "Bés bi ci topp, maire bi yonnee na ñu nettoyer maarse bi [The next day, the mayor had a cleaning crew down there]," Daba said with a smile. "Noonu la mel Mously, di maye, di jàppale ci jom [That is the kind of person Mously is—always giving and always finding ways of helping others with dignity]."

Ambitious Vulnerabilities

When I asked Mously what she worried most about regarding her campaign, she quickly responded, "Shame is what I really fear." Shame is an important social lubricant in Wolof society. In chapters 1 and 2, I discussed the importance of the proverb *xaalis moo faj gàcce* (money cures shame), meaning that gifts to one's family-in-law keeps one's honor intact and free of shame. In the political realm, shame can be a potent weapon against an opponent; it is also something to be feared and guarded against. As part of the campaigning strategy in Mously's district, the party asked that she and the other candidate, Ndey Fatou Diouf, campaign together. "Dama faral di wax samay jigéen, Macky Sall moo bëgg Yarax ndaxte tànn na ñaari soeur-u Yarax ci parti bi [I always tell my women that Macky Sall loves Yarax because he chose two of its daughters for the party]," Mously said. Ndey Fatou had been chosen by the president as number two on the party list, whereas Mously was much further down. Mously was uneasy about Ndey Fatou and worried about her own chances for reelection because it was advantageous to be as far up the list as possible. On our way home from visiting families alongside Ndey Fatou, Mously elaborated and said what she feared most was the potential shame of people in her district not voting for her, especially after all of her investments. One's political livelihood depends on the social capital that someone like Mously can gain, and to lose in her own district would be a clear rebuke of her as a person and her investments.

When the final counts were announced, the coalition Bennoo Bokk Yaakaar, mostly dominated by Macky Sall's party, the APR, won 125 seats of the 165 available. Mously and Ndey Fatou were elected as representatives for their districts in the department of Dakar. Although Ndey Fatou was elected as part of the party majority, she did not win in her own district, precisely what Mously had feared for herself: to lose one's own district meant their neighbors and possibly family members did not see them as a viable part of their community. For Mously, who did win a seat in her district, her long-term participation and investment in the women's associations allowed her to remain close to those in her neighborhood and to ensure their support.

In order to put Mously's story into comparison while reasserting the importance of women's associations and politics, I will turn to Awa Ka. Mously's story has demonstrated an ideal of a woman who has risen through the ranks of associations into a coveted position in the government and became a patrona in her own right. Awa's story and a few perspectives from some of her members, however, show the complex efforts from within the associations to be relevant to a political party and use this connection for personal and communal gain.

Awa Ka

Cambérène, Dakar, June 12, 2017, at the Home of Awa Ka.

Fifteen or so women sat together on a woven mat, each with their various items to sell such as mint, fabric, or handmade soap, as they did every Monday. One woman was busily making *àttaaya*, the sweet mint jasmine tea that was a staple for afternoons among friends. They drank tea and chatted while waiting for their association leader, Awa Ka, to arrive with a special guest from Pikine, Awa Niang, a current parliamentary representative of President Macky Sall's coalition, Bennoo Bokk Yaakaar. When Awa Ka arrived with Awa Niang and introduced her to the group, everyone stood up and began clapping while one woman sang out to mark their arrival, "Awa ñëw na, da ànd ak honorable député [Awa has arrived, and she came with the honorable representative]." Awa Ka presented the representative to her association. "Samay jigéen lañu, liggéey nañu bu dëgër, amuñu lu bare waaye dañu liggéey lu Macky Sall bëgg [These are my women. They work hard. They don't have much, but they work for whatever President Macky wants]," she said as the women chose poignant moments to cheer, "Amuñu leneen lu dul loolu [We have nothing else but that]." In a plug for her association, Awa Ka said to Awa Niang, "Loo ci mën baax na. Balaa Macky eg président, nu ngi woon ginaawam te jotunu dara. Yaw xam nga ndimbal la waa Cambérène joxoon. Yaw ak man yàgg nanu [If you can do anything. Since before Macky was president, we have been behind him, and we haven't received anything. And you know the support people in Cambérène have given. You and I have been together a long time]." She emphasized, "Xamunu leneen lu dul nit [We don't know anything else but people]."

Beginning Where the People Are

Awa Ka, similar to Mously, was also born into a religious family and community. The Laayeen are one of the five main Sufi communities in Senegal. Like the Murīds, the Laayeen community was founded in the late 1800s by Seydina Limamou Laye, who the Laayeen believe is the second coming of the Prophet Muhammed. The Laayeen are located among the fishing villages of Yoff, Cambérène, and Malika that run along the Présqu'île coastline in present-day Dakar. Awa, like many in Cambérène, is a devout Muslim and Laayeen.

Upon arriving at her family's home situated in the central neighborhood of Cambérène, first built by her father, there is a distinctive mural of the second khalif of the Laayeen, Seydina Madione Lahi. The portrait depicts a man in white clothing with a large black turban wrapped around the top of his head and a white cloth wrapped and tucked under his chin. Most families in Cambérène, an original Laayeen village, have similar paintings or photos hanging in their homes, images of a particular khalif who has special importance to the family. Beyond the gate was a beautiful tile courtyard big enough for a car and a long hallway leading into the house. This is where the women sit—along the wall of the hallway on the floor or in plastic chairs reserved for guests.

Awa's family and social life revolve around her identity as a Laayeen, as do her politics. She is a state employee who does not hold political office but has the attention of the ruling party based on her activities and support for the party via her associations as well as the importance of capturing the Laayeen vote. She is a self-declared idealist and has a picture of President Macky Sall next to her bed. She speaks about her allegiance to Macky Sall, even when it is not beneficial to her. A childhood friend recounted that her home has always been a place to gather after school because her mother would always have leftovers for anyone who was hungry. Awa herself espouses a similar policy, seen by those who know her as the mother figure of many, with a home that is open to anyone, in the spirit of Seydina Limamou Laye and the principles of the Laayeen as well as her personal conviction of being at the service of others. "Ku ñëw ci moom du leen mësa rejeter [Anyone who comes to her, she never refuses them]," says Khady Ka, one of Awa's mbootaay members. I was told by other community members that she was the woman who organized Laayeen women for Bennoo Bokk Yaakaar and held the key to women's activities in Cambérène. When I met her in 2017, she was hoping to be honored with a spot on the party's list for all of her help ensuring a victory for Macky Sall in Cambérène and neighboring Yoff. Although Awa had not been given the opportunity to serve in the parliament leading up to the 2017 election, her participation has been a pathway for steady investments from the party, which serves her associations.

Most members of her associations are women in the neighborhood, close friends, or even distant relatives such as Khady Ka. Khady shared with me that Awa always shared and never kept money to herself. I pressed further, wondering if she had had previous experiences that were not as positive as she made Awa Ka out to be. "Waaw dëgg la, amoon nanu kenneen, waaye daan na denc xaalis ci boppam. Lu ñu ko joxoon ak lu mu nu jox moo tuutiwoon. Kenn xamulwoon ñaata la gagnewoon moom [Yes, in fact, we had another leader who just kept the money to herself. She didn't share as much as she received from outside donors, and we never really knew how much she was given]," Khady said. "Nu bare bàyyi nanu ko dem ci Awa [Many of us left her and went to Awa]." In the case of Khady, although she is a cousin of Awa, according to her it was not their family connections that brought them together; instead, it was Khady's recognition of Awa as an honest, generous, and good person. It was Awa's characteristics and dedication to her members that she showed through teraanga and more official associational transactions that attracted these women to her.

The example of members from Awa's association choosing her over another leader for reasons of mistrust demonstrates that patrons don't always have absolute power over those in their circle. The former president of the association they refer to was not transparent in her management of associational funds and did not act as though she was in a reciprocal relationship with her peers. Therefore, her leadership was put in check by her members as she was not sharing the resources of the association and was much more dependent upon them than she was able to simply enrich herself.

Power in Numbers

I first met Awa at one of the association meetings on a Monday evening. I was introduced to her by a mutual friend who said she was the one to see about women and politics. It was difficult to find time to sit down and talk with her as she was always on the go. This is probably not surprising seeing that she was president of several women's associations in Cambérène. One evening, we chatted about her associations. "Semaine bu nekk, danuy joxe 500 cfa te yoon yu bare damay yokk 25,000 cfa bu sama xaalis [Each week we contribute one dollar, and every once in a while, I add another fifty dollars of my own money]." She manages three separate *leket*. Two are for aggregating money over a year's time to then withdraw a large sum at the end of the cycle. The third group was named after Awa by her peers so that she would invest in what they called a "social" group—one that is for more immediate needs such as paying for a ceremony. Similar to most associations, members choose a leader and then name their group after the individual or group, so as to solicit investments from them.

Awa was in charge of all three but named as a sort of godmother for the particular association I was attending. This was the same technique families employed when naming a child, often doing so with the idea in mind that their namesake would be someone of means to help support the child. I asked Khady Ka how she had come to know Awa and what interested her about politics. She replied that she had not known Awa very well, despite being cousins, until

Awa brought her into the fold of various political activities. "Politique moo nu boole [Politics is what brought us together]," she said. When I asked what she meant by politics bringing them together, she said, "Su Awa demee fenn, mu inviter nu, nu daje këram, te altine bu nekk nanu daje leket bu Awa créer di nu dimabli. Machallah, bëgg na nit, bëgg ñéppa benn. Damay ñaan Yàlla mu defal ko députée te may ko wàllam [If Awa is going somewhere (supposedly a political meeting), she asks us to go with her; then we meet at her house, and every Monday, we gather for our leket that Awa created to help us. Machallah, she loves people, wants us all to be united. I pray that God makes her a representative and gives her her due]."

What I found curious about Khady's statement was there seemed to be a seamless connection between what she called politics and the money-pooling activities for the purposes of development led by Awa. Politics, therefore, was simply another strategy for weathering the economic storms that had become even more viable an option with the increasing number of women in positions of power. For Awa to succeed in obtaining a position within parliament would mean that those who supported her efforts and benefited from her help would also see an increase in funding.

Selfless Ambition

In the weeks leading up to the deadline to submit party lists, people like Awa Ka were running around meetings with party leaders, holding association-sponsored events, and attending large gatherings such as a religious ceremony held by the main group Femmes de Bennoo Bokk Yaakaar (Women of Bennoo Bokk Yaakaar, or FBBY) with the presence of her members. FBBY was in charge of gathering and supporting the women's groups associated with their party, such as Awa and her members. Despite being reimbursed only slightly for travel to and from the event, which was often the case when attending party-sponsored events, Awa and others hoped their presence would add to her chances of gaining a place on the list.

On the evening the lists were announced, it was as if the whole of Dakar was tuned in to the radio as the names for each party and coalition were read off. I saw people parked and huddled around cars or plugged into their earphones, one person for each side. I called Awa to see whether she was on the list for Bennoo Bokk Yaakaar, only to find that she was not. Understandably upset, she said, "Dootuma campagne pour ñoom, tegnañu nit ci liste bi, nit ñoo xam ne amuñu mbooloo, dinañu am jafe-jafe ci Dakar [I won't campaign for them, and they placed those on the list that don't have people. They are going to have problems in Dakar]." Her words were indignant. For Awa, Macky Sall had made the wrong choice, preferring women who, in her mind, didn't have the people power in the city to gather a majority for the party. Not only this, but she felt the party owed her something for her dedication and crowdsourcing. Her frustration was palpable, and her members were also disappointed, saying the party had let them down. However, when catching up with Awa in the summer of 2019 on the back of the presidential election that saw President Macky Sall reelected, she had changed her tone. In the place of earning a seat in parliament with the president's coalition, she mentioned, she had become much more involved in First Lady Mareem Faye's charity organization *Servir le Sénégal* (Serve Senegal). "Mois avant election bi wax naa Première Dame bi, il faut nu campagne leegi [Months before the election, I told the first lady that they needed to start campaigning right away]," Awa said. She lobbied with other presidents of communities across Dakar involved in the organization for money that would go to her members as they organized the campaign.

> The first lady told us that each community receives 30 million CFA [$51,000] to share among the various associations, of which they calculated ten for each community. I said no, make it 50 million. She said OK, dropped 50 million CFA [$85,000], and the rest came from the Ministry of Women's Affairs, for a total of 95 million CFA [$160,000] to be shared evenly with each community. The thing with Cambérène is, we are a community that shares everything. You can't give to some and not to others. The other thing is, Cambérène has a lot of associations [*leket*], religious groups [*dahira*], and so when I called on all the associations in Cambérène for their lists of members, there were forty-eight groups instead of ten. There are women who join several associations in order to receive more. You know that road in front of Mbaye Seck's house [asking me about a large open area near our mutual friend's place]? That couldn't even hold all of us. No one knows how many people were there.[9]

Awa played a video of the meeting that featured the first lady and several ministers, and to my eyes and ears, it seemed a lot like a Laayeen religious gathering with the distinctive *zikr*, or religious chanting, and all of the women dressed in white. Although Awa did not get what she wanted in 2017, she found other ways of remaining in the political arena in order to keep her associations going. She took advantage of the benevolence of the party that seeks to invest in associations such as hers that need funds for moneymaking projects and have their finger on the pulse of the voting bloc. Their countless stories attest to Awa's generosity through advocacy for members as well as her own investments in their activities. "Ci Tabaski bi may na ñépp pombiteer ak soble, te loolu yombul. Loolu du xaalisu politig, xaalisu bopp la. Loolu mooy teraanga [During Eid al-Adha, she brought everyone potatoes and onions, which is not easy (inexpensive), and that is not political money; it is her own money. That is teraanga]," said Khady Ka. Awa's selfless ambition meant that she not only sought funding through her political contacts but also used them to help her members. Something Khady made clear was that this was not the case with their former leader, who was ambitious as well as selfish. Awa, on the other hand, saw no difference between her own successes and those of her association.

Conclusion

Associations steered predominantly by women have been historically central to the successes of male-led political parties. Since the 2010 passing of the parité law, there has been a noticeable shift. The stories of Mously and Awa demonstrate how the correlation between women's increased active presence in political life and their involvement with various associations provides women with upward mobility and rewards them with people power. These benefits are created and nurtured in many ways by prestations of teraanga that seem much like part philanthropic ventures, and others political maneuvers. Women's associations are also an important source of supporters, voters, and visibility. People like Awa Ka who manage an extensive network of women also lean on politicians with whom they have connections for intermediary support. At the same time, her members place hope in her ability to ascend to a position of greater power as it may translate to their own access to funds. At the heart of these interactions is the investment in social capital that takes place through instigating and continuing a circulation of money and constant support. Mously's participation in women's associations is one of continual renewal that relies on the circulation of social and financial debt. At the same time, members of these associations see leaders such as Mously and Awa as both role models of morality and gatekeepers to financial opportunities.

Mously is one of many female politicians that gained their start in politics from within neighborhood associations that have sought support and resources from microcredit institutions. Their membership is contingent on pooling money and creating a community of interdependence between members that goes beyond the association itself. She sees her investments in the associations as a result of her political status to be a viable alternative to the untenable debt women accrue from "the banks and other micro credit institutions that want to kill them [with debt]" (Diakhaté 2017). They do not share the same pity for the social realities of financial demand and reimbursement with which Mously has firsthand experience. Instead, their debt to her is a social one, paid by showing up to her events and creating the lively atmosphere so desired at political rallies and the voting power to bring a party majority. The courage that Mously and Awa demonstrate adapts to changing needs in the community and is expressed through the performance of teraanga in its smallest and most visible forms. These processes ensure that women like them continue to gain the support that places women in positions where they can overturn unequal access to resources based on gender.

Several of my interviewees, be they representatives for various parties or those aspiring to break into politics, expressed a hierarchical and circular type of social and financial debt, placing them either at the end or at the center of an interdependence for access to resources and power. Many scholars have tended toward calling this form of patronage politics or clientelism (O'Brien 1975; Fatton 1986). However, what Mously's and Awa's stories show is how patronage networks are taking on new forms as women move from clients to male-led parties, to leading associations and leading parties. As women like them gain access to new resources as well as legislative powers, it allows them to pay attention to issues important to women and the households they manage. This is to say that involvement in politics is one of many strategies these women utilize for overcoming oppressions in terms not just of gender inequality but of economic oppression that affects their entire family.

As is apparent from Mously and Awa's stories some are successful in attaining their goals of political power, and others fall short. In either case, what attracts their members to them is a shared kinship in the struggle for economic stability and relevance. In other words, they now have someone to help women. Mously's members reference to her as having *jom*, as Kitane (2010) notes, is a recognition of her using her position of power to affect change, which she (as a product of similar associations) is well placed to do. Similarly with Awa, her members are loyal to her because she has shown a selfless strategy for using politics by way of these associations to improve her and her members' lives. The dignity that Mously and Awa demonstrate is adaptive to changing needs in the community and is expressed through the prestation of teraanga.

5

Good Women, Good Deeds
Religious Identity and Political Ambition

July 26, 2017, field notes, taxi ride with journalist Papa Ismaila Dieng, Dakar, Senegal

After my interview with Papa Ismaila Dieng, we shared a taxi as I was going to Mously Diakhaté's house for a visit, and he lived close by. The taxi driver was friendly and talkative, as they usually are. He had the emblem of one of the Murīd *sëriñ* hanging from his rearview mirror, so I assumed he was a Murīd *taalibé* (disciple). Papa Ismaila was sitting up front, and I was in the back. There was an accident somewhere, and so we were stuck in a long line of traffic. Papa Ismaila started talking to the driver about the election, and the driver said he was backing Khalifa Sall (the mayor of Dakar at the time). Thinking about Ayda and Aysata, I asked if he would support a woman who was the head of a party. He said, "Jigéen mënul jiite. Jigéen mën na jiitle jigéen ñi mais pas jiite [Women can't govern. Women can lead women, but they can't govern]." He said, "Jigéen ñi dañu bëgg àdduna moo tax mënuñu jiite [Women love this world, which is why they can't govern]." He then started talking about marriage and how he wanted to find a good woman, but it was hard to find one, and he didn't have enough money to pay for a dowry. Papa Ismaila started talking to him about how it wasn't just about money and told him the story of an acquaintance who had all kinds of money, and his two wives were both equally given a ton of money, and yet they hated each other, refusing to even acknowledge one another at parties they both attended. He used the example to say that men also have a part in making sure their wives feel respected. The driver listened intently, reacting every once in a while with "wax nga dëgg! [You're so right!]" They talked about how men need to be a little bit more patient and not just put everything on the woman.

149

At one point the driver said he wanted to marry a Catholic woman because they seemed less complicated, more organized, and maybe less wasteful. Papa Ismaila then reminded him that Catholic women still spent a lot of money on ceremonies; they just planned better. They both laughed.

Besides the fact that this anecdote always makes me laugh—partly for the memory of our laughter during such an honest and funny conversation—it reflects several stereotypes about women that I heard often. The first was that women were capable of being leaders only among themselves and within their own associations but incapable of governing a country (not to mention the differing definitions between leadership and governance). The second was that the reason women could not be trusted to govern was that they were irresponsible with money or too concentrated on this world's pleasures (*dafa bëgg àdduna*). The phrase *dafa bëgg àdduna* (he/she loves this world, or he/she enjoys the riches of this world) is common and used in many different situations. It can be in reaction to someone's expensive taste in clothing or during elaborate displays of giving money during a lavish party. It refers to someone who likes to show off their wealth in public. The driver's use of the phrase toward women echoes the countless critiques of women and family ceremonies mentioned throughout the book. The third stereotype was the reference to *àdduna* (this world), presumably juxtaposed with paradise, *àjjana*, which assumes a prioritization of material wealth over spiritual piety. Someone who is too focused on this world is not adequately preparing themselves for the next.

These critiques were especially common during the 2017 legislative elections, when several women headed up parties and the parité law was on everyone's lips. During the campaigns and after, women politicians spent a good portion of their time countering these critiques by attending religious ceremonies where they emphasized their relationship to the religious community and took on the complex debates about parité and about women's roles in society in subtle ways. In addition, these women politicians performed public—and often mediatized—displays of teraanga as expressions of piety and femininity. In this chapter, I investigate the dialectic between objections to women as political leaders due to gendered perceptions of work and piety and the praxes of Ayda Mbóoj and Mously Jaxate's identities as Muríd taalibés (disciples), constructed through their negotiations of being *jigéen ju baax* (good women) and *jigéen ju mën góor* (women who are more capable than men).

However, and more importantly, the taxi driver's comments about women's inability to govern beyond their associations are tied to presumptive critiques of women's frivolous expressions of wealth that directly question their piety. Beyond critiques of frivolity, women's motivations and faith are constantly under a micro-scope. Being attached to the riches of this world means one is disconnected and distracted from ensuring one's success in the afterlife. This chapter examines the dialectic between objections to women as political leaders due to perceptions that women's domestic work is more suitable and desirable and the public perfor-mances of piety and gendered work by them. Like the distinction between *tra-vailler et bien travailler* (to work and to do good work) (Adjamagbo, Antoine, and Dial 2004), another common comparison was made between *jigéen ju mën góor* (a woman who is more capable than a man) and *jigéen ju baax* (a good woman). Ayda and Mously are devout Murīd taalibé and yet were often confronted with these distinctions during visits to religious conferences held in their honor.

I consider phrases such as *jigéen ju mën góor* and *jigéen ju baax* expressions of varying interpretations of gender, religion, and definitions of equality and equity. Thus, women's political participation, and the critiques of it, highlight the changing parameters of gender as a marker of possibility. Moreover, the strategies for the parité movement and continued advocacy for women's po-litical inclusion also demonstrate the complexity of diverse forms of claims to authenticity. In one way, the acceptance of parité within a specified political arena represents a universal cultural hybridity, what M'baye (2019) calls Afro-politanism, that is at once connected to global ideals of democracy and equality and embedded in Sufi Muslim philosophy intertwined with Wolof and other ethnic ideas of power dynamics. On the other hand, as the taximan highlights, the aversion to parité as a potential stand-in for gender equality demonstrates persistent "colonialities of gender" (Bertolt 2018) from a legacy of seeing gender as crucial to maintaining imperial power (McClintock 1995) in a society such as Senegal, where previous gendered divisions were not as significant.

Performances of teraanga demonstrate its significance to one's political pro-cess as an expression of social and spiritual connectedness and the connections between local Wolof ethics, Murīd doctrine, and women's fight for political power and parity. In this chapter, I suggest that women like Ayda and Mously rely on their Murīd identity and education for political capital and inspira-tion. They also utilize Wolof ethics to invest in the financial and social projects of women's associations that then also become important partners in their political campaigns. This chapter focuses more exclusively on the religious connections they make as part of their political strategy. I use various sources such as interviews I conducted, television and radio interviews, personal ob-servations of campaigning and more intimate time spent with the two women, religious sermons, and analyses of passages from Mously's autobiography, *Du Daara à l'Hemicycle* [From Qur'anic Schooling to Parliament] (2017). In all of these sources, reoccurring patterns show the constant manner in which their speeches, everyday discourse, and praise from others refer to acts of teraanga, their links of kinship—or mbokk and a faith and commitment to religious leaders and their teachings. Public events allowed them to reiterate their status as generous, trustworthy, and faithful while also generating new positive images. As the title of Mously's book suggests, Mously's political trajectory did not begin with a French education. In our interview as well as in television appearances, she proudly highlights the fact that she learned French later, through a combination of night school classes and her own self-education. "I think what is important is to learn. It's not studying French that is important," she said. Many people testify to their admiration for Mously's abilities as an autodidact and for choosing to conduct political activities in Wolof such as her interventions in parliament. In the testimonial section of her book, Dr. Cheikh Tidiane Gadio says, "No matter her level of competence in international languages, she chooses to express herself in a language that people can understand. This demonstrates two things: she is conscientious that the role of a parliamentarian is to represent the people and that this means understanding their views and knowing how to correctly translate them" (266). Her Islamic education is an asset that gives her legitimacy within the Murīd community and humility to employ French when needed among her colleagues. Many of her colleagues, being Murīd or devout taalibé in other Sufi orders, understood the significance of this type of education.

Another important aspect of Mously's autobiography has less to do with what is in it than what it represents materially. While talking about her autobiography in our interview, Mously mentioned that she had paid for its publication herself. She wondered whether she had a copy to give me and realized she needed to print more: "The publishers sold a few copies to the Ministry of Culture, but the rest I gave away. I did that so the generation after me would believe in themselves. It is important that people know where they come from but also where they are going. If I could print more, I would give them to universities and high schools so that people who want to be in my position know how to behave."[1] The book itself is an opportunity for teraanga. By giving the book away for specific public educational purposes, she is both demonstrating her munificence and promoting a kind of religio-political identity.

Trip to Tuubaa: The Holy City of the Murīds

Mously invited me to go to Tuubaa on a summer visit I took to Senegal in 2018. I met her at her house in Dakar, and we stopped on the way there at a fish shop for fresh cuts of swordfish and tuna to take with us, as fish is hard to come by in a desert place like Tuubaa, so far from the ocean. We arrived at dusk. Her immense three- to four-story home in Tuubaa was under construction, with sparse amenities except for a full wall-size print of Sëriñ Abdu Lahad Mbakke, which she touched affectionately upon entering the house. "I am the representative of Sëriñ Abdu Lahad. It is the work of my family, from my grandfather to my father, now to me to work for the people. That is the mission. Sëriñ Abdu Lahad is the reason."[2] The kitchen was barely equipped, but the cabinets were full of mugs with the Sëriñ's portrait on them for entertaining guests. She was preparing for the yearly commemoration of the Sëriñ and to receive fellow disciples who would gather to celebrate his birth and legacy.

Her father had been good friends with Sëriñ Abdu, and Mously was a devoted follower. Her brother, Sëriñ Abdu Lahad Diakhaté, was named after the Sëriñ and said that "when my father received guests, he would ask them questions about the Sëriñ. Depending on the responses—whether the guest expressed a liking for him or not—he would either break out all the goods to ensure they had a pleasurable stay, or he wouldn't break his neck for them" (Diakhaté 2011, 159). Therefore, the very instrument of teraanga is embedded in religious and political affiliations. Mously frames herself and her political career similarly, seeing herself as representing the principles taught by Sëriñ Lahad Mbakke and the interests of his followers in the political spaces of parliament. Her home and the celebrations she holds there are therefore a way of marrying her political and religious worlds through teraanga. Mously showed me the rest of the house; there were two floors and a large sitting room surrounded by bedrooms for guests. On the ground floor Mously pointed out her plans for a large kitchen that spilled out into an open courtyard designed for cooking and assembling large quantities of food to feed attendees breakfast, lunch, and dinner for several days. Just as for family ceremonies, many relatives would travel from the rural areas and stay for several days to benefit from the hospitality. (Ayda Mbóoj's house, like Mously's in Tuubaa, has several floors designed to accommodate guests.) Rooms are normally left empty or with furniture covered with sheets to protect them from dust, but can be quickly transformed into living quarters by a young woman who traveled from Dakar or the guard who is paid to stay and look after the house when no one is there. In a place like Tuubaa, where the houses of Dakar residents are habitually empty, the guards of neighboring homes gather at night to share a meal under a lone streetlamp on what is a mostly deserted street.

After the quick tour and unloading our bags, we immediately went to pay the family members of Sëriñ Abdu a visit. One house was right next door, as it

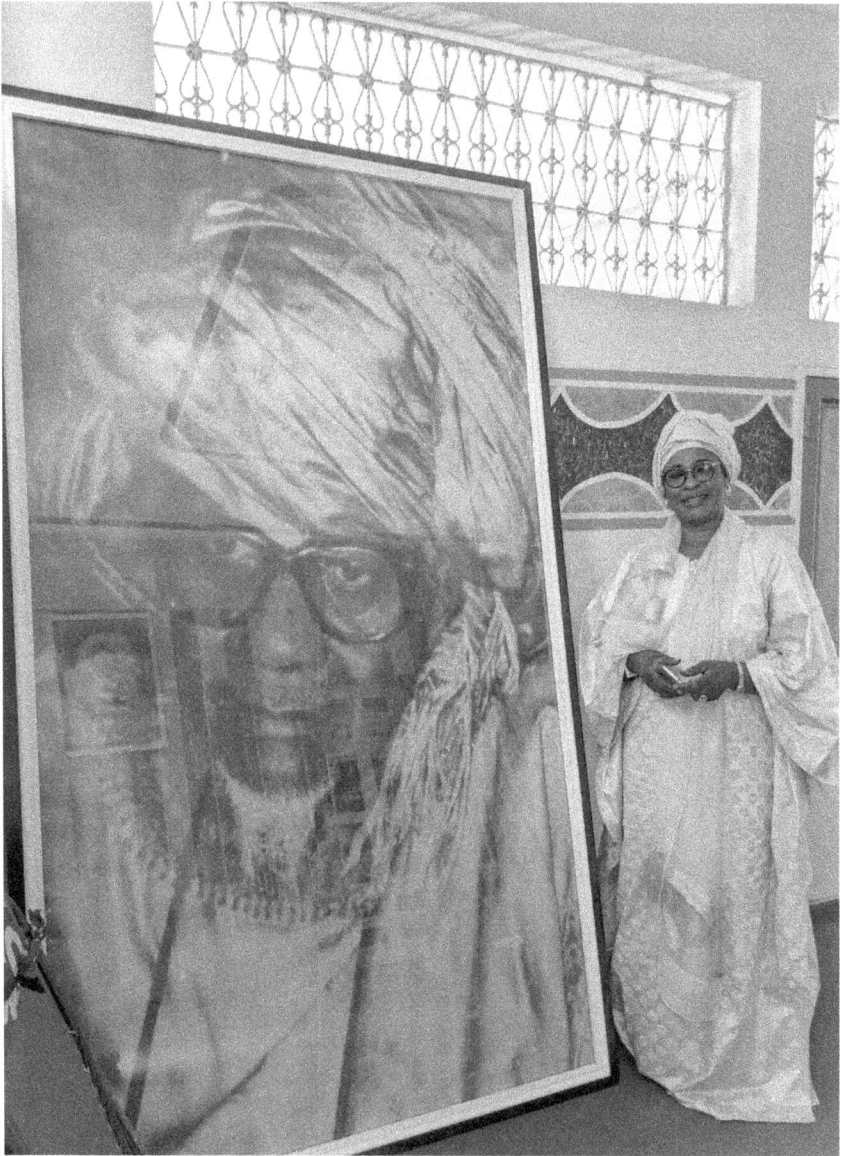

Mously Diakhaté in front of a photo of Sëriñ Abdu Lahad Mbakke, the third khalif générale of the Murīds and her spiritual guide, at her home in Tuubaa, Senegal. *Photo by author.*

was the Sëriñ who had given Mously the land to build her home. "Mënuma ñëw Tuubaa nelaw balaa may nuyu samay guides religieux [I can't come to Tuubaa and spend the night until I have greeted my religious guides]," she said. This included a visit to Sëriñ Sidy's house each evening as well as a large lunch with him and other followers at the home of his father, Sëriñ Abdu. Sëriñ Sidy was Mously's first husband. I very hesitantly asked why they were no longer married. "Mënunu amoon doom, Yàlla moo ko dogal [We couldn't have children together; that is just what God wanted]." However, the mutual appreciation and affection they shared was obvious. One comment she made struck me as particularly interesting. During lunch and most other interactions with religious guides, taalibé sit on a mat slightly below the sëriñ or next to him on the ground. Women must sit with their legs tucked to one side in order to preserve some kind of discretion since most are wearing wrap skirts. Men are afforded more flexibility. I always found it extremely uncomfortable but assumed it was my egregious lack of flexibility and practice. When we left to get back in the car Mously was driving, she let out a sigh, rubbing a sore knee from the long period of sitting and said, "Dafa metti pour les femmes. Sama yaram lépp mooy metti. Je suis trop vieille [It's so hard for women. My whole body hurts. I'm too old for this]." At the time, Mously was a mere fifty-three years old. What she was alluding to was sacrifice. Mously saw herself as having dedicated her money, time, and body to Murīd principles and expectations of women that included sacrifice, submission, and helping others. When we arrived back at the house, she gazed upon her house and said, "Maa ko liggéey. Mérité naa ko [I have worked so hard for this house. I earned it]." The house, after all, was a physical representation of the social, religious, and political labor she invested in her communities and the balance she struck between being a formidable politician and a jigéen ju baax (a good woman).

Teraanga as Gendered and Spiritual Performance

Two years after my visit to Tuubaa with Mously, I sent her a text message wishing her a peaceful Màggal. The Màggal commemorates the day Ahmadu Bamba, founder and spiritual guide of the Murīds, was arrested by the French colonial army and exiled to Gabon (Ngom 2016, 190). It is the most important gathering of the Murīd community. Her response was to forward a video from Hann TV, a local television station in her neighborhood of Hann Bel-Air back in Dakar. The camera accompanied Mously to her home in Tuubaa during the Murīd celebration of Màggal 2020. The video begins with the host, Sister Diez, at the main entrance to Mously's home, explaining that they will be speaking with "Honorable

Women walking in front of the main mosque in the city of Tuubaa, Senegal. *Photo by author.*

Mously Diakhaté ku nu gis nii ci wañ wi dina nu won nu muy préparer Màggal Tuubaa [Honorable Mously Diakhaté, whom we will see in her kitchen, and she will show us how she prepares Màggal Tuubaa]" (Hann TV 2020). We find Mously sitting on a low stool in her kitchen—remodeled—cutting and cleaning meat over a large plastic tub. Others working with her are doing the same or cutting fresh vegetables. It is clear they are preparing for a large feast. Mously begins by giving thanks to Allah and Sëriñ Tuubaa as well as to the camera crew and to those watching. She then talks about the circumstances of the COVID-19 pandemic, which meant the main mosque and other gathering places were drastically limited to small crowds; therefore, most families were celebrating from home. Mously is dressed in a relaxed and simple outfit for cooking and working in the kitchen—distinct from her normally elegant and elaborate dresses. Her demeanor demonstrates she is a woman of the people, a devout Muslim and Murīd, and generous, as her statement makes clear. The statement also illustrates the connections between her expressions of devotion to Allah and Murīd teachings and helping those who are less fortunate.

The Màggal Tuubaa, we do it in a different way from others, but we thank Allah. We praise Allah because when the occasion arises, whatever we have or don't have, we help our neighbors who don't have much, we share this day [the Màggal]. What is important is that when you die, Allah, you praise him by showing him that he created the children of Adam differently. And even if you are more privileged than them, even if you don't have a lot, you have more than them, and you should give them and show them that you share it together, that you own it together. Because after the rituals of sacrificing [a sheep], whatever is left we give to fellow children of Adam.[3]

She continued showing Sister Diez around the house, where children were studying the Qur'an. She talked about her strong and faithful connection to Sëriñ Abdu Lahad Mbakke and how her dedication to him has outlasted his physical presence on earth; in fact, the grandchildren of the Sëriñ celebrate the Màggal, as well as his birthday, at her home. Her demonstration of her life embedded within the Murīd community in the context of welcoming a camera crew and providing hospitality bestows on Mously a reputation of teraanga, femininity, and piety that has great purchase within the religious and political circles she inhabits.

Ayda was also astute at using media sources to stage scenarios of giving charity or demonstrating her abilities to cook. One such occasion was a television special on the channel Groupes Futures Media (iGFM) for the Tamxarit holiday (Ashura in Arabic), which celebrates the tenth day of the new Muslim year. The classic dish made is *cere*, a millet couscous with a tomato-based sauce, symbolizing hope for a plentiful year. The meal is often shared with neighbors, family, and the needy, in the spirit of sharing and solidarity. In the dining room of Ayda's Dakar home, she was being filmed making the cere, a process called *arrow*, or affectionately named *bomb*. As she vigorously swiped her hand under the millet flour while her daughter Mame Diarra (named after Shaykh Ahmadu Bamba's mother), visiting from Canada, slowly poured water to help give it the right consistency, Ayda's griot Mame Seydi began a verbal praise from behind the camera.

Look at my queen Ayda Mbóoj. She's working the couscous. Putting it in the calebasse. This is tradition, Mbóoj! She takes the couscous when it's ready and adds sauce. She sifts it with her hands, works it until it's mixed. She puts in seeds and raisins, keeps working it. Puts in beans and more sauce. Everything is in there, yes! Ayda, you taught me to make couscous. Women should be inspired by you. Ayda, you'll have a wonderful dinner. You'll spoil your mother-in-law, she will smile, make sure you are well taken care of, and pray for you. You'll show women so they know how it goes. Look at this couscous. My master, you made me couscous, Mbóoj. Good work. But this is not today but yesterday [history]. Mbóoj, you started this when you were little, learning to work then go to school, get your degree. Young women should learn, learn women's work—that's how I like it. Those who hear Ayda Mbóoj, you should know her. You are able and a hard worker. I'm happy with this.[4]

Mame Seydi was present during all of our trips to ceremonies and political rallies alike. She mixed descriptions of what Ayda was doing along with a stylistic way of telling the audience that she is a woman who is to be emulated as a good woman who can cook and whose mother-in-law would feel loved and taken care of with her teraanga. In addition, it shows a happy mother-in-law is one who will advocate for her daughter-in-law with her son and provide important spiritual protection. "Young women should learn women's work" is a direct message to Ayda's followers that she understands and assumes the role of an ideal woman and wife. Although I never witnessed her cooking, I assume she did cook in her earlier years, when her children were younger. Now, as an older woman, she has the help of her daughter-in-law and younger girls who came from the family in Bambey. This staging of hospitality skills with narration from her personal géwël was crucial for Ayda's reputation as knowledgeable and relatable yet also as someone to be admired for holding powerful positions while remaining a woman of the people.

Equality, Equity, and a Woman Who Could Be More Than a Man

One objection to parité, as I discussed in previous chapters, was often about women not being qualified to work in politics. However, the debate was also about whether the sexes can be truly equal, as we saw with the taxi driver. In other words, although parité was more about equal opportunity in political contexts, it was interpreted in moral, religious, and social terms that questioned an idealized gendered identity. It frequently became a battle of semantics: equality vs. equity, good and pious women vs. women who sought to undermine men's authority, or generous vs. wasteful. Even beyond references to politics, parité became a buzzword that men and women used to talk about gender relations. If a woman felt oppressed about something in her daily life, she spoke of parité as a declaration of her rights. For men, parité was synonymous with women looking for ways to gain more authority where it was seemingly unwarranted. For many, hearing the word *parité* meant women were arguing that they were equal to men. Therefore, women in politics had to be creative about how they portrayed the very idea of parité: arguing for a seat at the table but highlighting their roles as wives, mothers, and Muslims as assets for political representation. As Sylvia Tamale highlights in her study of women parliamentarians in Uganda (1999), "women had to emphasize their femininity in order to win over the electorate. Particularly for the affirmative action candidates, appearing and acting feminine augured well with an electorate that was dominated by traditional and chauvinist men. . . . Many had to bring their husbands to campaign rallies. . . . As acts of deference were tactical strategies that women candidates employed to circumvent patriarchal authority" (95). Similarly, part of how I imagine the diverse strategies that Senegalese women politicians of the Teraanga Republic employ in order to remain relatable includes portraying themselves as good and pious women and wives.

A 2012 newspaper article regarding parité workshops in Sedhiou, part of the Casamance in southern Senegal, represents well this conflict of interpretation. A woman is quoted as saying, "It is high time that people, women especially, live parité in our societies because we have noticed that it improves their authority. Equity can happen in the home because what a woman can do, a man can as well." Another leader of the organization giving the workshop objected to this representation of the meaning of equity and made a clarification: "We are of the opinion that it is time to give voice to women because they also contribute to the social and economic threads. But it would be presumptuous to want to establish equality, but equity is possible" (Drame 2012).

Often the distinction between equality and equity is used by parité advocates to convince religious leaders and other skeptics that parité is about representing women's causes rather than arguing for their equal status, and there are certainly men and religious leaders who support the cause. At a ceremony celebrating the publication of Fatou Sarr's book on the first parité generation, entitled *Les Premières Héritières de la Parité*, Sëriñ Sidy Mansour Sy Djamil, the vice president of parliament and advocate of parité, shared religious insights. Djamil is a longtime political and Muslim religious figure who has been both a member of the government and one of the leading family members of the Tijāniyya Sufi order from Tivaouane. He led a progressive citizen-based political party, Bës du Ñakk (Seize the Day), that took seriously the call for female leadership by working closely with the Catholic parliamentarian Elène Tine. Sëriñ Mansour said a few words to mark the occasion.

> I'd like to say something regarding parité as the vice president of parliament and as a religious leader. Because I often hear on the radio those who oppose

[parité] without any basis in scripture, the Qur'an, or the Sunna. The day before yesterday I presided over a graduation for students of the Qur'anic school Seydi Djamil who had memorized the Qur'an by heart. Out of nineteen recipients, eleven were girls. And among those eleven, five had just passed their high school exam S1 and S2.[5] So that is the most relevant example to see that [these girls] are successful not only in high school but also in the Qur'anic schools. I want to cite a passage: God said, that among Muslims there are those who have completed their contract with God. I told the students that we cannot talk about being gifted [academically or otherwise] without talking about rujula. There are two concepts in Islam: we speak of *dhukura* and *rujula*. *Dhukura* is the biological fact of sex. If you see a man you know he is a man, and if you see a woman you know she is a woman. Then there is *rujula*, which to me is the fulfillment of human perfection, which is sexually indifferent. Masculinity can embody it, and femininity can embody it. So I told the children that today I finally understand this passage because the contract that you have with God—that is, the message he sent you—you have mastered and accomplished it. So no one can say it's only men. It is the fulfillment of a person who is sexually indeterminant.[6]

Essentially, God sent the message that the accomplishments of doing God's work do not depend on sex. The two Arabic terms, *dhukura* and *rujula*, normally refer to masculinity and manhood. Or, to be more specific, Mahadeen (2016) argues that dhukura signifies maleness and rujula manliness, and given that rujula is the "completion of dhukura" its definition can be used for nonbiological attributes such as bravery and authority (450). While describing the value of generosity among market workers in Cairo, Elyachar (2005) defines a generous person in Arabic (*gada'*) similarly to Shryock's definition of hospitality (*karam*) among Jordanian Arabic speakers as "nobility of character and integrity." The gada', as she points out, is "a persona from the popular classes who has the characteristics of 'manhood' (rugula)," meaning a set of characteristics such as someone "who watches out for those near to him" (137–38). Djamil's inference that the female sex can also do what tends to be reserved for the male sex, such as leadership and authority of knowledge, is quite like the frequent uses of the popular Wolof saying *jigéen ju mën góor*—the woman who is more capable than a man. The Wolof word *mën* is quite versatile and complex, however. *Mën* can signify a capability as well as a stronger sense of domination. If I were to say *mën naa jiite* (I can lead), I am simply saying that I am capable of leading. However, if I am referring to leadership in a comparison with a friend, I would say *maa la mën* (I am more capable/powerful than you) to mean that

I am more capable than you; I have surpassed your abilities. In the context of women politicians, there can be confusion as to whether women employing this phrase mean that they are equally capable to men in politics or that the woman has surpassed the man in terms of abilities or knowledge.

The saying gained popularity with the stories of Aline Sitoe Diatta, a Joola woman in southern Senegal known for her mystic powers to make it rain, among others. The national Senegalese imaginary decontextualized and essentialized her story to relate to a mostly urban Muslim and Wolof population in the 1980s, since the Senegalese state was starved of (female) idols to promote national unity. The narrative of Aline Sitoe Diatta as a colonial resister was more about cultivating a national unified identity against the French while ignoring regional disputes that the Senegalese state preferred not to address. Instead, jigéen ju mën góor eclipses the complex history of gender that has to do with labor and marriageability. Toliver-Diallo (2005) argues that making her story into one that serves an urban national identity erases the ethnic, regional, and religious differences throughout Senegal. Seeing Aline Sitoe as a woman who was more than a man in this context allowed for her to be understood as heroic because she accomplished extraordinary feats normally attributed to men, which for the national audience reified the notion of the patriarchal state. This phrase and Diatta's history are often cited in the context of women in politics in order to describe powerful women who have proven themselves to be capable of the actions typically assumed to be masculine. The phrase has since been appropriated for several women's campaigns, for the way in which people talk about individual women in politics, or for those who display particular power or leadership qualities (Baum 1999).

Not everyone agreed that the phrase conveys a positive way of thinking about women's contributions to politics. Rokhyatou, the director of COSEF, expressed serious concerns that framing women's worth as contingent on behaving like men is a disservice to women politicians. In fact, framing women's worth based on simply playing at a man's game is not the progress they seek.

It's very cultural [the use of this phrase]. It goes back a long time, even before Aline Sitoe Diatta, to the women of Nder, so we have a lot of references. So there is jigéen ju mën góor, or we say ki méngale na ak góor [those who are confused with being a man]. In my opinion that has been used against our objectives. Because a jigéen moo mën góor [another way to say jigéen ju mën góor] means a woman has surpassed in terms of behavior and power. Meaning that our society tells us that their aggressive behavior [assertiveness] doesn't belong to them, it belongs to men. So if a woman wants to make it to a certain level, society pushes her to think that if you want to have a seat at the table you have to be a man. This type of aggressive behavior worked when women were beginning to attain power. The women who represented us initially got out the big guns [biceps]. They acted like men, and men said, "Oh yeah, they are lions." The reference to lions means that she has a way of speaking and behaving like this animal. And it is not a subtle animal but aggressive. That's where I'm not in line with this phrase because women need to take guidance or reference from themselves and not from men.[7]

The connections of women with strong and aggressive animals had even become part of their campaign strategies. In radio or television interviews, Ayda was referred to as the Lioness of Baol (*La Lionne de Baol*[8]), the region she is from. During one campaign event, when she was campaigning to be a national representative rather than representing her hometown of Bambey, as the géwël introduced her as the Lionne de Baol, Ayda corrected them: "No, I am the Lioness of Senegal." It was an attempt to connect her reputation as being strong to her ambitions of a presidential bid in the future. It was one thing to be popular in Bambey and among Murīd communities; it was another to win over a diverse national electorate. I began this book by positing that women in Senegal live with constant contradictions they must negotiate, and their political character is no exception. Rokhyatou spells this out very clearly: "The double standard is, they [men] say as long as you aren't like us you can't be at our level. We will recognize you if you are like us, but if you go too far we won't recognize you. In essence, women who attempt to navigate the male-dominated sphere of politics must *mën* (be capable) like men but not *mën* (surpass men) to question their dominance."[9]

Jigéen ju mën góor and Jigéen ju baax

The phrase *jigéen ju mën góor* was often at odds with *jigéen ju baax*, meaning a good woman or a woman with good qualities. Much like the distinction between to work and to do good work/work well (Adjamagbo, Antoine, and Dial 2004), these two phrases symbolize the desired gender roles of women (jigéen ju baax) and those who deviate from that mold. For as much as jigéen ju mën góor solicited national narratives of honor and feminine courage, many of the examples of jigéen ju baax that I came across in the context of religious meetings also spoke of good women as honorable and courageous for their demonstrations of patience and submission to their husbands, as well as for their reputations of generosity and hospitality.

Among the Murīd Sufi community, to which Ayda and Mously were dedicated, the famous stories of the founder Ahmadu Bamba's mother, Maam Jaara
Buso, were lessons in submission. Maam Jaara (as she is affectionately called)
was said to have stayed outside all night in the rain and wind because her husband had asked her to hold up the fence in their courtyard while he found
a rope to hold it up with. Although he forgot and went to bed, Maam Jaara
stayed in an act of obedience. She stayed outside, as it rained, until the next
morning when he found her there. This story is repeated as a lesson for women
to emulate. While with Ayda at two different religious gatherings during the
2017 campaigns, I heard another story recounted about the cousin of Maam
Jaara Buso. The first was a stop in the community of Dinguiraye in the Keur
Massar part of the Dakar sprawl, to attend a women's *jàng*, or religious conference, where Ayda was an invited special guest. We visited family members and
disciples of Maam Cheikh Ibra Fall, himself a disciple of Ahmadu Bamba, and
then went on to the event taking place under a large tent in the sandy courtyard
of a group of houses. As we arrived, Ayda and her entourage were announced
over the speakers and seated in large cushy chairs meant for special guests and
members of the religious family. Audience members sat in plastic chairs facing
the panel of guests. Sëriñ Mansour, the religious guide who was giving the ser-
mon, welcomed Ayda and announced that they had been discussing the theme
of the conference, which the Sëriñ announced was *Jigéen ak taxawaay, bi mu
wara taxaw* (woman and the role she should play). He began by discussing the
female role models of the Murīds and their desirable behaviors of selflessness,
teraanga, and submission.

> We were talking about the subject of jigéen ju baax. We often say jigéen ju
> mën góor, but if we want to take an example, we talk about Soxna Jaara. Soxna
> Jaara was a gift from God. No woman in the world was like her. To be able to
> manage a husband while waiting outside in the wind and rain all night until
> the sun comes up. A close second might be Soxna Anta Njaay Mbakke. She
> was known for her courageous act and self-sacrifice when a young woman in
> her home was to be married off to a man from a lower-caste family. The girl
> disappeared, and to save his honor and that of her family, Soxna Anta offered
> herself instead. She even provided for her own dowry as the man had no
> substantial wealth.[10]

He offered another example of Soxna Anta's generosity, calling her *jigéen moo
ëppoon teraanga ci àdduna* (the woman with the most teraanga in this world).
She had come to be a very prominent businesswoman who traded in gold jewelry and was known not only for sharing meals with less fortunate neighbors

but also for discretely wrapping gold in a piece of cloth and hiding it in the bowl of rice she sent them. A child would then take it to a family in need so they could *faj seeni soxla* (heal their needs/pay their debts).

The significance of her story and the timing were striking. It was the eve of the election, and there was a lot of talk about parité and about the law turning women away from religion and their duties as women, wives, and mothers. It was the first election with so many parties led by women as well as discourses about women's inclusion coming from male-led parties. Sëriñ Mansour continued with citations from the Qur'an to back up his assertions of the nobility of a "jigéen ju baax, a woman who knows how to manage a home and take care of her husband."

"A woman, a jigéen ju baax, who cares for her husband and assumes her responsibilities in the home is said to receive half of the blessings needed from God. That is no small thing. And we are not just talking about housework but cultivating and work in the fields. The Qur'an also says that the responsibilities that men have, women also have. Fifty/fifty," he said in English first. Ayda and others echoed his confirmation of parité in the background: "Sounds a lot like parité." He wrapped up his speech, and Ayda asked him if she could respond because she wanted to address the issue of parité.

> Greetings to all, to the men and their wives who came to this event. Sëriñ Mansour, what you said is true. Women should be in men's homes. My father taught me that the responsibilities that you have to your marriage [*néegu séy*] he taught me that when your husband looks at you his mind goes to his mother and his mind is at ease. It is the woman's responsibility to make sure her husband is well. And this is not a contradiction with parité. When I first started fighting for parité there was so much noise about it that a government official (*sous-préfet*) called me and said, "You are causing issues between men and women, husbands and wives, and now women are saying they won't do anything because we aren't paying." I didn't say that! Then one day they came by the house to find that I was serving my husband, taking care of him and was all dressed up, *sañsé*. . . . God sanctioned our union. . . . We say "*liggéeyu ndey* [mother's work]." There is a religious explanation and a scientific explanation for this phrase. We have a role in society to have children and care for them. Back to parité. Shaykh Sidy Makhtar sent his eldest son, Moustapha Mbakke, to see me. He is my friend. He came because there was all this objection and he wanted me to speak to it. I told him that just like we were talking about earlier, if a woman has success from something, so does her husband. If a woman receives *cër* [honor] from politics, so does her husband.

A woman gets in a car, so does a man. We have equal investment. But that all has its context. We are talking about parité in the context of politics. We aren't saying parité to reject religion. We aren't saying parité to corrupt our disciples. We aren't saying parité to replace our husbands. Marriage is very important. God sanctioned it. My marriage has not ruined my education or my leadership. To the contrary. I want to be a role model, so they see that when it is time to pray, I pray. When it comes to my husband, I respect and take care of him. And that when people come over, they know who the head of the household is.[11]

Conferences of this kind are common among all the Sufi communities in Senegal. They gather groups such as the leket featured in this example, as well as *daayiras*, religious associations tied to a specific sëriñ or cheikh who teaches themed lessons from the Qur'an and other Islamic texts. It is common to use the histories of prominent figures from the Murīd religious family as the Sëriñ did with the example of Soxna Anta Njaay Mbakke. Soxna Anta demonstrates the ideal of a good woman who gives teraanga to those in need and does so with *sutura*, the Wolof word for discretion, but also benefitting from the fact that it becomes common knowledge that they are indeed generous. In fact, a popular Wolof saying, "the left hand should not see what the right hand gives," expresses the idea that true teraanga is known only between the two immediate parties. Once it is made public, the sentiment changes. Politicians are often invited to attend and help with expenses in exchange for an opportunity to speak with the attendees about their party, giving envelopes of money in an act of discretion. In Ayda's case, she wished to clarify the meaning of parité. The noise and objections she refers to have come from religious leaders, politicians, and journalists spreading ideas that parité is antireligion and encouraging women to refuse their husbands and their responsibilities to the family. In essence, parité was said to promote the identity of a jigéen ju mën góor and therefore does not need him, in place of a jigéen ju baax, the ideal that Sëriñ Mansour preached about in which a woman's world turns around the needs and wants of her husband and his family. Ayda specifically referenced her own work as a jigéen ju baax, serving her husband and getting dressed up (sañse) on his behalf. She also made connections between the importance of marriage and the religious significance of both men and women having responsibilities and shared successes. Finally, she made the point that parité has a specific context that is formal politics and does not negate the centrality of marriage and certain gender relations. In fact, parité can be a way for Murīds to fulfill the religious ideals laid out by Ahmadu Bamba himself. In the next sections I will discuss the Murīd philosophy and how women like Ayda and Mously negotiate their own identities as Murīds and its connection to their politics.

The natural difficulty that Ayda encounters in situations like these is that she attempts to align herself with the figures of Maam Jaara and Soxna Anta, women whose revered images stem from their sacrifice for and submission to their husbands. Although Ayda and Mously perform the ideal tasks of a good wife—including hospitality and religious piety—and talk about submission to one's husband, in reality they are independent women who have images of not depending on their husbands. Their messaging is effective, however, in that it demonstrates a legitimacy within the Murīd community and a recognition of its principles.

Work, Reciprocity, and Human Investment: Murīd Philosophy and Politics

The ideas of work, struggle, and investment in others come in many ways from Mously and Ayda's interpretations of Murīd doctrine. This section will discuss how they incorporate these interpretations into their discussions and practices of development and politics.

A crucial element of Ayda's political strategy was her identity as a Murīd taalibé. As a proud Murīd, similar to Mously, she framed her philosophy and practice with the teachings of Ahmadu Bamba and the *yoonu Murīd*, or the Murīd way. When I sat down with Ayda for our first interview, I thanked her profusely for the opportunity to interview her, and she responded thus: "You know, I am a taalibé, and that's [hospitality] why it's important. It is part of being educated in the Murīd way. Another dimension of it is humility. To not have an ego, and who ever calls upon you, you keep them in mind. Because whoever you bring into your life they will also love you in return. This is also a lesson for doing politics."[12] Her thoughts on humility—"to not have an ego," or to be among the people, signifies a reverence for others, bringing someone into her world as a part of a sense of mutual connectedness—are key aspects of Ahmadu Bamba's writings and philosophy.

In the second half of Mously's autobiography, *Du Daara á l'Hémicycle*, she features testimonials from colleagues in parliament, family members, and religious leaders. They speak to her character and faith that are both part of her family's genealogy and her identity as a Murīd taalibé. Late Sëriñ Atou Diagne, a moral representative for a small but powerful Murīd organization called Hizbut Tarqiyyah, recounts Mously's history as an indication of her personality: "She is someone who defends what her parents defended: the popular cause, dignity, and the social needs of others. . . . It's very important that to represent one's people is to know them well. . . . She came to parliament to represent, beyond her party, all Senegalese by way of a symbol of the kingdoms in Fuutaa, Cayor, and Jammbuur. She has origins in each region." He notes that on her father's side her family were Islamic judges resolving conflicts between Muslims and French colonial administrators. Her mother's side is characterized by faith, theological knowledge, and generosity. Kings would rival one another with gifts to her great-great-grandfather in exchange for prayers as they prepared for battle (Diakhaté 2017, 149–51). Sëriñ Atou Diagne continues to talk about her Murīd identity: "Sëriñ Tuubaa . . . taught his taalibé to refine their personality so that no one can change who you are. Mously is this kind of taalibé. That's why all those in parliament can't sway her. Her guide didn't have weapons or an army, but his strong personality and spiritual dynamism made him stand out" (153). Other contributors paint her as a "real soxna," or a real Senegalese woman, "always elegant" (328), and the historian Penda Mbow notes that Mously doesn't appear to have done any skin lightening, and therefore "she symbolizes the beauty of the Black woman, of the Senegalese woman. I think we should make a film; Mously could incarnate the Senegalese woman" (256). Seydou Diouf, a fellow parliamentarian, described her as "a woman who is very Senegalese, meaning that beyond the political battles . . . of parliament . . . she preserves her human dimension with her colleagues in parliament. That is extremely important" (221). Therefore, elements of sénégalaisement are an elegance of dress and presence as well as a spirit of kindness in an environment of political tension.

Righteous Deeds

The most important of Ahmadu Bamba's Ajami poets, Mbaye Jaxate, has a poem that captures a principle among the Murīds that Fallou Ngom (2016) calls "righteous deeds." "People with material wealth will end up losing their wealth. People with crowds will also end up losing their crowds. Whatever you seek here will leave you, or you will leave it one day. Owners of wealth will be separated from their beautiful wealth. But owners of deeds will not be separated from their deeds. Take good care of your deeds [because they] will always accompany you, and perfect them, for no one has anything except their deeds. Know this." In many ways, the idea and practice of righteous deeds are synonymous with teraanga. Its basis in local Wolof knowledge is important to Bamba's religious philosophy and pedagogy. In fact, what Ngom (2016) calls the "Ajamization of Islam," the use of modified Arabic script to write in African languages such as Wolof or Mandinka, brings local African moral philosophy to the heart of Murīd religious thought and practice. *Jëf ju rafet* (beautiful actions/righteous deeds) (Ngom 2016, 208), according to Ajami sources, are the most important spiritual investment in order to achieve salvation. They give great meaning to Wolof proverbs such as *am alal, am nita ko gën* (to have wealth is good, but to have people is better). Righteous deeds such as giving money to those in need, being welcoming and hospitable, or offering gifts during ceremonies fulfill an obligation to others that is then rewarded with salvation. Mously explained this in her television interview during the Màggal: the disruption of COVID-19 in fact highlights that it is not the official celebrations that matter in terms of praising Sëriñ Tuubaa and Allah; it is providing support to others through sharing. One of Bamba's own writings recounts a conversation he had with a taalibé who confided that he feared poverty. Bamba's response was simple: "Share whatever you have with your fellow human beings" (224), suggesting that investing one's material wealth in relationships with others ensures one will never be wanting because they will have those they can count on. In essence, real poverty is a lack of human relationships. Uley Samb (see chap. 2) talked about the importance of *teg sa xaalis ci yoon* (using your money wisely), referring to using one's money to invest in others, responsibly of course, with the idea that such an investment would serve better than hoarding one's wealth. In other words, generosity given is generosity received. But that sense of giving gifts must come from a place of unconditional generosity, as another poem by Mbaye Jaxate notes. He addresses Lady Aminata Mbakke, Bamba's sister, and offers her some advice: "Your duty is to be grateful and to emulate your brother's faith. Offer your gifts to anyone you see and be indifferent to theirs" (Ngom 2016, 212).

Although Mously and Ayda were also nurturing their political prospects, they framed their actions as a fulfillment of social and spiritual obligations. Ayda, for example, always visited friends and participated in family ceremonies by providing money and moral support as much as she provided support to local daaras and *daayiras*, religious associations. In fact, Ayda's philosophy about teraanga and responses to perceptions of corruption in politics speak to her understanding of how social and spiritual relationships are built on these kinds of reciprocities. I detail this further in the next chapter.

Parité as the Fulfillment of Bamba's Teachings/Goals

Women like Ayda and Mously, who are more self-reliant with their own salaries, see themselves as examples of hard work and faith even beyond the limits of being a woman. At the same time, they understand their unique positions to help other women who are dependent on these rituals of teraanga for their own survival. In essence, the engagement in the political economy of teraanga is always political, whether for women like Ayda and Mously who are negotiating positions in state politics or for other women who are negotiating their status among their family, friends, or business prospects. Interestingly, Ayda and Mously frame their positions as politicians and women of a certain status and success who have fought for parité as not at odds with religious principles but rather as in line with Bamba's teachings of righteous deeds and equality. In fact, they push back on claims that parité is somehow un-Islamic by citing that Ahmadu Bamba advocated for women's equality in education and that hard work makes a person successful and not their family name (and, one would also assume, one's sex). Ayda offers an example from a visit to a mosque in Dakar near her home.

> It's difficult for women to be considered. In terms of religion we say that for women the hardest part is the people who haven't studied properly. For example, at the mosque in Sacré Coeur, Imam Cissé, he speaks English, Wolof, and French and is very open-minded. One day it was Qadirs, the twenty-seventh night of Ramadan. He invited me. When he invited me, I was minister at that time, and he took me up to the tower. There were people protesting and saying, "Look, he takes this woman, he must love money and life's riches." He listened and then got out a passage from the Qur'an to cite. "God said, when a woman attains a certain level of power, I say, God is the one who did it. Because power, God owns it. So I say, God gave a part of his power and gave it to this woman so that she is free and can sit with men. Because she has studied and her culture and her openness has afforded her that."[13]

Ayda refers to the difficulties women have with religious interpretations of their roles in society. In this example, Ayda places herself in a position of considerable power, which then makes her equal to men in the eyes of God. Another example she gives refers to a time in 2004 when the town of Médina Gounass in southern Senegal was badly affected by fires, and in her official duties as minister she headed down there in a rented plane to provide beds and other supplies in addition to a large sum of money that President Abdoulaye Wade had approved. Médina Gounass is a religious community whose members have "exiled themselves within the bounds of the Senegalese state in an attempt to create a space uncorrupted by secular colonial and postcolonial governments" (Glovsky 2021). They are known for being particularly conservative. When she arrived, they told her that the sëriñ would not see any women. She thought it odd but decided to return home without giving them the aid. Before her plane could take off, the governor of the region begged her not to go, saying the sëriñ would see her. "Donc su ma faibloon tuuti duma gisantee ak sëriñ bi [If I was weaker I wouldn't have seen the religious leader]," she said. "Te pour man, su ma nekkee maa ngi yor ay fonction yoo xam ne damay fàtte sax ne jigéen laa. Parce que un certain niveau de responsabilité dangay fàtte sax jigéen nga [You know, for me, if I hold certain governmental office, I even forget I am a woman. Because at a certain level of responsibility you forget that you are a woman]."

These two stories from Ayda refer to issues of religious interpretation and to her belief that God chooses who is to be endowed with specific powers that obfuscate identity based on gender. Her possession of power and her demonstration of state-sanctioned charity go hand in hand. Her power enables her to provide for others, which then is the greatest fulfillment of a Murīd taalibé: righteous deeds in the form of aid. Mously speaks in a similar tone about her work with women's associations and investments in their projects as a kind of religious fulfillment of charity to others.

In many ways, Mously and Ayda see themselves as transcending gender norms and yet also demonstrating these norms in order to remain relatable. Where Mously cooked in her home for the TV cameras, so, too, had Ayda done television spots where she showcased her cooking skills with a popular dish for an upcoming religious holiday. Although I'm sure that both had spent their fair share of time cooking for their families in their younger years, I had always seen younger girls doing the cooking. While Ayda could "forget that she is a woman" due to her status, she, Mously, and others could perform their femininity when necessary. They framed themselves specifically as champions of women's causes while seeing their own identities as flexible. For all that Ayda spoke about her ability to transcend her gender to be equal with men, in the spirit of Bamba's teachings on equality and rejection of the hierarchy of nobility customary to Wolof society, she also has deep pride in her family's status as nobles, frequently referencing the Mbóoj family connection to Njëmbët and Ndaté Yàlla Mbóoj, queens of the Waalo Kingdom.

Work, Education, Agriculture, and Bamba's Teachings

In 2017, ahead of the legislative elections, Ayda Mbóoj had just started her new coalition following her break from Abdoulaye Wade's PDS, which caused a media stir because she had always been known for her loyalty to Wade and was seen as his golden girl. In fact, just about every framed picture in her three-story Dakar home was of her and Wade or Wade at diplomatic visits from the French president or others. Following his defeat to Macky Sall in 2012, Wade left Senegal to live abroad, as is common with most former presidents, and the party functions were taken over by Oumar Sarr. Ayda's defense for leaving the party was that she remained loyal to Wade but no longer found space for herself in the party, and she had her own ambitions. She had ample experience to lead a party; as she said, politics was in her blood, something she learned very early from her parents. Her father, El Hadj Amadu Mbóoj, attended a private school in Saint Louis under the colonial government and later worked for the French-controlled peanut industry. Her mother, although formally uneducated, was a leader among the women of Senghor's Parti Socialiste. Many women of her generation were the backstage organizers of political parties, and as a child, Ayda benefited from shadowing both her mother and her father in their political activities. In Bambey where they lived, Ayda's father worked for the local municipal government and was in charge of voting processes, a memory that stands out for Ayda as a young girl: "Mes premières écritures ci ginnaaw cartes yi, ci politig laa ko doon def [My first writings were on the front and backs of voting cards. I was doing politics]."

During the 2017 campaign, Ayda did an interview on the SudFM program *Janoo bi* with the Islamic teacher and radio host Oustaz Maodo Faye. She spoke about her coalition and its formation, emphasizing women's labor and the religious connections.

> The coalition is called Ànd, Saxal Liggéey [Work and Grow Together]. Work is what we know, and we want to do politics differently. Doing politics differently means the way that we were using women to simply applaud is over. We want to work [*saxal*, meaning to plant a seed]. *Saxal liggéey* [plant the seed] refers to ongoing work that we help to grow. We have always worked; we have never stopped working. We are workers, so that is why we called it this, so that women can do politics in a different way. A kind of politics that stems from their empowerment. This whole thing of stuffing women in cars so they can applaud, that's over. We will help find them resources for their projects and help the youth with training in social development, especially for the most vulnerable.[14]

Ayda's emphasis on work is important, as is her identity as a Murīd taalibé. Her insistence on women's tradition of working and her reference to agriculture speak to a history in which women's and men's labor in rural areas was complementary. The work women had done for men's campaigns, although crucial, was superficial in terms of what it afforded women. Work has always had strong hierarchical implications in Wolof society, determining one's labor roles and access to power, as we saw in the introduction and chapter 2. One of the essential aspects of Ahmadu Bamba's teachings is the relationship to agricultural practices and linguistic references. Ngom (2016) points out that "work ethic and vigor, which are rooted in the local ancestral agrarian moral philosophy, have been elevated into devotional obligations through the cultivation of *himma* [inner strength] ... and with Islamization, they acquired a new religious significance" (208). Part of the new religious obligations of labor, suffering, and patience meant one's hard work and striving for success were more important than arbitrary hierarchies.

Conclusion

In this chapter, I have explored the connections between women's political work, hierarchies of work, and political strategies. The role of religious leaders, personal faith, and tapping into religious networks are key to these processes. Mously and Ayda demonstrate a deep connection to the Murīd community, and they demonstrate its importance to their personal and political lives. In many respects, despite the objections to parité, they find ways to navigate their spiritual and political identities that in some ways rise above the limitations of gender and in others play to their gendered identities. Their public displays of teraanga reinforce their image as pious and good women who value the expectations of women in Senegalese society, even as they are actively political. As Murīd disciples, they both situate their social and political lives within the religious community. This has allowed them significant support from men among both the Murīds and their male colleagues in parliament.

As they construct their identities as both good women and women who can rise to the ranks of men in politics, they base their political strategies and messaging within a particularly Wolof and religious sense of ethics. These include agriculture, hard work, and good suffering that extend to what it means to be a woman in society and politics. In the next chapter, I examine the contested forms of politics with examples from Ayda, who embodies all that is teraanga as political strategy, and Aminata Touré, who rejects many of the principles of the Teraanga Republic.

6

Political Economies of Teraanga

With homes in Dakar and Bambey, Ayda Mbóoj spent many weekends travel-ing to Bambey. On one trip I asked her what she planned do while in Bambey, to which she replied, "Damay politique [I'm doing politics]." Our trip consisted mainly of first making an appearance at the funeral of a neighbor then on to the wedding of a loyal supporter's son. At the funeral, we also went with a large delegation, as Ayda called it, to pay our respects to the family of a local digni-tary of the party in power, Macky Sall's Alliance pour la République (APR). It also seemed like a political move encroaching on her political rival's territory. First we all huddled in to visit the women who were grieving and left a small amount of cash for symbolic purposes. Ayda's family géwël, El Hadj Aly Niang, announced her presence in the tent outside where others had gathered. As important figures shouldn't shout or raise their voice, Ayda spoke softly while El Hadj theatrically echoed her words. Through him as a medium, she shared a little bit about her relationship with the deceased. "Ajaa Ayda ne na," said El Hadj to get people's attention, "Sëriñ Ngom dafa ma mësa faral balaa may nekk maire-u Bambey te membre-wu APR la [Sëriñ Ngom has always supported me even before I was mayor of Bambey and he was a member of APR]." While he echoed Ayda's words, she handed out money to mourning family members and to El Hadj for his work. As he finished his presentation of Ayda, a politician from APR showed up with his delegation, accompanied by a quick-witted and energetic—and much younger—géwël. When he began to speak, it was like a round of thunder hit us, as he had people clapping and on their feet with joy with his projection and rhetorical style. After a few moments we left and got back in the car, where members of the entourage commented on his skills, even as they seemed annoyed by being upstaged.

In this chapter, I consider the political and personal trajectories of Ayda Mbóoj, Aminata Touré, and anecdotally Ndey Sukkey Géy. In the spirit of Diaw's assertion that women's quest for power is intertwined with problematizing these borders of public and private, I argue that Ayda and Ndey Sukkey are such examples. They are part of the majority of governing women who are reinventing relationships between gender, space, and authority through a political economy of teraanga, a system of redistributing resources that places social relationships typically seen within private spaces at the center of public economic and political transactions, thus bringing the power of public resources to home dynamics and vice versa. I also discuss the former Senegalese prime minister Aminata Touré as a representative of certain kinds of French republican values, such as seeing the individual and the nation as abstract and thus drawing a clear line between the private and public; her espousal of these forms of governance means she does not threaten this division but instead seeks to enhance it. But it is too simple to say she disbelieves in important cultural values such as teraanga. Through the examples of Ayda and Aminata's politics, I highlight their similarities in epistemological understandings of teraanga as well as their differences in how teraanga factors into their governing philosophies. Given the distinctions in governing styles and philosophies, in this chapter I discuss the question of opposition to women in politics and accusations of corruption as a matter of women muddying the lines between private and public rather than actual misappropriations of government funds, which I cannot speak to with any certainty.

"Doing Politics" Senegalese Style

"La politique existe au Sénégal il y a longtemps, et la participation des femmes aussi [Politics have existed for a very long time in Senegal, and so has women's participation in them]," said Ndey Sukkey. Ndey began telling me about the rich history of the women of the great kingdoms in the Senegambia and their roles in ruling their territory and people. Such historical references of national heroines of Senegal are part of a national imaginary, representing collaboration with and resistance against the French colonial project, destabilization in the region, and women's powerful roles in history (Toliver-Diallo 2005; Baum 1999).

Ayda certainly made good use of her shared heritage with Ndaté Yàlla and her sister Njëmbët as early representatives of female leadership. "Leadership yàgg na ci jigéen ñi. Il y a des femmes ñu xam leadership [Leadership has a long history among women. There are women who know leadership]," Ayda insisted as she pointed out the family relations with Ndaté Yàlla, who was from the Mbóoj family, a notable factor for Ayda's genealogy as a political figure and as a member of the Wolof majority in her region. Ayda herself has occupied some of Senegal's most prestigious and influential governmental positions. She has been instrumental in the parité movement, and she is well known for her fiery rhetoric yet charismatic demeanor. In 2020, she received her doctorate in international relations from an online program, with a thesis entitled *La gouvernance territorialisée: Modèles de développement des territoires* (Territorialized Governance: Examples of Territorial Development). Ayda has remained popular even with those who disagree with her politics, evidenced by her many political appointments and her reelection to parliament, despite being in the opposition party following the PDS's defeat in 2012. In addition to being mayor and house representative of Bambey, she became the first female president of a departmental council of Senegal following the local elections of 2014. And after forming her own coalition in 2017, she was close to being a candidate for president in 2019 and 2024. "Doing politics" (faire de la politique) is translated by Bayart from the Wolof word *nguur gi*, which he says means a devotee to a leader or faction (1993, 212). However, nguur gi is most commonly used to describe the governing body, the state in everyday parlance. Cooper (2014) describes doing politics (50) in terms of a pivotal historical moment in 1945, following the hard-fought battle for Senegalese women's suffrage under the French empire. Their new voting power led to sweeping legislative gains for the Socialist Party and inspired fresh calls for "the application of republican principles" and benefits that French citizens enjoyed. Thus women's suffrage and the workers' strikes of 1945 and 1946 exposed the "fragility of a colonial order" (53) and questioned the legitimacy of republican values. Other accounts of this time and especially of the fight for women's suffrage note the savvy ways in which women mobilized through social networks and associations funded by pooling money or holding social events (Sylla 2001). As I have been building this argument throughout the book, the role of associations and teraanga to women's politics has been recognizable for a long time, as have their negotiations between French republican visions of governance and those of the Teraanga Republic.

One of the main ways Ayda was doing politics was by cultivating relationships, giving back to her supporters, and being present during their family events, such as the wedding of a son, the birth of a grandchild, or the death of a supporter or someone in their family. Just as family ceremonies are crucial to the functioning of social and familial relationships, they are also central to political processes, and Ayda is a perfect example. I accompanied her to weddings, naming ceremonies, funerals, and religious ceremonies in Bambey and

Tuubaa. One wedding took place in Bambey, not far from her family home. The scene was always a familiar one, a lively gathering of mostly women celebrating the union of a man and woman, as well as of their families. Guests sat in rented plastic chairs for the occasion, in a hollowed-out circle that made room for géwëls and those facilitating the gift-giving process. We arrived with Ayda, her entourage (comprised of friends and family), and me in tow. Amy, the mother of the young man getting married, had been part of this same entourage for years, always accompanying Ayda to the social and religious events of her partisans to bring gifts and words of support. Ayda was named as the *Ndeyale* (honored mother figure), a symbolic gesture that demanded financial support from Ayda and provided a spotlight for Ayda to display her generosity and closeness with friends and constituents.

Wearing an elegant blue-tinted dress with gold embroidery and gold earrings with a matching necklace, Ayda walked with gracious calculation, greeting everyone by shaking hands or waving while her bodyguard remained alert a few steps behind. As we all sat around the circle, Amy stood in the center to thank Ayda for her presence and for the large sum of money she contributed. Her sentiments were amplified by the family géwël, who echoed the pronouncement of the praises and family relations: "Ayda, jërëjëf, yal na la Yàlla may ndam! [Ayda, thank you, and may God grant you success!]" Turning to other guests, Amy pointed at Ayda and offered an emotional testimony of Ayda's generosity and loyalty, saying, "Ayda mii, dafa maa mësa may teraanga [This Ayda right here, she has always given me teraanga]." It is commonplace for a friend or family member to honor a person's generosity, friendship, or gift with a vocal reply of praise so that everyone may hear and take note. It also offers a way for those gathered to share similar feelings while Ayda passes around bank notes to the géwël and those who offer public expressions of support, in her own form of reciprocal teraanga. One by one, women jumped up to shower Ayda with kind words and remind her of their long-standing relationship or of a time when Ayda was good to them or helped them.

Ayda's tactical use of generosity has created a vast network of supporters, which she calls her base. A base is the foundation of any politician's success, but as Ayda demonstrates, women are particularly adept at securing supporters as they are most often present during social events such as family ceremonies. Many who become part of the base have personal connections or have been positively affected by the politician's work in the community. Even if no original connection exists, the relationship is fostered through a system of reciprocity between the politician and their base. Politicians cultivate this relationship through visiting and hosting social events, providing financial assistance to community members during trying times, and offering support to party sympathizers. In return, the base provides the politician with a public forum to gain publicity and further their reputation as generous and charismatic. Ayda's rhetoric during speeches or television interviews shows she is adept in personalizing her interactions. In television appearances, after she is introduced, she acknowledges God and greets everyone individually with some kind of association, as a mbokk or *doomu ndey* (a distant cousin of her family or, in some cases, someone who shares her last name). She makes everyone around her feel special and seen. She is always sharing anecdotes about one's connection to her family or pointing out the successes of those present. Her participation and offerings of teraanga to Amy and others are semiprivate yet also public displays of affection that add to Ayda's reputation as giving and present in the lives of those who support her.

"To Be a Leader, It's about Character": *Generations of Family Leadership*

Ayda was born into a political family, originally from the north of Senegal, who ultimately settled in Bambey, a city in the heart of the country, close to Tuubaa, the holy city of the Sufi Muslim group the Murīds. Ayda got her start in formal politics with the Parti Socialiste but said, "PS moo ma ralenti ci sama politig [The PS delayed my political career]." Many women of her mother's generation were the backstage organizers of political parties—"my women" (sama jigéen)—and as a child, Ayda benefited from shadowing her mother and father on their political quests. "Xam nga, ci caractère la dépendre [You know, it's about character]," Ayda said in response to my question about what it was like to be a Senegalese woman in politics. "Benn xaritu sama pàppa, c'est un paysan, dafa ko daan tooñ di ko wax ni "sa jabar jii bu jangulwoon école sax leader lay doon." Mën nga toog ci sa kër di yore sa leket ngay tànn ceeb kese, mais dangay nekk leader' [A friend of my father who is from the country was teasing him saying that 'your wife, even if she hasn't studied in school, is a leader.' You can sit in your house just gleaning rice and still be a leader]."

In Bambey, Ayda's father worked for the local municipal government and was in charge of voting processes, a memory that stands out for Ayda as a young girl. "Donc bi ma nekkee xale sama tur mu ngi woon ci carte UPS yi parce que bloc de carte yi sama pàppa di jënd dañu ci bind sama tur. Kon ci environment boobu ci laa judo, ci laa yaro [So when I was a child, my name was all over voting cards for the Senegalese Progressive Union because they were cards my father was buying. We would write my name on them. So I was born into and grew up in this environment]." She snickered. Early on, Ayda was recognized by prominent figures who passed the house, such as Pierre Senghor, the first mayor of Bambey and the brother of Senegal's first president, Léopold Sédar Senghor. He told her mother that Ayda was going to be a leader because she was noticeably open and generous. When I asked her what it means to be a female leader in Senegal, she said it depends on the woman's character and personality. She told me an anecdote from her childhood: "When I was a child, I would baptize every sheep that was born. If a sheep were born, I would call all my friends from the neighborhood and have a naming ceremony just to gather people together. We would pretend to cook and serve the meal to everyone. They would put down the mat. It was from this I got my sense of politics."[1]

Even as a child, then, Ayda was assembling peers and creating an inviting space, mirroring a ceremony where her peers could engage in an exchange of food, talk, and gifts—teraanga. Undoubtedly, many of Ayda's longtime friends became supporters in her bids for political office. To support an opponent would be a direct violation of their bond. Linking this ceremonial space to practicing politics demonstrates the crucial role that teraanga plays in her identity and practice as a politician. In many ways, she has re-created these types of gatherings in her professional life, using family ceremonies as spaces to offer hospitality to neighbors in Bambey and at her home in Dakar. During weekend visits to her mayoral home, which is down the street from her mother's house, she welcomed residents at all hours of the night to visit, give their regards, and ask for help with particular issues and activities.

Ayda understands the place that rituals of exchange, obligation, and reciprocity hold for her process, something she learned from her mother. Ayda's mother was also known for her generosity and ability to assemble people, especially other women. She showed how central women were to politics leading up to and following independence, even before they occupied official positions in the government. Within the Parti Socialiste, men often employed women to organize and animate rallies, to cook, and to provide music and general ambience. Women wore ribbons and a *musóor* (head scarf) in party colors to show party affiliation. At the time, women who were involved in the party were only informally associated with a male politician, known simply as the leader's *jigéen* [woman], yet they were an integral part of Senghor's ability to gain supporters in the rural towns throughout Senegal, and they continue to be so. "Sama yaay moo faral di njëkka xam poste administrateur bu vacant ndaxte moo nekkoon ca dëj ba [My mother was often the first person to know when a local administrative position was vacant because she had attended the person's funeral]," Ayda said. Women like Ayda's mother often had more of a finger on the pulse of the community, whether through mbootaay or ceremonies, which would serve men politicians; they hosted the men during campaign touring and served as a supportive network, demonstrating hospitality to the political party members. During her mother's time in community politics, their home often served as a base camp for politicians to rest and also to hold campaign rallies or small gatherings. Social groups were natural environments to create alliances and exercise them during each other's celebrations.

Just as important as the official celebrations or political gatherings were women leaders who assumed this role in all aspects of their lives. Being a leader meant being intimately involved in the lives of others, providing services, counsel, and help in good and bad times. Ayda expressed this about her mother:

> My mother once told me that having gone to school doesn't mean you are a leader. You are born a leader and then your behavior, your education, your generosity are the reasons you can assemble all these women so that they follow you. Then you will stand up, have a presence/importance, because there are a lot of people who came to Bambey as newlyweds and are members. My mother is the reason they were able to stay married. She would counsel them and tell them to be patient, that if women had problems with their husbands, that they come see her. They would visit my mother, and she would tell them what to do and talk to the husband too. At the same time, she would tell them, "You shouldn't do this" and tell their husband what to do, telling him, "If you must help her, help her." Maybe if a woman's husband wasn't working she would help them with the family. There were people whom she had helped who would tell others, "Go visit our mother, Ajda Aminta, and honor her because if I am sitting here it is because of her." And that [lesson] has been very useful for my politics. So now when I come to do politics in the area or wherever I go, people will come up to me to say, "I want to help you very much because my father told them that your mother was a godmother to my mother. So, my father is your uncle." So then I joke with her that we are related, or that she is the child of my mother. Even the other day, a young cameraman came to film me in my office for Tuubaa TV. He said, "You don't know this, but your mother cradled me and baptized me."[2]

When Ayda speaks of the woman who approached her with details about their relations, she uses the word *mbokk* to describe a fictive kinship she has with someone she doesn't know but with whom she shares a kind of kinship, one based on the good deeds and teraanga of her mother. She also uses the term *doomu ndey* (siblings from the same mother) to express a fictive kinship of siblinghood. *Doomu ndey* is often used between good friends with different parents. Within polygamous families where siblings can share a father but not a mother, they refer to one another as *doomu baay* (siblings from the same father). Her reference to the cameraman for a Murīd TV channel demonstrates the ways she benefits from her mother's teraanga and the deep connection with the Murīd community. The anecdote serves as a reminder that reputation is also inherited. Much of Ayda's power comes from her mother's reputation that is known locally and that she uses in discourses more broadly. The Wolof saying *doom ja, ndey ja* (like child, like mother) refers to this very fact, that the stories of parents are also the stories that their children carry with them—for good and for bad. Thus legacies of generosity are taken very seriously. Events such as family ceremonies where géwëls relay these stories are important for the public oral record of one's reputation and therefore future possibilities for personal social advancement as well as that of their children. The anecdote also shows, importantly, that the line between local leader, marriage counselor, hostel owner, and midwife is rather fuzzy. Being a leader in this context, from which Ayda draws inspiration, creates a holistic relationship with community members.

This section shows Ayda a bit more in-depth and shows also the ways in which she does politics. Her understanding of politics and leadership comes from a deep respect for a genealogy of women leaders such as the queens of Waalo and her own mother. From an early age, politics for Ayda have naturally been connected to the social expressions of teraanga, whether in relation to naming ceremonial sheep as a way to gather and host friends or cultivating a political base through reciprocal relationships nurtured by day-to-day and ceremonial prestation. The stories of her mother paint a picture of how Ayda was inspired by her leadership but also how to instrumentalize her legacies of generosity and care to build upon her own similar reputation. Ayda's use of media and the more traditional communication styles of her géwël allow her to show off as a pious wife who can relate to, as well as be a reference for, women. These elements are parts of a whole and show how women understand governance and representation. The next section considers the different tactics and governance philosophies of Aminata Touré.

Doing Politics Republican Style

Aminata, the Senegalese Iron Lady

Aminata "Mimi" Touré, one of eight children, was born to an accomplished family. Her father, Madiou Touré, was a pediatrician and president of the medical doctors' union of Senegal, and a World Health Organization senior staff member; "and he was in his younger age a member of the PAI, Parti Africain de l'Indépendance [African Independent Party]," Aminata said. The PAI was a communist party forced underground during the 1960s by a repressive one-party system. The politician Landing Savané, also a founding member of the PAI, chose Aminata to lead his campaign for president in 1993 when she was just thirty-one years old.

Aminata's mother was a midwife. "My mom was among the first generation of girls to go to school. Her father was very progressive and believed in girls' education. He was very involved in politics in Kaolack. My parents were very dedicated civil servants. That's how I grew up," she said. She was born in Dakar, but her early years of schooling were in Tambacounda and Kaolack, cities in central Senegal. She was a successful soccer player in Dakar, where they moved due to her father's career; she notes that this is where she got her sense of competition.

Aminata received a master's degree in economics from the Université de Dijon and a doctorate in international financial management from the Université de Bourgogne, where she wrote her thesis on women and microfinance in sub-Saharan Africa (Fundación Sur). After having spent much of her adult life outside of Senegal studying in France or working for the United Nations Population Fund in New York City, she returned to Senegal in 2012, when she was assigned by the Sall administration as the minister of justice. She helped initiate the controversial Cour de Répression de l'Enrichissement Illicite (CREI), a special court in the justice system to track down illicit use of government funds. This court was established following a public uprising against Abdoulaye Wade, who sought an illegal third term, which some suspected was to install his son, Karim Meissa Wade, as a successor. Aminata became the anticorruption poster child as she took on many politicians from the Wade era, including Karim Wade, who was accused of corruption, and even her own ex-husband, Oumar Sarr, a senior member of Abdoulaye Wade's PDS party. Aminata was determined to take anticorruption measures seriously, often being referred to as *La dame de fer* (the Iron Lady), likening her to Margaret Thatcher and her austere persona and policies. However, her efforts were mostly met with criticism as many people found it difficult to comprehend a woman who would seek to prosecute and humiliate an ex-husband, and so publicly at that. Most Senegalese felt the bond of families and kinship was much more important than laws. Ayda Mbóoj was one of the harshest critics of the process against Karim, saying that Senegalese believe in *maslaa* (dialogue/diplomacy). I speak to this concept later in the chapter.

Aminata was chosen to succeed Abdul Mbaye as prime minister in September 2013 due to her performance as justice minister. The press questioned her fitness for the task given her reputation for being stern and distant yet with character. An article in the magazine *Jeune Afrique* said she was "too rigorous to meet populous demands when it was necessary, too methodical to fall prey to simplicity, and those who came across Macky Sall after his victory in 2012 recount a woman who was distant while also warm, smiling and measured, who, for her simple presence imposed self-control" (Carayol 2013). I attempted to attend Aminata's highly anticipated first speech to parliament as the newly elected prime minister of Senegal in October 2013 in Dakar. Unable to get a seat inside, I wandered among the crowds of her supporters, who were blowing whistles, cheering, and holding banners with sayings like "Avec Mimi, on passe à l'essentiel [With Mimi, we focus on the essentials]"—a slogan that addressed the core of her anticorruption mission but also felt symbolic of the austere nature of her own personal choices of dress, demeanor, and public policies. (It was also one of the few slogans in French, with no Wolof equivalent.) All the television stations were outside covering the arrival of deputies as they ascended the red carpet, lined by pristine blue pools cascading away from the main entrance. On my other visits to the National Assembly these fountains had been turned off. In order to watch her speech, I rushed to the home of Aicha, one of my research participants, where I found her and family members crowded around the television in the living room. As Aminata approached the lectern, Aicha and the women of the house cheered with elation, shouting, "Waay, xoleen musóoram ak maquillage bi! [Wow, look at her headwrap and makeup!]" Pleasantly shocked, the women remarked on the contrast between what they described as Mimi's normal drab outfits and "same-old wig"—a short bob—and her new bright yellow and purple dress with makeup and a stylish headwrap, or *musóor*. One woman observed, "She actually went to the salon to have the headwrap pinned in place." Aminata spoke about the priorities of the Sall-Touré administration in the midst of a global economic crisis: "This current context demands the efforts of all countries for courageous rationality and reforms to fight against wastefulness and direct primary resources towards programs designed to improve the life conditions of its citizens."[3] Although her reference to the "fight against wastefulness" was directed toward government spending, it is hard not to make observations about her choice of words in relation to the campaign mentioned at the beginning of this book, especially given her reputation as being indifferent to the behaviors and preferences of the majority of women. While putting effort into one's appearance is an expected practice for women on special occasions, especially for family ceremonies or public functions, in the eyes of my friends watching her speech, it was apparently remarkable for Aminata. Aicha commented that she admired Aminata for her intelligence and bravery: "Boppam dafa pleine, waaye xamul sañse [Her head is full, but she doesn't know how to dress well]." At the same time, television reporters captured the arrival of politicians on a red carpet leading to the main parliament doors, with an awards-style commentary on the fashion, pointing out Ayda, who was present for the speech, as the queen of fashion— "always elegant," as one reporter noted. "Oh, look at how beautiful Ayda is," said the woman I sat next to, who had mocked Aminata for her lack of style but now commented in approval of Ayda's dress and poise.

News outlets scrambled for Aminata's personal information, one saying, "At 50 years old, 'Mimi' Touré becomes the second woman to occupy this job [of Prime Minister] in the country of teranga. It is an opportunity for Jeune Afrique to make known her rich career, her passions and hobbies, her militantism, her fight against corruption, her reputation" (Kibangula 2013). Another article called her a "strong head . . . not exactly what we would call a passionflower [*pasionaria*]: too strict to gain popularity when the need for it is palpable" (Carayol 2013). Two DakarActu TV journalists, apparently uninterested in her ideas about policies, referred to the criticisms of her actions as justice minister, noting, "You have been called the mastermind behind the *traque des biens mal acquis* [the search for illicit goods] and become known as a strong woman, a woman of force. Can you tell us whether that corresponds with the woman we see in front of us now smiling?" Aminata replied, "I believe in determination. . . . It has nothing to do with the individual. And this is the confusion with gender that we should avoid. Institutions are disembodied. Individuals come and do their job the best they can, we hope, and then leave. Institutions stay for our children and grandchildren. So I am determined." Unsatisfied with her answer, the other host asked her to reflect on the image the Senegalese public have of her. "But beyond institutions, what can you tell us about Mimi at home with the family? Is Mimi sentimental?"

Aminata is therefore represented as a strict and all-business politician even as the latter journalists try to humanize her by bringing up gender tropes such as wanting to know about her private life and her feelings rather than focusing on her political ideas. Her response is out of the French republican playbook of seeing individuals, whether they are politicians or not, as obscured and abstract. Portraying an institution as disembodied means she understands it to be impersonal, not sustained by any particular individual but by the individuals' ability to see themselves as just part of the greater project. The fact that Aminata separates the sentimental from her public duties is unsettling for some as they are arguably more accustomed to the "hyperpersonalization of power" (Mbow 2008) espoused by the former president Abdoulaye Wade, and many politicians who understand personality to be equally important as policy.

The journalists, still unsatisfied, transitioned to a question about politics, although shrouded in the same inquiry about her reputation: "Can you tell us why you decided to migrate from Grand Yoff to Kaolack? Is it because, as some say, you couldn't make enough inroads in Grand Yoff that you preferred to move to Kaolack?" During the local elections in the summer of 2014, Aminata lost her bid to become mayor of Grand Yoff, the Dakar neighborhood where she lived. Following her loss to Khalifa Sall, mayor of Dakar, Macky Sall removed her from her position as prime minister. One can only speculate why she could not gain adequate support. On the one hand, perhaps Khalifa Sall had too much money and power behind him, and she never really stood a chance. On the other hand, perhaps she was unpopular because she had not made a splash in the public scene. Part of this might have been due to her image as socially detached and not exhibiting a charismatic personality, as Ayda and others did. Possibly this is an example of the political peril of shunning practices of teraanga for Western discourses of law and order; perhaps Aminata had failed to conform to the norms and expectations of women, making it difficult for people to relate to her. Some said that she was *ku xamul teraanga* (one who doesn't know teraanga), which could be seen in her minimalist fashion sense, lack of public showings of generosity, and rhetoric that was more technocratic than the personalized messaging that makes connections with important past and present public figures or references members of her team. In fact, around the time she lost the election in Dakar, Papa Ismaila Dieng, the journalist mentioned in chapter 5, recounted gossip about how Aminata was someone people understood to be ku xamul teraanga because she would not stop to greet people in her own neighborhood, a serious social infraction that could lead to a reputation of being elitist and generally disliked. These pieces of gossip were insidious in public discourse. Despite whether the images painted Mimi as being stingy, unfriendly, or too serious were true, the public decided she did not represent the ideal Senegalese woman who is sensuous, generous, and deferential.

I experienced Aminata very differently. She was very generous with her time and in according me an interview. When I admitted to her that my French had become complicated by learning Spanish—having moved to Mexico a year prior—she gladly suggested we speak in English. She was in fact very personable and self-reflexive, making me think that one-on-one conversations were more her cup of tea than large gatherings. She easily switched between talking about Senegalese Wolof soap operas as a suggestion for me to keep up with my Wolof—although she admitted not having time to watch them—and talking about global politics. Having lived in New York City for almost ten years, she was very aware of and interested in talking about racial politics and immigration in the United States, providing examples about her own siblings who had moved to the US with nothing but were able to work their way up to a middle-class lifestyle. She spoke proudly of her childhood and her parents and about her group of close friends. And Aminata herself sees her legacy as not about personality but about her ability to inspire younger women, referencing her own place among women who came before: "You know I was the second woman to be justice minister and second woman who was then appointed as prime minister. Mame Madior Boye was also." She sees her legacy as simply one link in a chain for which there are antecedents and future women in power.

Curious, I asked Aminata what her impression was of these kinds of interviews where the journalists probed her about personal questions. "I mean, the stance that I had [referring to the Karim Wade dossier] was unusual for a woman [taking on a man in court]. So I guess the stereotype they had about women is not to be that strong, not to stand, not to be able to make your case. All the stuff in the press [about her], that was quite a surprising profile; they [the Senegalese public] had never seen that." She seemed to find some glee in having been a source of bewilderment, telling me another story about perceptions of her: "When a friend of mine who was working on a project with my husband mentioned to a builder that they were working with Mimi Touré's husband, the guy was like, 'Hunh? I have to see this guy,' apparently needing to see who could be the husband of *THAT* woman. He was expecting someone who was three meters high and three hundred kilos. He had to be an exceptional man to be able to deal with a woman like that." She laughed at the prospect of being seen as such a difficult woman to deal with.

"And it seems like these journalists wanted you to offer them some kind of proof that you are this feminine character that they could relate to," I said, hoping she would give her reaction.

"Which I assume that role. I'm like any woman," she responded with a big laugh. "And actually for a long time people didn't think I was married. Until one day I went to a show with my husband and the press was like, 'Mimi, the newlywed,' to which I was like, I've been married to the same man for twenty years, man, come on." She mentioned that her reputation has evolved over time to where she has become more accepted, yet, more importantly to her, "Either you like me or you don't like me." She preferred to let her policies and politics speak for themselves. However, in the landscape of Senegalese politics, standing out, not blending in, matters more.

Therefore, Aminata's reputation is obscured by gender stereotypes about what it means to be a good woman and wife, which she mostly shrugs off as having nothing to do with her political duties. She celebrates the legacies of women who were in politics before her and seeks to set a positive example of good governance for young women who wish to also participate in politics. The separation between her personal matters and her position in politics is quite stark when compared to the governing tactics of Ayda Mbóoj. Doing politics republican style for Aminata is respecting the boundaries between private and public conduct—or the person and the office—as well as seeing the individual, including herself, as an abstract representation of the nation. In the next section, I discuss how these differing governing philosophies take shape with regard to the question of corruption in Senegalese politics.

The Clash of Two Governing Philosophies

Aminata and Ayda represent the complex negotiations between values and practices of a French Republic and those of a Teraanga Republic. For Ayda, politics were personal while Aminata appeared to systematically separate her public and private lives, including how she understood the concept of teraanga itself. And yet, Ayda's reaction to the juridical case of corruption against Karim Wade is an example of how politicians in modern Senegalese society negotiate and manipulate these two different governing styles.

The rivalry between Ayda and Aminata is mostly a public imaginary hyped up by the media. They are depicted as enemies from the former ruling party and the new administration that under Aminata's leadership within the ministry of justice sought to prosecute cases of corruption against former Wade loyalists including his own son. The trial that eventually put Karim in jail was followed by a campaign headed up by Ayda against "arbitrary detention" (Mbóoj 2015) where Ayda accused the government of targeting Karim Wade because he was the former president's son, not because he was proven to have stolen government funds. Accusing Aminata and the prosecution of being arbitrary, Ayda fought for his release on the basis of preserving the character of the Senegalese nation as peaceful and forgiving. She argued that his detention was arbitrary because others who were equally accused of corruption went without punishment because they were of little public interest. She attacked the process as lacking transparency, but Aminata argued that the justice department needed to fulfill its duties away from public influence or away from arbitrary mediation from outside actors such as Ayda.

In a letter published in the online journal *Dakaractu*, Ayda quoted Montesquieu's well-known phrase "injustice done to one is injustice done to all" (Mbóoj 2015), urging readers to sign a petition to force the government to reconsider Karim Wade's case. Ayda was certainly not the only one criticizing Macky Sall and his administration of making an example of Karim Wade, and her use of French political philosophers such as Montesquieu, the father of the theory of separation of powers, demonstrates a savviness of using republican-style language to speak directly to the legal processes concerning Wade. In many ways, this is a perfect example of the ways in which politicians negotiate politics via engaging with French institutional philosophies and laws that formally prohibit arbitrary rule while the day-to-day governance and popular understandings of justice are nothing if not arbitrary. In the end, Ayda's campaign was able to help Karim get out of jail on conditions that he would leave the country and pay back a certain amount of the money he was accused of stealing, a luxury not afforded to those she said did not receive the same treatment as Karim Wade. Ayda demonstrates an example of negotiating between the two worlds of French justice and republican governance and a Teraanga Republic where ultimately family connections and social governing rules determine an individual's fate.

During my conversation with Ndey Sukkey Géy at her home in 2017, she reflected on her friendship with Aminata and on some of the advice she had given when Aminata was named prime minister. Having grown up next to Aminata as a child in the town of Thiès, when Aminata's father was sent there for work, and having worked with her while Aminata was the program coordinator for the Gender and HIV in West Africa United Nations Population Fund, Ndey held her in high regard. However, Ndey Sukkey said she worried Aminata was seen as being too Westernized and out of touch with Senegalese values and too harsh in her campaign against corruption. Her affinity for justice, as Ndey pointed out, was not how most Senegalese saw the world, and her education seemed only to distance her further from the average person. Aware that female politicians are heavily scrutinized for their behaviors and persona, Ndey said, "I sent her a letter of congratulations upon her nomination in 2013, also warning her of the potential pitfalls of being too lawfully minded."

I want to bring Aysata Tall Sall into the equation to give her legal perspective on what Ndey means by being "too lawfully minded."

The modern justice system, quote unquote, is not well regarded by Africans and by Senegalese in particular. Why do I speak specifically about Senegal? Because there is always the topic of religion that intervenes. Justice, it is poorly viewed because it applies rules that no one understands. For us, these legal rules were inherited from the French tradition who inherited it from the Roman tradition, and it is the antithesis of our cultures and our African civilizations. So, people think that justice is a foreign game played by people who don't understand the social rules in which people live. Because for us, what is justice? For us, for Africans, justice is regulating social tension. It is not a referee or a judge; it is always trying to mediate and find a balance. It is not justice. For example, if I do something wrong, and they call upon us, and because I am older than you, in front of everyone they will not say "Aysata, you were wrong." They will say, "Well, Emily, after everything, Aysata is your older sister, and there are some things you need to accept." Now, when you leave the room, they will tell me, "OK, but Aysata, you kind of messed up." Because there is something more important, which is seniority, the rights we give to elders. That is more important than giving justice to Emily.[4]

According to what Aysata offers in the previous quote, in Senegalese society, French ideas run against "le fait social" (social rules/governance) of Senegalese understandings of justice because it obscures the important personal relationships and hierarchies that allow for social harmony. Therefore, Ayda demonstrates a creativity in her ability to navigate both worlds while Aminata is painted as not "understanding the social rules in which people live." When Aminata was still minister of justice and handling the Karim dossier, Ayda accused her of being biased against Wade and his family, citing rules of French republican law, while in reality it is Aminata who plays by the book and is often "too legally minded," as Ndey Sukkey says. Part of what has made Ayda more popular than Aminata with the Senegalese public is her ability to function in the two republics while Aminata sees the idea of teraanga as a governing style as part of what prevents Senegal from emerging into a modern state. Aminata's focus on legal frames as both the way in which justice is served and as how development and resources serve people runs against how most Senegalese understand relationships. While Aminata believes that relationships are best supported by state structures that eliminate the possible discrepancies or contradictions of human biases, Ayda sees them rather as a tool to mediate the core of the issue: human relationships.

Sharing Is Caring

As is quite clear, politicians such as Ayda Mbóoj have successfully employed teraanga as a specific tactic of doing politics that demonstrates their flexibility of character and acute knowledge of situational requirements, including amid criticism of and controversy over their actions. For example, following my field research in 2013 and 2014, Ayda was elected as the first female president of her departmental council but was subsequently deposed by the president on the principle that she unlawfully held too many governmental positions since she was also mayor of Bambey and a representative in parliament. Although this law has not been applied to many politicians, men and women alike, Ayda seemed to have been made an example of due to her high-profile status and for being a member of the opposition. Perhaps it was also a way of challenging her growing authority. Ayda acknowledges the criticism against her and yet stands firm in her belief in the role of such actions to her political process. These ways of doing politics are effective but also attract criticism that possibly stems from not validating teraanga as an appropriate strategy that is seen as connected to the private sphere or, in Ayda's case, not seeing the lines between politics and other social expressions.

Ayda herself recognized that her style of doing politics attracts criticism, particularly about corruption. She said:

> If giving teraanga to those in need is considered corruption, then, well, call me corrupt. Those in civil society who say there is corruption in politics just don't understand. They don't know that it is teraanga you are giving. You give a lot of teraanga, always giving teraanga. Because the day that you need someone they will help you because you gave them teraanga. It's not corruption; it's teraanga. You mutually give teraanga even if you aren't doing politics, you give teraanga. So, the day you start doing politics you go to them and they help you. Even more, to show it is not corruption, when I campaign around the country in rural areas, people welcome me and give me teraanga like sheep, chickens, peanuts, beans that will fill up your car. You know, that is ter-aanga. Then when they come to Bambey, I cook them rice, they eat, and when they leave I give them money for transportation. Teraanga is what connects two people. An exchange of civility between two people. If you get married, see the mother of your husband or the big sister of your husband, you give them teraanga. She too, when she comes and finds your child, she gives them teraanga. Or when you have a beautiful cloth, or she has a nice present, they give it to you, give you teraanga.[5]

She rejected the idea that her investments could be understood as corruption. When I asked her about the use of the term *teraanga* when referring to gifts, she said, "We say *teraanga* so that people know it wasn't given by force." Or *teraanga, kenn du ko xëcco* (no one fights over teraanga), as we saw in chapter 1. Obviously, the distinction between forceful obligation and general obligation to others is muddied and complicated. The proverb I shared in the introduction, "teraanga moo dox sunu diggante, nde lu du ñaaw [it is honoring one another that brings us together, for it is not ugly]," shares a similar sentiment that teraanga signals a positive expression of interpersonal relationships that is neither forced nor outside the norm, or at least in principle does not seek to harm, but rather unite. It is in many ways the greatest preoccupation: trying to balance social relationships with individual desires and needs in a context of local systems of hierarchy and its expressions as well as with Sufi teachings of "communality and religious spirituality" (Ngom 2016) as an expression of faith against the "modern era shaped by individualism, rationalism, and secularity" (Babou 2007). Ayda speaks about the distinction between corruption and teraanga in terms of a moral obligation to others, a necessary social lubricant to keep relationships moving along smoothly. Her assertion that politics is simply one kind of relationship shows how she functions by "always giving teraanga," so for her, why would politics be any different? It can be seen as forceful or corruption only if one doesn't see oneself already operating within a world driven by teraanga. The example of Ayda's mother shows us that the holistic nature of being a community leader means that teraanga is a way to repair relationships, care for others through housing and food, and generally keep the peace.

Furthermore, women's discourses about power and elected positions are framed in a way that focuses less on personal enrichment, as the politics of the belly suggests (Bayart 1993), and more on their ability to provide aid to others and demonstrate themselves as part of a larger community. Ayda even frames her sense of community in terms of sharing food: "Even now, I eat with everyone because I can't eat by myself. If everyone has left the house I wait until evening to eat as I won't have an appetite. . . . When there are a lot of people I can eat well. What I really like is to eat with others around a bowl and to give them something to drink. That is my inspiration for politics."

Ayda's description of eating with others and providing food for others as a model for her politics means that she sees her actions as teraanga, not corruption, which in this case means the sharing of wealth or seeing one's wealth as also for others. Always being available to share a meal is to make sure others feel that you feel them, *yég nañu yég nga leen*. Therefore, Ayda's insistence that because her politics are based on daily acts of hospitality, sharing of food and resources, and investing in those in need, they cannot be classified as corruption. Corruption disproportionately benefits the taker whereas teraanga is using the wealth one has in order to better the situation of those around them.

Ku xam teraanga *(Someone Who Knows the Meaning of Teraanga)*

Aminata sees corruption differently, as a matter of social injustice.

> I was very revolted by injustice as a child. In fact, I have a little story. One day, an old lady came to visit my mom. I was maybe six or seven. And she was poor, and I guess she needed some help. And when she arrived, my mom was having a nap. So she waited to see her. I looked at her shoes, and I said, "Auntie," and I forget her name, "your shoes are so old. Why don't you change your shoes?" She said, "well I don't have money." I said, "Just wait, I'm gonna solve this." I went to my mom's closet and took her nicest shoes and gave them to the lady. You can imagine what followed after that. I got a nice spank. My mom told me, "You know, if you want to be generous, you have to work and have your own stuff so you can be generous with stuff you own. You can't be generous with people's stuff."

A combination of this type of lesson and her parents' roles as civil servants inspired her to work for social justice. Very early on, she was taught that generosity must come from what one owns and not from what others own or, in this case, public money. Still, she was portrayed publicly as "Mimi is good, but she is so stingy." She laughed; "and I was like, no, I'm not stingy, I just don't have money to distribute to you. But it takes a lot of pedagogy and education for people to understand that if they want public services to be well managed, you cannot distribute as you wish. I'm generous, but where am I going to get the money?"

In an interview entitled "La corruption au Sénégal: la source du mal" (Corruption in Senegal: The source of evil) on 2STV, a local Senegalese TV channel (2020), Aminata spoke frankly about the status of corruption and a proposal to combat it—what she calls dematerialization. She talks about the responsibility of citizens and not just politicians to fight corruption: "I see a direct connection between corruption and gifting. For corruption to exist you have to have those who ask and those who give." She and Ayda agree that there is a mutuality when it comes to teraanga, but Aminata understands its utility differently. "Li ma gis ci de-materialization mooy, manam, nga dem wuuti say kayitu juudu. Li nga wara xam, ki ñu fa teg sa impôt la ko faye. Kon moom service bi la wara joxe, fay nañu ko pare. Kon timbre bi nga wara joxe parce que loolou la loi bi wax waaye amuloo yekketi di ko jox, amul itam laaj. Timbre rekk nga wara séq ak moom. [The goal of dematerialization is that, for example, you go to get a birth certificate. What you should know is that that government worker, your taxes have paid for them. So, the service they provide you, they have already been paid for. So, the fee you must pay is regulated by law, but there is no giving and no asking (referring to corruption). The fee is the only thing that ties you to them.] It's all on the computer." In essence, the problem with "little corruption," as she calls it, is that government functions are too personalized, meaning the identities of the two parties become subject to personal interpretations "because if we sit down together, the person will think that they need to give teraanga and that you as the government worker feel you need to also do something." Her use of teraanga in the example is telling. She is not saying outright that teraanga equates to corruption; in fact, she is acknowledging that because most day-to-day interactions involve some kind of teraanga, one may think that this particular instance is no different. But the issue for her is a lack of understanding about citizens' role vis-à-vis the state and vice versa.

In our interview, I asked Aminata about the links between teraanga and politics.

> It's a tricky one. Teraanga means . . . teraanga is something I would define as a kindness. Into kindness you put a lot of things: hospitality, welcoming, caring, exchange of good services. And as you know, teraanga has a cost. When you get to a wedding transaction, that is when you know teraanga has a big cost. And when it comes to politics, people expect their leader to know what teraanga means. Meaning you have to be generous. But where are you going to find the money to do that? So I have to sit down with my fans, as you call them, and explain to them that, you know, people believe I am doing the right thing when it comes to public resources. So, it comes with an inconvenience because I don't have money to distribute to you guys. I mean like I said, you can fit a lot of content in the word *teraanga*, but when it comes to giving teraanga to a civil servant it's called corruption. Because you don't need to give them anything for that service because they are already paid by the state. But you make it look nice by calling it teraanga. It's a very general word, and you can twist it to make it seem nice when you are not doing something nice. But when we are talking about Senegalese teraanga, we are talking about welcoming. You can hide behind the word to do things that are not the nicest. It's kind of like a transaction most of the time. You know, *ku xam teraanga la* [he/she who knows teraanga] means someone who is generous. But he is generous with money, or he is generous with public money? That's where it gets tricky within politics. A politician giving teraanga, where does the money come from? A guy who is running his campaign and giving you teraanga, that is money that was supposed to be for a new hospital or something like that. So, when people don't want to know where the money comes from, they call it teraanga.

Aminata makes the distinction between teraanga and corruption when it comes to politics, a distinction that is also about keeping the private demonstrations of generosity separate from public politics. In his book *Moral Economies of Corruption*, Pierce (2016) argues that the discourse of corruption has more recently shifted from a lack of moral competency to acknowledging the importance of "local systems of knowledge" and therefore seeing corruption as a default primitivism (13). In other words, corruption is a sign of political and developmental immaturity. In the same 2STV program, Aminata speaks of corruption as being something innate to all humans, saying that "scandale yu gëna réy ci gé ci adduna ci dëkku toubab lay amee. Ëppuñu kenn moralité, ëppuñu kenn éthique. Doomu Adama moo bindee noonu. Mais, li nga xam ne ñoom lu nu ci jël, dañu fexe ba am de-materialization [The largest scandals of corruption in the world are committed by those in the West. They are not morally or ethically better than anyone. Humans were made that way. But what we can take from them is that they found a way to dematerialize (their institutions)]." In an article Aminata penned for the French newspaper *Le Monde*, she reflects upon her contribution to the fight against corruption in Senegal: "Corruption is well understood as a global phenomenon. However, the impact of corruption is felt more in developing countries where resources destined for collective infrastructures, education, health, and other critical sectors are misappropriated by those in power for personal enrichment" (Touré 2016). As her interview with Dakaractu and many other examples show, her understanding of corruption aligns more closely with the idea of "a failure to live by the mores of a particular kind of bureaucracy" (Pierce 2016), a bureaucracy that "naturalized distinctions between public and private and delegitimized political motivations on the basis of 'private' interests" (12). As we have seen with Ayda's example, the question of morality is about respecting not institutions but people. This is not to say that Ayda does not see the value in institutions. She is a civil servant in some of the most important institutions in Senegal, but her understanding of politics is also about a loyalty to people. Aminata disagrees. In fact, even after she was fired by Macky Sall after a short tenure as economic and social adviser to the president in 2020, she said, "Men and women come and go, but institutions remain" (Ba 2020). It is not about the individual, as she demonstrates. It is instead about the ability of institutions to continue beyond the individual. Even as she was fired from her position she maintained her philosophy of strong institutions temporarily steered by abstract individuals. In her public denouncement of Macky Sall's refusal to outright clarify his position of seeking a third term, Aminata went against him and defended the constitution.

Conclusion

Even while postcolonial countries such as Senegal have adopted democratic policies and capitalist economic structures, the day-to-day workings of society still more closely resemble a gift economy, or rather a political economy of teraanga. And as McNee (2000) points out, modernization and development have not led to the demise of a gift economy. If anything, it has somehow strengthened its presence as a balance to the inequalities of modernity, and women in politics have taken advantage of this. The cases of Ayda Mbóoj and Ndey Sukkey Géy, as compared to that of Aminata Touré, demonstrate the frictions between these political philosophies in the context of doing politics in Senegal. We remember from chapter 2 that Ndey Sukkey Géy spoke about the importance of teraanga to a woman's social and political processes as well as to demonstrate authority against overbearing mothers-in-law. She argued that doing politics sénégalaisement was the surest way for women to make space for themselves in state politics. Many Senegalese view teraanga as the core symbol of Senegalese national culture and collective identity. Such an economy holds together extensive networks that are modeled through processes of "generalized exchange" (de Sardan 1999; Sahlins 1965), such as gift giving and hospitality. Money and social relations are two sides of the same coin (Moya 2015), and gifts are significant as powerful symbols of the strength of social relationships (Mauss and Halls 1954). Hospitality reaches beyond an object: it is an embedded social transaction that connects the individual to the community through small and large gestures of generosity and openness (Candea and Da Col 2012; Derrida and Dufourmantelle 2000). And the imposition of these social realities onto a republican framework of government allows for women like Ayda to succeed and for Aminata to find it difficult to break into elected positions to represent her fellow citizens.

The comparison between Ayda and Aminata therefore serves as an entryway into discussions about perceptions of governance, democracy, and postcolonial identities. Symbolically, Ayda and Aminata represent two different realities of the Senegalese postcolonial experience, one that embodies local and traditional knowledge systems and practices, and the other characterized by Western education and therefore disconnected from Senegalese cultural practices. This is not to say that Aminata is against local cultural practices but rather that she casts a critical eye on their mobilities. Ayda's and Aminata's contrasting identities are constructed through popular discourses and debates about what it means to be a real Senegalese woman and citizen.

Drawing on and developing themes from the first chapter about the centrality of teraanga to marriages, reputations of generosity and femininity, and female agency, I have shown how these complex relationships translate to the political arena and how this translation is the source of both success for many women politicians and resistance against them. I have argued that the connection between women's involvement in the social reproduction of families by way of ceremonies and day-to-day prestations creates both political possibilities in elected positions and accusations of corruption. And yet it is important to see the theme of corruption through women's different experiences and approaches to the art of government. Ayda's issues with naming her actions as corrupt have to do with her overall philosophy of leadership, which is tightly connected to holistic expressions of teraanga. Moreover, she sees the components of politics as no different from the reciprocal relationships that make up a political economy of teraanga. Aminata, on the other hand, views government as separate from private choices, understanding teraanga as a socially unifying factor of family and other relationships. In this sense, teraanga cannot translate to politics because as a state governed by French-inspired republican principles, the presence of teraanga personalizes the individual and the political process.

Therefore, as a response to their testimonies, we must consider whether our definitions of governance make room for women's alternative governing styles. The common denominator between shifting political systems of feudalism and democracy and modernity, the art of government, has been the continued exclusion of women not just as citizens but as governors. Does the idea of a Teraanga Republic allow us to consider Senegalese women's legacies of leadership as tied to a political economy of teraanga—or doing politics Senegalese style—that have consistently been a kind of parallel type of governance in the absence of women's authority in formal state politics? In the preceding chapters, I explored these questions by examining the connections between women's associations, international and national development policies, and the parité movement; women's involvement in religious communities; and the women-driven patron-client networks that have allowed for women to keep their families afloat during times of economic crises.

7

Is Senegal Ready for a
Female President?

A month before the 2019 presidential elections in Senegal, all forms of media were ablaze with the news that Aysata Tall Sall—presidential hopeful, member of parliament, and veteran politician of the Parti Socialiste—had decided to back the sitting president Macky Sall for another term. She had been known as a stark opponent of Macky Sall and his agenda since the beginning of his presidency in 2012 and had even critiqued those who couldn't win the battle against *transhumance*, or the act of switching parties or alliances, of which she was now being accused. Aysata sought to run for president until she was disqualified for lacking the amount of initial support to be a viable candidate; a controversial change to the electoral code adopted earlier in 2018 required a certain number of signatures to appear on the ballot, called *parrainage*. It was questionable whether she and the two other female candidates, one of whom was Ayda Mbóoj, lacked the number of signatures needed or whether there was an effort by the government to prevent them from running. The law required a specific number of signatures from potential voters living in at least seven of the fourteen regions of the country. It was controversial and the media accused Macky Sall and his administration of using the law to limit the competition. In fact in 2021, following the elections, the Communauté Économique des États de l'Afrique de l'Ouest (CEDEAO) justice department ordered the law be struck down on the basis of it preventing free participation in the democratic process. And yet, in 2024, the parrainage law was still in place, and the same issues Aysata faced had befallen Ayda Mbóoj and Aminata Touré, also disqualifying their candidacies.

The media's reaction to Aysata's decision to back Macky Sall was at times vile and uncivil, and at best full of disappointment. One headline read, "After her transhumance, Aysata Tall Sall got lynched on social media" (Ndiaye 2019). The Twitter account of a young journalist equated her decision with the death of women's political hopes: "I have seen on this Monday, 28th of January many dreams destroyed. Especially those of many young women, whether politically active or not, who saw Ms. Aysata Tall Sall as the most elegant and eloquent, and patriotic of what was to be the Senegalese woman in politics"[1] (Ndao 2019). Her slogan, Osez l'Avenir (Dare to Face the Future), became a source of ridicule, with headlines saying, "Aysata Tall Sall a osé la transhumance" (Aysata Tall Sall dared to switch sides) (Dieng and Diamanka 2019) and Twitter posts rebranding her slogan as "Osez Transhumer" (Dare to Switch Sides) or "Osez Trahir" (Dare to Betray). The word *transhumance* refers most commonly to the migration of sheep to greener pastures, an image of following the herd in search of sweeter returns. In Aysata's case, she was accused of abandoning her morals and her values, which were highly gendered, as well as deceiving her supporters who believed in her movement. There was a great deal of speculation reported in the article: Was she pressured by her religious guides and family, or perhaps possessed into making the decision? Was she bribed? Was she offered a position in the government? These questions consumed the media for weeks before the election, which took place on February 25, 2019. Macky Sall, her once rival, won a second term and later named Aysata his minister of foreign affairs.

During a visit to Dakar that following summer, my friends and research participants asked disappointedly if I had heard about what Aysata had done—knowing that I had spent time with her and her campaign during the 2017 legislative elections, when she launched her movement and consequently won a seat in parliament. One friend told me they were disappointed and that she had always been the exemplar of a Senegalese woman in politics and another lamented that she was unfairly castigated for being a woman. A Twitter user said about Aysata, "she was one of the rare women politicians who was respected and admired" (AiichaBamba 2019) and another said, "she was always an important figure of the modern African woman. A pity, I admired her so much" (Hawoye 2019). Certainly, as this comment suggests, many men in the history of Senegalese politics have made similar choices to back a once stark opponent or to change parties due to pure ambition. And yet they were not met with such vitriol and accusations of deception. So why was the reaction to her political strategy so strong and full of disappointment?

In the months leading up to the 2017 legislative elections, Aysata had a meeting with select supporters to gather their thoughts as to whether they should join another coalition of parties and individuals or if they should go it alone with her own movement. Men and women gave testimonials about Aysata, saying she was a "woman of value" and a "woman of quality." One man said she was a "sellable product," given that she was seen by the public as "*jigéen ju mën góor*," or a woman who is more capable than a man. Others said it was time that a woman emerges so that they may do politics in a new way.

Doing politics another way, or *faire de la politique autrement*, was one of the catchphrases of the election. Throughout the campaign it became obvious that many parties employed this discourse to mean they were the "female-friendly" party fighting for women's rights. Male-led parties were using the second on the list, a woman, as a sign of their progressive ideas, implying that having a woman on the ballot (even though it was mandated) showed their respect for women and that they were doing things differently in terms of new ways of governing. During the meeting with Aysata's supporters, there were also warnings that they were truly looking for a different kind of politics, most likely including politicians who remain faithful to their party and the supporters who helped get them there. One woman stood up and said this was the first political meeting she had ever been to because all other parties had disappointed her: "Dama am yaakaar ci Aysata. Loolu moo ma fi indi . . . waaye [speaking directly to Aysata] soo andee ak yeneen parti yi, du ma la topp [I believe in Aysata. That's the only reason I'm here. But (speaking to Aysata), if you go with these other parties, I will not follow you]." Not surprisingly, two years later, on the eve of the presidential election, women who had seen her as an inspiration felt betrayed, and others saw it as a sign of the failed experiment of women in politics. Another Twitter user responded to Fary Ndao's letter of deception by saying, "Quel gâchis d'avoir donné à une femme politique sénégalaise ma confiance et mon amour. Une chose que je regreterai toute ma vie [What a waste to have given my confidence and love in a Senegalese woman in politics. Something I will regret for the rest of my life]"[2] (Sarine 2019).

As these media posts demonstrate, her choice was interpreted as quashing the image of a strong woman capable of leading on her own, which had been her battle cry and that of many other women's campaigns for parliament or president. Many perceived her so-called treachery as a sign that women could not be trusted in politics because they were unprofessional and incapable of thinking for themselves; in other words, they were used as pawns in men's political games. Beyond these gendered tropes about leadership, another narrative emerged that exposed the different burdens that women like Aysata bear, such as the legacy of women's fight for equal participation in national economic development and political decision-making. Furthermore, it highlights a similar legacy of centering gender in Senegalese political and developmental policies and practices in ways that circumscribe women's possibilities.

In this chapter, I discuss the major advances in women's political authority while recognizing the societal and strategic limitations of prioritizing gender and personality as markers of political valor. I also demonstrate how the ties between femininity and teraanga as a gendered practice continue to shape the expectations of women's political campaigns and political identities. This chapter will examine the messaging and strategy behind Aysata Tall Sall's establishment of her coalition and 2017 campaign. Based on my observations during campaigning and conversations with Aysata and Mareem Sow, a member of the coalition, I demonstrate the complexities of basing one's political image on distinctly feminine identities as an argument for a woman's place in political office. I argue that although these strategies have worked to some extent, more often than not, they have disallowed women politicians from creating a political identity based on anything other than these feminine ideals. Or, as Butler (1999) argues, "insistence on a stable subject of feminism, understood as a seamless category of women," reveals instead a stringent coercion to abide by these categories even if their "construction has been elaborated for emancipatory purposes" (7). It limits the parameters in which women can identify themselves. In this light, Aysata's decision to back Macky Sall's campaign felt to many not just like an abandonment of her party but as a defeat for the women's movement for national equal political representation, which had been largely constructed on these same principles. I also discuss the complex relationships between Aysata and Mareem, a woman she chose for her party's list and who helped her campaign in 2017, as well as Ndey Mbóoj, the niece of Ayda Mbóoj who helped organize her coronation ceremony we saw in the introduction. Ndey demonstrates another side of the female patronage relationship that played out during the election.

Courage as a Feminine Trait

Aysata launched her coalition, Osez l'Avenir, in 2017, after years of vying for a more central role within the Parti Socialiste. I asked her where the name for the coalition came from, a name that perfectly explains the contradictions that Senegalese women face about the nature of generosity in teraanga and in politics.

> Osez comes from our mutual experiences. I understood very early on that one of the most important things in politics is to have courage. If we don't have courage, we can't make it in politics, especially as a woman. This is why women speak to you about courage because they know they must transgress

barriers. There is a social barrier and you rise above it to dare doing politics. Everything that politics demands is refused to women. To be strong, a woman shouldn't be strong. It is regarded poorly. To speak in public, a woman shouldn't speak in public. It is regarded poorly. To lead, a woman shouldn't lead. To look for power, a woman shouldn't look for power. It is regarded poorly. So, when women get into politics, courage is the first thing because she is leaving a world that was designed for her, knocking down a barrier, and entering into a world that is not made for her. A world that is made for and by men. The game of politics is defined by men. And, when we want to succeed in politics, we have to play like a man while remaining a woman. If not, we can't win. It's also directed at men to have the courage to break with the past. Men have controlled politics to this point, and it is time to do politics a different way. It is a question of doing [politics] more seriously. It is time to bring something for people, instead of generosity. We don't do politics to have a position. We do politics because we believe that we can change things. That is the idea of generosity. It is to say to oneself that I have my life, I can live it carefree, but no, I won't be passive. I will leave my house, leave my comfort zone, leave my luxury to go give something to those who have not had the luck that I do. That is where the idea of generosity comes from within our campaign. So, after courage, there is generosity. And generosity without the participation of those you are helping is charity. Politics is not charity. Politics is a collective action, a collective effort that we make because we feel it is going to help everyone. That is where courage, generosity, and participation come from for Osez l'Avenir.[3]

Aysata describes Senegalese women as being up against a great deal of adversity. In fact, Senegalese women in society and politics are at constant odds with a male-dominated public that overwhelmingly rejects their presence. They are either too feminine and therefore unprofessional or too masculine and threaten men's dominance, or they cannot be taken seriously, because they do not embody the ideal and relatable Senegalese woman. In addition, women are limited to being good women and good workers in the private sphere or being courageous disruptors trying to make it in a man's world. They are generous—or give excessively—therefore embodying teraanga, or they are stingy and reject teraanga, making them unrelatable. They are also up against the overarching debate about what relationships and governance should look like. Her comments about the importance of limitations to generosity, as well as its textures, signal this debate. How to be generous and social yet judicious in what one is willing to do for the sake of the collective? In her comments, Aysata identifies a kind of generosity—most likely referring to political patronage—that has been the political norm and distinguishes this from a new way of doing politics in which generosity—of time, representation, and advocacy—translates as working for people's shared aspirations. As she mentions, "It is time to bring something for people. . . . Politics is not generosity," considering generosity not simply as providing money to supporters in order to gain their vote but to provide advocacy on their behalf. Part of the courage that she cites is about standing up not only to men or those who doubt women's abilities but also for women to self-govern in a way that is also self-preserving. As we have seen throughout the book, women are under a great deal of pressure to satisfy the needs of everyone around them. As Kiné noted in chapter 4, she wished that women had the courage to stop participating in the futilities of ceremonies as they have become such a looming factor in how women relate to one another and set the tone for their economic and political possibilities among others. It is also curious that because of women's proximity to these acts of generosity, teraanga, and their critiques, the question of generosity and even corruption take on particularly gendered undertones.

Another aspect of Aysata's distinction between charity and politics is about advocating for women's participation in politics beyond their supportive role of *sama jigéen* to men's campaigns, which has reinforced women's dependence on men's benevolence. In this aspect, women's courage is about finding ways to have authority both among their families and within politics that is about equal participation and access to resources. The question and predicament that these contradictions imply is what governance looks like in a post-parité, postcolonial Senegal. Does it resemble a complex personalized and reciprocal relationship characteristic of a Teraanga Republic or a technocratic state that seeks to standardize ideas of governance and representation? Therefore, what do these strategies look like for women in positions of power such as Aysata and those seeking it? Have they been effective, or what limitations do they present? Next, I outline the 2017 legislative campaigns as to better understand the political context of campaigning and elections.

The 2017 Election

In the early part of summer 2017, parties and newly formed coalitions, such as that of Aysata, chose men and women for their lists. These were in turn submitted to the Ministry of Elections with a steep fee to achieve formal registration. For parliamentary elections, there are two types of representatives: those who represent a local district and those who represent national interests. The national list required sixty candidates from each party, and the departmental lists depended on population size. All lists were mandated to respect the parité law, requiring alternating male and female candidates. If a man was *tête de liste* (the head of the list), the second in line must be a woman, and continuing to alternate down the list. In 2017, there were a record number of forty-seven registered parties and coalitions; of these, four were led by women, with a male candidate in second position. Although the parité law was passed in 2010 and enacted for the 2012 parliamentary elections, parties in 2017 scrambled to find enough women to fill their party lists. I was told by male politicians this was due to a lack of qualified candidates or few women who were interested or known to party veterans, although this assertion was constantly disputed by women I spoke with. To find women, most male-dominated parties sourced the thousands of associations, mostly directed by women, in strategic neighborhoods throughout Dakar. This process was often haphazard. One freelance journalist told me that on the eve of the deadline to register party lists, people were scrambling to meet their quotas minutes before the deadline, asking others if anyone knew the names of women they could add to their incomplete lists. Because they are possibly unaware of or disconnected from the sophisticated women's associations throughout the city, the general population of men and women still find it challenging to take women in politics seriously, not just as placeholders but as valuable contributors to state political decision-making.

There was a specific three-week period in July before election day for authorized campaigning, but that year's campaign (2017) was thrown off by the tragic collapse of several stands in a soccer stadium in the city, killing several people. As a sign of solidarity, the government called for a day of mourning and a two-day moratorium at the beginning of the campaigns. Once we got started, our first tour was throughout Dakar and its outskirts. We coordinated our movements with vans, cars, and trucks full of enthusiastic coalition members. Supporters sang, "Osez, Osez, Osez! Buur Yàlla nu ngi lay ñaan! [Dare, be brave, God, the King, we are seeking your help!]" while hanging off the sides of what looked like hay-baling trucks. The song was a mixture of Aysata Tall Sall's party slogan, Osez l'Avenir, and a generic prayer. In between singing and chanting, music boomed from seven-foot-tall speakers stacked across the bed of the truck. Campaign signs were taped across it and on the windows and sides of cars that were also part of the *caravane*, or parade. The music was prearranged and played on a loop. In between communities or neighborhoods, the playlist began again as a way to announce Aysata's arrival, with intervals of direct messaging coming from the microphone. One song specifically commissioned for the occasion featured a rapper spinning a message about Aysata as a strong woman. The caravane lasted for hours, weaving through Dakar and eventually into other urban and rural areas of Senegal. I found myself in the comfort of party members' cars or in the bed of a 4×4 while members danced, and I held on for dear life as we sped up between sections of a planned route. One of the young women in the back with me, Mareem Soda Ndiaye, was the youngest member on Aysata's list and was handpicked by Aysata to take over her seat in parliament when she was appointed as foreign minister. When we slowed or reached the home of a specific supporter who had gathered a crowd, campaign workers, who wore T-shirts and baseball caps with Aysata's campaign photo, jumped out of cars and off the truck to pass out fliers and chat with onlookers. They played the song "Jàmmi Senegaal" (Peaceful Senegal) by Coumba Gawlo Seck, a famous singer from a griot family; it was like a wave of electricity that made people in the streets dance, wave, and run out of their homes to see who was passing by. Coumba sang, "Senegaal, sama réew mi, dëkku teraanga bi, teraanga Senegaal, teraanga Senegaal! [Senegal my country, land of Teraanga! Teraanga Senegal!]" Ayda Mbóoj also had a recording of Coumba Gawlo singing about her as an example of a woman who could wear the pants in the family; the song was played when she entered the stage for a rally. At specific opportune moments, Aysata emerged from the sunroof of her SUV to wave at supporters and say a few words through a megaphone.

Candidates reached their audiences through campaigning across the country or throughout the district they hoped to represent. From Dakar, Aysata's group went down south to the Casamance River and back up through the middle of the country, to her hometown of Podor. Many politicians espoused the tactic of these caravanes, or what Foucher (2007) calls marchés bleus, a method of campaigning that allows for parties to get maximum exposure for less money. During stops at strategic homes where supporters had family, the politicians would "draw upon family celebrations where they pose as a benevolent relative" (116).

Gendered Messaging

Women's campaigns mirrored the tactics of most men's campaigns but also had messaging that was particularly gendered. This was a theme most of their campaigns shared in an effort to address the classic critiques of women as not being strong or capable enough but also to demonstrate their feminine sides. Much of the language used for party slogans or descriptions of the women leaders featured sayings such as Aysata's theme, "Une femme forte pour le Senegal [A strong woman for Senegal]," or a chant heard at Ayda Mbóoj's rallies: "Jigéen ju mëna baax [A woman who can do/be good.]" Other chants made a distinction about jigéen ju mën góor (a woman who could do as a man could).

Posters, designed in Wolof and French, with the photo of the party or coalition leader, were plastered throughout cities, on billboards, and molded around cars and light posts. Aysata's slogan, "a strong woman for Senegal," was on posters, hats, T-shirts, and even cell phone covers. Despite the visual presence of campaign materials, the majority of the messaging was done via music, documentary-style recordings, and megaphones repeating bite-size chants in order to reach a wide and mobile audience. Aysata played not only Coumba Gawlo's song about Senegal but also a rap song specifically written for her campaign, with the apt title of "Osez!" While creeping slowly throughout parts of Dakar's more affluent neighborhoods, a professionally recorded documentary in French played from the speakers. A man's silky voice began, "Aysata Tall Sall, an iron lady. A woman of action and conviction, attached to her home and her country, and a dedicated Muslim." With the sound of an old film roll running in the background, the man's voice said Aysata was a woman of courage, power, and perseverance. As he narrated her political biography, Aysata added that "being a woman, or an African woman, it's not that. If you have political ambitions that is the most important thing."

The documentary is interrupted by the artist Viviane and her popular song "Ku ma neexul [To those who don't like me]." Lyrics like "to those who don't like me, continue on your way; to those who don't like me, follow a different path" offered an interesting combination with the documentary and the general message of the campaign. The song reflects the flexibility of identity required of women to demonstrate strength, faith, and a kind of irreverence in the face of other's critiques: at the same time that Aysata wished to rise above gender, she chose to run a campaign that highlighted her qualities as a brave woman, as if to suggest to men that she shared the same qualities necessary for governing while serving as a role model to women who might be afraid to speak up.

When I asked Aysata to assess the outcome of the campaign and election, where she was the only person from her coalition to win a seat in parliament, she struck a positive note. "Oh, Emily, the campaign was so interesting. I learned a lot. I was so tired, and I ate so poorly because we were always on the go. I'm fasting right now because I am thankful to God and because I need to cleanse my body from all the cookies and soda I had," she said with a little giggle. "You have to be pretty strong to get through a campaign like that. Not everyone can. Not all men can." The campaign was indeed grueling. We were up early getting everything packed and ready for the day, and then the caravane lasted most of the day, requiring a great deal of energy and enthusiasm that went into the early hours of the next day. We jumped in and out of slow-moving cars, often jogging beside them or gathering alongside Aysata's car, where she sat atop the roof waving to onlookers. It continued this way for three weeks.

Certainly, one of the concerns people had about women in politics was the time commitment and the stamina it took to not only campaign but also govern. Governing in this sense meant that politicians spent long days traveling to their regions from Dakar to attend a funeral or other ceremony of a supporter or meet with their local collaborators. Most representatives are based in Dakar in order to work at their offices in parliament or attend official sessions but spend significant time on the road. Someone such as Aysata, who was a representative and the mayor of Podor, a good eight or more hours' drive from Dakar, spent a great deal of time traveling between the two. However, she did not seem to feel that it was too tiring, and even if it was, her resolve to show strength of character and physical ability was greater, possibly as a result of such concern and criticism. Due to her children's education in Dakar, Aysata was often absent from home. "I prepared my children early on that I would be gone a lot. They understood that was the sacrifice I was making," she said. In many ways the absence from home was due to this commitment to campaign members or supporters in the districts. Part of the intensity of their schedule was the expectations from supporters to have a piece of her time. And although many women dedicating their time to Aysata's campaign did so initially for their belief in the person and what they stood for, there remained an expectation of some kind of reciprocity. Knowing how to manage these relationships was also the courage Aysata mentioned. Next, I consider the case of Mareem Sow Ndoye.

Mareem Sow Ndoye

One tactic employed by most parties was to include supporters from specific regions on the party list. This would ensure they campaigned with their family and community members in places the party leader couldn't reach. This was the case with Mareem Sow, also Pulaar, whom I accompanied to her family home, Gede Chantier (Gede Fields), in the department of Podor in northern Senegal. Mareem managed her own business in hospitality services as well as working for the administration in the Ministry of the Interior, managing everything that had to do with paperwork for the ministry. She had also been named an adviser for the municipality of Point E, which oversaw a cluster of Dakar neighborhoods where she lived. In such unpaid positions, Mareem and others served as the eyes and ears for the mayor, advising on issues needing to be addressed or helping spread the word about initiatives from the mayor's office. This had been her first foray into politics, and she liked being helpful. In

Mareem Sow during the 2017 campaign, Dakar, Senegal. *Photo by author.*

fact, if you took one look at Mareem, you could tell she was motivated. A short woman with a spring in her step, Mareem flawlessly anticipated the needs of others, never sitting long enough to be idle.

Her name was on Aysata's list of candidates, but since the coalition was so new and Mareem was nowhere near close to the top, it was unlikely she would be elected. "Pour être honnête, neuvième position ça m'a surpris, mais agréablement. Dama foogoon ne dinaa gëna nekk ci suuf. J'ai été honoré franchement [Honestly, ninth position, I was surprised, in a good way. I was expecting to be way further down the list, so I was honored, really]," Mareem said. She was always positive like that. She decided to help Aysata because friends of hers were supporters and suggested Mareem to Aysata. Although Mareem was given money from the party for campaigning, she put a lot of her own money and effort into posters, travel, and the customary *saricé*, the kind of teraanga given following a trip or visiting someone out of town. Because she was also campaigning among aunts and uncles she had not visited in quite some time, it was necessary for her to reciprocate their hospitality and provide financial aid to her family who had little access to the abundance of choice in the city.

Mareem's family home was a small group of villages in the northern Haal-Pulaar region of the Fuutaa.

Upon our arrival to the village, Mareem had to call to ask for directions, and she giggled, finding it funny that she was a bit lost. It had been so long since she had visited. When we arrived, there was a welcoming party of young and old who greeted us warmly. Mareem acted as a translator for me and her Wolof-speaking husband. Sitting under a large mango tree for shade, Mareem explained that she was campaigning for herself and Aysata Tall Sall, also Haal-Pulaar, in the upcoming elections. She was asking for their votes. After a while, we walked with her uncle and other family members around to various houses, hung posters at the health clinic, and visited the Senegal River that divides Senegal and Mauritania to the north. I was struck by the contrast of the bright pink and white posters against the earth-toned buildings. We finished our visit at the *penc mi*, the thatch-covered meeting space where men of the village gathered to make decisions, rest, socialize, and receive guests. Mareem's uncle mostly spoke for her, reminding others who she was and giving some genealogical background on her parents and other elders who had lived in the village. This context was crucial: they might vote for her depending on the reputations of her family members over the generations, and it offered their community national recognition if one of their own were to be in parliament. As the elders listened, they nodded their heads in agreement and shared a prayer to bless Mareem's cause.

Mareem's lineage also became relevant when her uncle suggested she should run for mayor of Gede Village, the governing district of several villages, also known as Medina Feressbe. In fact his language was much stronger than telling her to run in an election; rather, he told her to claim a position of power that was already hers to take. "Danga wara ñëw fexe nga jël mairie bi, parce que sa pàppa, seen lignée, yeena wara jël mairie bi [You should come back and take the mayor's position because your father was from here and your lineage means you should govern]," Mareem said, citing her uncle. She clarified that "aux temps, quand il y avait des rois, sama pàppa ci lignée royale la bokkoon. Mais comme leegi roi amul, et tout est lié à la politique, et comme man maa nekk kiy def politig ci sama famille moo tax ñu wax ne maa wara dem jëli [mairie bi] [In the past, when there were kings, my father belonged to the royal lineage. But now since everything is about politics, and I'm the one in the family doing politics, I should go and assume the responsibilities (of mayor)]." I asked whether there were issues with her being a woman in terms of being able to campaign there and potentially be mayor. "There is no problem," she replied. "There are some prejudices. But whatever women do, men do. There was a time when no one would have thought that women would be doing politics, but now the time has come. People have evolved and matured. Look at my village, Gede Village in the department of Podor, where the mayor is a woman—my leader, Aysata Tall Sall. And she has been mayor for two terms."[4] Mareem's comments about her family's royal lineage and the evolution of access to authority in society, including the increased inclusion of women, reveal further questions about the role of gender and succession in politics.

During the campaign and election day, Mareem seemed happy to hustle about trying to get as many people to vote for Aysata's party as possible. Her pitch was strategic. She aligned herself with Aysata for those who had previously been or remained in the Socialist Party or who were fans of Aysata. Among women, she framed Aysata as a champion for women's causes. And for her family members or friends, she argued their support was an acknowledgment of their relationship with her. However, when I spoke with Mareem several months after the 2017 election, she had a different tone. "I didn't even receive a phone call of thanks after she won," she said indignantly. "I won't campaign for her again. I was just doing it because she put trust in me." She mentioned that it had turned her off to all politics, even the potential of becoming mayor of her family's municipality. "I don't think I'm cut out for politics," she said. When I spoke with her years later, following Aysata's appointment as Macky Sall's minister of foreign affairs, she was even more discouraged. She mentioned an event she had attended where Aysata was present. "She didn't even say hello. I'm not sure our relationship has much of a future." She was disappointed that Aysata hadn't acknowledged the hard work she had put into the campaign back in 2017. She felt it was a sign that Aysata didn't understand the importance of maintaining her relationships in the *longue durée* of politics. Just as the woman had said when they were launching her campaign, if Aysata went elsewhere or abandoned her party members she would not follow her. Therefore, although some of the indignation expressed about Aysata's transhumance had to do with what some saw as her turning her back on the cause for women's equality, it was more about her failure to maintain her ties with her supporters and demonstrate teraanga.

Mareem's experience raises an important issue: no matter what form of politics is involved, a functioning and sustainable political operation needs personal feedback in order to ensure continual support. In other words, *kollore* (loyalty) in the form of Aysata recognizing Mareem's sacrifices would have meant a great deal. Maintaining a campaign involves personal demonstrations of teraanga in the forms of loyalty and generosity. In other respects, this is an impossible endeavor. On more than one occasion, I overheard parliamentarians receiving phone calls from supporters asking for help with family issues, monthly allowances, or other financial emergencies. The politicians vocally expressed frustration at the pressures put on them to constantly help others and how to manage it.

Recognizing and Rewarding the Hustle

Mareem Sow's experience during and following the 2017 election was one of many I encountered among the women who were part of elite women's campaigns. Another is that of Ndey Mbóoj, niece of Ayda Mbóoj. When I first met Ndey, she was unmarried and Ayda supported her and some of her informal commercial activities. We kept in touch over the years while I was not in Senegal, and a great deal of my time during research visits was spent with her on Ayda's campaigns and on trips we took to Bambey. Ndey worked tirelessly to help Ayda campaign, visiting people and places Ayda did not have time for or doing menial tasks such as picking up official documents or running other errands. Ndey was a spokeswoman for Ayda and in return received funds for her herself and shared development projects, as she was the leader of several women's associations. Ndey's affiliation with Ayda allowed support for her associations as well as keeping herself afloat.

Ndey was an educated divorced woman who was good at many things but had not managed to turn any of them into something concrete. She had traveled extensively and received a master's degree in Morocco. Tall, skinny, and gangly, Ndey was unconventional. She was always hustling for one thing or another, changing residences or jobs in the city. She was an expert at *lijjanti* (the art of hustling), always full of ideas about how to create moneymaking activities for herself and others and working her contacts for personal debts as well as to help them resolve issues in return. She was either producing a pamphlet for Ayda's campaign or flipping through magazines in Chinese to buy food processing equipment for her associations to be able to grind millet or peanuts to sell for baking. She had impressive and extensive networks within the Murīd community that helped women with development projects and religious associations. She was even a member of the 12ème gaynde (12th Lion) troop, the traveling fan club of the Senegalese national soccer team, the Lions of Teraanga.

During Ayda's campaigns throughout the years, Ndey was one of her biggest cheerleaders, utilizing her own networks of women to promote Ayda while using the occasional money she received from Ayda to invest in the projects of these associations. As a divorcée she was the black sheep of the family, but her travel-loving nature was ideal for helping Ayda with campaigning or last-minute needs. Ndey's big break came when Ayda chose her for her party list, Ànd, Saxal Liggéey. As the president of the coalition, Ayda oversaw choosing running mates. Ndey was quite far down the list but was honored to be given such a formal recognition of her support, just as Mareem Sow Ndoye had been. Their dependence was reciprocal yet vertical. Ndey depended on Ayda for financial support, and Ayda depended on Ndey for everything else. Although Ndey and Ayda are from the same family and considered to be of royal blood, Ndey is very much subordinate to Ayda in terms of class, age, and marital status. In fact, Ayda's family and close party associates often call her *mère* [mother] as a sign of respect. Ndey's association with Ayda and her campaign also afforded Ndey important social capital; especially since she was without a husband, she leaned on Ayda as a way to cultivate her own kind of teraanga networks. When it came time to campaign for Ayda's coalition and for her own potential seat in parliament, Ndey took it as a sign of her hard work and dedication paying off and was indefatigable in her efforts.

During the beginning of the campaign, I accompanied Ndey to her family home in Sibassor, just outside of Kaolack in central Senegal, so we could campaign among her family and friends. Sibassor was along one of the main highways and bustled with economic activity. Ndey and I began in the neighborhoods, visiting friends and family that Ndey knew well, bearing party flyers that listed the candidates in rank order, giving their full names and professions. Upon receiving the flyer, a woman who was familiar with Ndey said, "Waaw kay, Yal na la Yàlla dimbale, Ndey Mbóoj, yaa ko mérité! [Yea! May God help you, Ndey Mbóoj, you deserve it!]" Ndey agreed: "Oui, sama cër la, ginnaaw at yu baree bare di jàppale Ayda. Xam ngeen ni maa sonne ngir moom, di ko lijantil nit di jàppale ci campagne bi [Yes, respect after all these years of hard work for Ayda. You know how much I have hustled for her, bringing her new supporters and helping to run her campaign]." She used the word *cër* to express what she was owed, a word that is often associated with the reciprocal side of teraanga, denoting a specific social debt, or a kind of respect. Ndey used it here to express a sense of honor or acknowledgment from Ayda for this work. As we continued the campaign, I would also find out that for Ndey, *cër* also meant a vindication of sorts.

I heard *cër* again when we ran into one of Ndey's brothers on our walk around the neighborhood. He was visibly angry. In so many words, he accused her of not respecting him because she had missed the naming ceremony of his new baby, despite naming Ndey as the première njékke, an honor that came with certain responsibilities such as providing gifts of clothing and diapers. "Kenn mënula wax ne joxewuma teraanga [No one can accuse me of not giving teraanga]," Ndey said with an indignant tone of offense. On our ride out to her family's home, Ndey expressed her frustration: "Comme amuma jëkkër te amuma doom, dama mëna joxe *teraanga* rekk te duñu ma ko mësa delloo. War na am yeneen options, waaye ci xew yi ngay mëna dabe li nga mayeewoon [Because I am not married and have no children, I can really only give teraanga and not receive it. There should be other ways, but unfortunately ceremonies are the best way to recover from your investments]."

These investments are meant to be paid back with interest at the occasion of Ndey's ceremony. However, without a marriage or naming ceremony of her own, she would be unable to recuperate those sums. It was about money but also about prestige. As we have seen throughout the book, married women accumulate social as well as financial capital in their marriages by way of participating in ceremonies as well as hosting them, or the instances of teraanga given to a woman's family-in-law. Being on the campaign trail would be one way for her to recover some of her investments, as friends and family would contribute.

Ndey had no real chance to win a seat in parliament because she was too far down the list and Ayda's party was new and not well known. But that didn't stop Ndey from dreaming. She framed her political opportunities as social ones that would allow her the social and material capital to reinvest in her associations. She was particularly fixated on the benefit of a car and a driver given to representatives for their own transportation. A car, she felt, would afford her the ability to give people rides and a way to facilitate the work of those within her development groups. She spoke of it as form of teraanga, as many people did when thanking friends or family who went out of their way to lighten their burden of taking public transportation or paying a heavy fee for a taxi. Having a vehicle and driver would also allow her to visit family in Sibassor more often, not to mention being a physical manifestation of her change in status. It would demonstrate that her investments of teraanga with Ayda had paid off.

These framings of access to political authority are similar to those of Mously Diakhaté, who argued that her investments in the money-generating activities of her women's groups were ultimately more sustainable and humane than the bank loans that had no mercy for their clients. These women see themselves as alternatives to immoral banks, impersonal development funds, and male politicians who don't have women's interests in mind. Women see politics not only as an opportunity to make legislative change but as a way to turn their political capital toward supporting women's social activities, a sort of female-led informal welfare program. James Ferguson (2015) argues that social welfare programs on the continent and globally are increasingly becoming the modalities in which governments distribute wealth to their citizens. As he also points out, with the gendered stereotypes of men as breadwinners in a world where wage labor is no longer a sustainable expectation, women have used governmental and nongovernmental handouts to create political mobility while for men receiving aid is often seen as less socially acceptable. It is the coordinated and methodized mode of teraanga that women in politics have been particularly adept at, in what Ferguson would classify as "new modalities of distribution [that] are associated with both new kinds of political claim-making and new possibilities for political mobilization" (14).

Differently from Ferguson's argument of specific government welfare programs, women politicians have taken it upon themselves to create a welfare system that is articulated through their person. This is, of course, not without its obvious issues; however, in this way, women see themselves as mediators between their supporters and state resources. Furthermore, women have been especially deliberate in making the connections between development and politics or, in thinking about Ferguson's concept of the politics of distribution, making their politics about who decides what is distributed and to whom. A central impetus of the parité movement was about not only women's representation in state politics but also the ability to have a say in how state funds are being handled—especially in the context of development programs that have overwhelmingly implicated women. Distributive politics are, after all, "specific claims to a share of material goods" (51). As one slogan of the movement said, "To elect is good; to be elected is better." One could also consider a similar notion that being given money is good, but to control where it goes is better. Or, as the parliamentarian Aysata Daouda Dia said, "You can't do development without politics, and you can't do politics without development."

Conclusions

Things didn't exactly pan out for Ndey Mbóoj as she had hoped. She did not win a seat in parliament. In fact, Ayda was the only person who won from her party. Just as Aysata had won only her seat, it was typical for new parties to gain the seat of their popular leader—a main reason for a boom in the number of new parties. However, Ndey did not completely lose out. Because of her association with Ayda, her work on the campaign, and being a member of the Murīd community, Ayda set her up with the son of an influential Murīd family in Tuubaa. They married shortly after the campaign, and she became the second wife in a polygamous household. This allows her to spend time on her projects and associations in Dakar while benefiting from the comfort and prestige of being married. Also because of her work with Ayda's campaign and new status, Ndey earned a position in the Ministry of Agriculture, traveling often to France and the subregion of West Africa. On the side, and due to her travels, Ndey takes part in small entrepreneurial ventures such as buying and selling fabrics, clothing, and beauty products in Burkina Faso or the Ivory Coast.

In the case of Mareem Sow and Aysata Tall Sall, there remain incongruencies about the nature of the patrona-client relationships. Mareem and other women on Aysata's campaign hoped that her focus on female power and solidarity would translate to specific consideration for the women who helped her in her rise to political office. On the other hand, the issue of Aysata Tall Sall's transhumance and Mareem's own disenchantment with Aysata raise several questions about the status and strategies of women in politics in Senegal. Why was the reaction to Aysata's decision so strong and so gendered? Publicly, her supporters blamed her for betraying their message about strong women; privately, people like Mareem accused her of a lack of recognition and solidarity. That she did not embody the strong woman who "knows teraanga" enough. Their deception—and that of the public—leaves open questions about the efficacy of framing a political identity on feminine qualities while seeming to discount the ways in which women have historically gained political authority.

Much like Aminata Touré, Aysata Tall Sall had hopes for women in government that go beyond teraanga, or charity, as she calls it. Hoping that they could move beyond generosity and teraanga as the prerequisites of governance. She was also named justice minister by Macky Sall in March 2024—the position that had begun Aminata's career in Senegalese politics. However, since the new Diomaye Faye administration took office in 2024, she has mostly been absent from public view. Upon an interview on March 8, International Women's Day, Aysata did not hide her ambitions to be president someday, saying, "I can assure you that my ambition to be the first female president of the Republic will never be behind me" (Camara 2024). Both have been successful at reaching the heights of some of the most important state positions in Senegal, and yet the question remains about how popular they are among the general populace and especially their female audience. In the political arena of the Teraanga Republic, what legitimacy do they have if they reject its very foundation?

Within the Wolof cosmology, teraanga is expressed as a set of amply defined performances that govern one's behavior that are symbolic and practiced. There are ñu xam teraanga (those who know teraanga) and ñu xamul teraanga (those who don't know teraanga). To "know teraanga" is to understand that personal actions affect the stability of the collective and can be expressed through the form of gifts, hospitality, verbal praise, and self-sacrifice. As expressed by the griot Jéynaba about the deceased woman in her neighborhood of Medina, "If in life no one thanked you, in death, no one will cry for you"—one's life forms meaning in the processes of working toward a shared future.

What I have attempted to demonstrate throughout this book is that while state structures remain a French Republican model, the reality, especially for women politicians, is that politics is a much more complex performance of social relationships. And in fact, it is a negotiation between the two. Politicians such as Ayda and Mously, although I would ultimately say they have embraced teraanga as political strategy, also take part in the democratic process of voting, deliberating in parliament, and the management of parties or coalitions. They employ the tactics of teraanga—a style of governance that depends on the personalities of its leaders instead of serving as an abstraction of the state—while also representing and advocating for their constituents and their needs within the state structure.

Much of the successes of the parité movement and women's style of politics has been their ability to translate the practices of teraanga and the networks they build and sustain into the public realm of state politics. Part of this is directly related to the ways that teraanga has become increasingly gendered. Employing teraanga as public political strategy, not unlike that of daily social governance, allows women to utilize to their advantage the complex networks that have themselves become reflective of the materialization of values such as solidarity. As the journalist Fanta Diallo mentioned in chapter 5, men in general do not have these outlets, and the kind of teraanga that is demonstrated by them is on a much smaller, less organized level than that of women, and more often expressed through women for their benefit. The example of Ayda Mbóoj seeing her own gender in politics as something flexible and malleable in certain situations, which she believes allows her to go beyond the confines of being a woman, especially when power is involved, is illustrative. The transformations of associations into machines of development programs were born partly out of economic necessity when men of the household no longer had access to traditionally male-dominant government or wage-labor jobs but has also served as a way for women to organize, develop leadership skills, and drive new patron-client networks.

Women like Ayda and Mously have been successful in utilizing teraanga as the central aspect of their governance. They are recognized by the public, whether supporters or political rivals, as representing an ideal Senegalese woman who is generous, pious, classy, and relatable. They conduct themselves via the guidelines of teraanga and have remained popular because of it. In the case of Aminata, although she has been extremely successful, having been prime minister, minister of justice, and now a presidential candidate and leader of her own party, she has yet to be elected by her compatriots. She is seen as representing an image of Western sociality that shuns the practices of teraanga both in and outside politics. To many, Aminata is unrelatable and too far outside the register of the idealized Senegalese feminine subject. As Mareem Sow Ndoye demonstrates, Aysata has in some ways failed to prioritize the relationships that made her feminized movement successful in the first place. The disappointment felt by her supporters symbolizes the hope they had for parité and also the potential dangers of making it about a specific gendered subject.

For women like Ndey and Codou, the benefits of being embedded in the political activities of Ayda and Mously are numerous. I have detailed a few ways in which Ndey's association with Ayda has allowed her new social standing among her family and several job opportunities. For Codou, her association with Mously launched her local political career—she ran for mayor of her commune in Dakar. She could also count on Mously's resources and support for their association. Moreover, even failed candidacies for political office or associational links with women politicians mean having access to resources and social capital that many women feel is not the case with men politicians. Women have expressed a solidarity with women politicians because they assume they would have empathy for a shared experience, which is potentially why the reaction to Aysata's choice to go with Macky Sall hit many supporters hard. After all, the parité movement was based on a hope for a different kind of politics with women at the helm.

The implications that these examples have for our appreciation of contemporary African politics are broad reaching. On one hand, the testimonies presented demonstrate women's keen understanding of various backgrounds, not only of the historical implications of their realities but also of the creative strategies they employ to navigate them. Their sophisticated debates about all types of governance—self-governance, governance among family and friends, and state governance—are about what kind of *pays de la teraanga* they wish for themselves and others. On the other hand, the women in this book make us question the separation of different types and spaces of authority and what those authorities produce. Through their political strategies of teraanga they have bridged several gaps between the private and the public as well as our understanding of how different forms of authority and legitimacy—patrimonial and bureaucratic-legalistic—coexist. The Teraanga Republic is where women negotiate and produce authority.

Epilogue

Is the Future Female?

In 2023, the Senegalese political landscape experienced a series of tumultuous moments having to do with the trial of opposition leader Ousmane Sonko, who was accused of rape and inciting youth violence. The trial was delayed several times and was followed by clashes between the state police and Sonko supporters, displaying an unprecedented level of state violence rarely seen in Senegal. As I walked the streets of Dakar in March 2023, I was shocked to see armored police trucks and smell the lingering effects of burnt tires and tear gas. Sonko was accused of raping and threatening a young woman, Adji Sarr, who worked in the now infamous massage parlor Sweet Beauty, which Sonko frequented. Sonko's supporters said it was a plot by Macky Sall to eliminate his strongest political rival. On June 1, 2023, Sonko was cleared of his rape charge but sentenced to two years in prison for "corrupting the youth." With his political future in question, he chose a close party member, Bassirou Diomaye Faye—also in jail for charges of incitement to insurrection—as his replacement for the party's presidential candidate.

In the first days of February 2024, just weeks before the presidential election of February 25, president Macky Sall shocked everyone by submitting a decree to parliament to postpone the election. There had been a fear of some kind of maneuver on his part to extend his term despite his commitment to step down. The parliament ratified the decree, and the new date was set for December of the same year. Massive protests broke out, and international media attention cranked up the heat. Despite significant interruptions of the internet, social media got the word out. Hashtags such as #doyna (that's enough) and #GASSI (it's over) filled social media posts denouncing Macky Sall and calling his actions a constitutional coup d'état. Before Sall could concretely act, the constitutional court deemed his decree unconstitutional. Upon further deliberation, a new date was set for the end of March 2024.

During these conflictive months, two processes happened that are relevant to the topics in this book. The first is the problematic reactions to Adji Sarr's accusations against Ousmane Sonko. The second is the overwhelming silence about the number of women running for president and their contributions to the race. Since going public, Adji Sarr has had to live under police protection and is living in basic seclusion. A *Le Monde* article called her "the most hated woman in Senegal" (Kane and Ollivier 2022) as many people accused her of ruining Sonko's chances to take down Macky. In some extreme cases, people have even blamed her for the deaths of protesters. On social media, users launched insults and death threats and implied that she would be the downfall of Senegalese democracy.

In an article published in *Le Monde Afrique* in 2022 by a feminist collective, scholars, entrepreneurs, students, lawyers, and journalists warned of a backsliding of the parité law. They argued that there had been a tendency to "discredit the parité law, making public opinion believe that it is a danger to democracy" (Sow et al. 2022). And of course, when one speaks of parité, one speaks of women, despite the law being about political equality between the sexes.

Following the passing of the parité law in 2012, there was much hope for women's future in politics. Yet in the 2019 presidential election, the candidacies of Aysata Tall Sall, Ayda Mbóoj, and lesser known Nafisatu Wade were rejected. In the 2024 presidential election Ayda and Aminata were again disqualified for failure to provide sufficient or legible signatures to validate their candidacy. "A joke," Aminata told me, reacting to the decision. Although Ayda and Aminata have mostly been on opposite sides of the political spectrum, they both decided to back Ousmane Sonko and Bassirou Diomaye Faye for president. However, in the midst of all the conflict surrounding the election, the main attention to women has been the vileness toward Adji Sarr. There has been little discussion about the record number of women running or their political ambitions.

As the feminist collective stated, "We observe an unrelenting desire to exclude women from decision making spaces, especially in politics. . . . Women's competence is systematically questioned, media spaces are dominated by men . . . and the latter are asked to give their opinions on subjects they are not competent to speak on." They further cited instances during every election cycle in which feminist groups must remain vigilant for party lists that refuse to respect parité. Many of the women elected in 2012 or after as beneficiaries of parité were not reelected. In the case of Mously Diakhaté, she was excluded from a party's list despite years of dedication to Macky Sall. Since the 2022 legislative elections, the percentage of women in parliament hovers around 45 percent. The collective also notes that "the machismo is the very fabric of men politicians who have no problem exploiting women's mobilizing abilities . . . but once elected, they show a contemptuous magnanimity, confining women to supporting roles with no real decision-making power." The initial successes of parité seemed to evaporate and lead to some women even being accused of political treachery, corruption, and general unprofessionalism. In an opinion piece for the blog *Africa is a Country*, Marame Gueye (2024) remarks that the hopefulness of Senegalese feminists for the Faye administration was short-lived with the announcement of the new government. Of the thirty secretarial positions, only four were women. Women's rights activists wondered if this "means a backward movement that excises women from leadership positions and confines them to the home and family," and Gueye asks, "Whose democracy is it anyway?" Therefore, the question remains as to whether we can say that the mission of the parité movement has been successful or stopped short of its goals. Has women's greater presence in parliament and other positions of decision-making had an impact on women's condition in society? Although it would be ideal to be able to answer these questions definitively, the objective of this book has not been to make such an evaluation. Instead, my aim has been to understand how women navigate the different spaces of politics that are often closed off to them and what kinds of opportunities these forms of authority allow them.

The objection to women in public space and particularly in politics lies in a deep sense that women's bodies and contributions to society should be confined to the private. And, as Diaw (2009) notes, women's crossing over into the public sphere brings disorder to it. It is no wonder, then, that Adji Sarr is seen as polluting the institutions that are said to make Senegalese democracy real or that the parité law and the women elected in part because of it are seen as a threat to democracy.

GLOSSARY

aawo	first wife in a polygamous union
àdduna	world
àjjana	paradise
ànd	togetherness, solidarity, consensus
añu njékke	a part of a cooked animal gifted to a sister-in-law during ceremonies
àttaaya	concentrated green tea served among friends and guests; the tea is brewed for a long time and served in small clear shot glasses
baadoolo	a peasant with low social status
bàjjen	paternal aunt
baay	father
Big manism	a political science term referring to male political leaders who abuse their power and display corrupt and totalitarian tendencies
Big womanism	female political leader who display similar tendencies to big manism
brak	king from the Wolof Waalo kingdom
buur	king
ceebu jën	rice and fish dish
cër	honor
daara	an Islamic school
daayira	an Arabic circle, a religious association
degoo	to come to an agreement
demokaraasi	Wolof spelling and conception of democracy
dhukura	Arabic for maleness, biologically

doomu ndey	brother or sister from the same mother; a friendly term for someone considered a close friend
feem	feminine tricks
fóot	gifts of items for a newly married woman to use in her home
gaal gi	pirogue, fishing boat
gaaruwaale	an indirect verbal attack; praise shrouded as criticism
gàcce	shame
gan	guest, visitor
gaspillage	wastefulness
géer	a noble within the Wolof social structure
géew	gift-giving circle
géwëlu juddu	a family's griot
góorgóorlu	doing one's best, manning up, make do
goro	in-law
griot (*géwël* in Wolof)	an important figure in many West African societies
hémicycle	the circle within parliament where voting takes place
jaami baadoolo	slave of peasants
jaami buur	slave of the king
jàppale	to help one another; mutual aid
jeeg	woman
jëf ju rafet	righteous deeds, good actions
jëkkër	husband
jii	agricultural cultivation; symbolic planting of a seed
jiite	to govern, to lead
jiitle	to walk one after another
jigéen ju baax	a good woman. A term often used in daily speech to signify a virtuous woman who respects her role as wife and mother and whose work is for the good of her family
jigéen ju mën góor	a term associated with Aline Sitoe Diatta, a Joola woman known for powers to conjure rain. Diatta led a religious revival that the French thought to be anticolonial. Her memory has been converted into a symbol of power despite her gender, and therefore women who display authority are compared to her image.
jom	self-dignified
jongama	woman of large stature
jonge	cognate for woman; feminine ways
joxalante	round of gift giving during family ceremonies
juboo	to come together, to resolve disagreements
karam	Arabic term for hospitality and to be generous and giving

kër	house
kersa	modesty
leket (calebasse in French)	a hollowed-out gourd with multiple uses: holding grains, storage, or for collecting a baby's shaved hair during its baptism. A leket is also the name of women's rotating savings groups as this is where the money is collected during their meetings.
lekku ndey	part of a cooked animal given to a mother during a ceremony
liggéey	work
liggéeyu ndey	mother's work
lijjanti	a persistent hustle and solicitation for solutions to economic and social problems
lingéer	a queen from the Wolof kingdom of Waalo
lingua franca	a common language spoken despite speakers' native language
Màggal	annual pilgrimage to Tuubaa to commemorate of Amadu Bamba's exile to Gabon
marchés bleus/ blue marches	a campaigning technique consisting of a caravan of cars and trucks that parade through cities and the countryside
maslaa	dialogue, diplomacy
may bu njëkk	a promissory gift a man gives to a woman he intends to marry
mbokk	a relative; a person who is considered part of an extended family; a member of a shared community
mbootaay	a money-pooling association
meen	maternal line
mën	to be able to, capable, powerful
méngale	to confuse between two things
mokk pooj	feminine wiles; knowing how to instrumentalize sexuality to seduce others
muñ	to be patient
musóor	stylized headscarf
mutuelles	a credit association
nàtt (tontine in French)	a rotating savings and credit association
Ndakkaru (Dakar)	the capital of Senegal and also a region along the Cap-Vert coast of the Atlantic Ocean
ndawtal	gifts of cloth; money given during naming ceremonies
ndey/yaay	mother
ndeyale	to honor a woman as the godmother of a child
ñeeño	a casted person within the Wolof social structure

ngente	naming ceremony for a newborn baby
ngor	honor, honesty
nguur gi	the state, governing body
njékke	sister-in-law or a woman considered to be a sisterlike person
noppil	shut up!
parité	the French word for equality of status between women and men. Parité, as it is known in France and Senegal, is the equal number of women and men in elected office
parrainage	demonstrated political support
patrona	a Spanish word meaning a female employer or boss
patron-client networks/ clientelism	a system of relationships where a leader or stakeholder and their followers are linked through exchange of favors and support
ràbb	to weave
rujula	Arabic for manliness
sañse	to dress up, to dress fancy for a special occasion
sama jigéen	my woman; a term used by male politicians to refer to women helpers of their campaign
sax	growing in terms of agriculture; symbolically, to grow a political base
sénégalaisement	to do something according to a Senegalese style or cultural code; to get by
sëriñ	marabout; a Muslim religious leader
séy	to marry; to tie a knot
soxna	a married woman
sukerukoor	sweeting of the fast; gifts of sugar, coffee, powdered milk, dates, and other items used during the holy month of Ramadan when breaking the fast
sutura	discretion
taalibé	disciple, follower
takk	to marry; to tie a knot
tamxarit	Islamic holiday of ashura commemorating the tenth day of the first month of the Islamic calendar. It marks when Moses parted the Red Sea and the salvation of the Israelites.
taasu	a laudatory and self-referential praise-poetry spoken at family ceremonies
tëgg	ironmakers within the Wolof caste social structure
ter	the moment of contact when a boat comes to shore
teraanga	hospitality, generosity, reciprocity; the generous and civic-minded qualities and actions of individuals

tête de liste	party leader at the top of legislative electoral party lists
transhumance	animal "grazing"; could be thought of in terms of the saying "the grass is always greener on the other side." In politics, it is the practice of switching parties to gain political terrain.
Tuubaa	a town in central Senegal, in the Diourbel region. It is the second most populous city in Senegal after the capital, Dakar. It is also the holy city of the Murīd community.
tuubaab	foreigner, particularly a white-skinned foreigner
uude	leathermakers within the Wolof caste social structure
wallu bàjjen	part of a cooked animal given to a paternal aunt
warugar	dowry; moral obligation
xëcco	fight over something; pull something toward oneself
yére wolof	Wolof-style clothing
yoon	path, law, rule
yoonu Murīd	the Sufi order called the Murīd

NOTES

Preface

1. The standardized spelling is Jaxate, however, because she is a well-known figure, I have chosen to use the common spelling of Diakhaté.

Introduction

1. "Thanks be to God" in Arabic.

2. May jëm ci sama andaando di gërëm waa coalition yeen waa Askan wi . . . war ngeen xam par la force aujourd'hui que nous sommes partis de la même famille. Que nous partageons les mêmes valeurs, te valeurs yoo xamantane ñoom lañu am, dañu leen wara am au plan social, sur le plan politique valeurs yooyu moom ngeen di défendre fi. Buur yooyu ñu ma jox message, ñu ne jigéen yi mën nanu ko segal (protect), mën nanu ko sutural (wax ju rafet) ci biir états de service di fa taxawaayal mbokkam.

3. Ndey Mbóoj, danga ma teral waaye teraanga dafa ma cee tiit, ndax dafa mel ni danga ma jox message, dafa mel ni danga bëgg ñi ma andal ci politig danga bëgga mu sax.

4. The Mauritanian band and the presence of a shotgun that Ayda possesses following the ceremony are representations that honor the special relationship between King Trarza of current Mauritania and the Waalo kingdom given his marriage to the most important lingéer, Ndaté Yàlla Mbóoj. Their marriage across the Senegal River is said to have prevented a war between the two kingdoms.

5. The distinction between the spellings *teraanga* and *teranga* (sometimes *teránga*) is mostly a stylistic choice. Despite Wolof being codified since the 1970s,

most people write it in the French orthography, given Wolof is not taught in formal schools. I have chosen to follow my colleagues by using a double *a* to represent the elongated sound that is made when speaking.

6. I outline the caste system later in this introduction.

7. For a more complete overview of their political trajectories, consult their biographies in the biography section of this book.

8. https://www.unfpa.org/data/world-population/SN.

9. Newspaper articles refer to Senegal this way, the official message of the Ministry of Tourism and Leisure cites Senegal as the Pays de la Teranga, and their monthly magazine is called *Teranga*.

10. The Wolof name for the monarchy is different according to the various kingdoms. The Waalo king was a *brak*, among the Jolof the king was named *buurba*, *dameel* in Kajoor, and *teeñ* in Bawol (Camara 2008, 95).

11. The word *baadoolo* has transformed greatly in present-day usage. It often is used to signify someone who is useless or of bad blood.

12. Spelled with the French version of Baol elsewhere.

1. One Wedding and a Funeral

1. Mokk Pooj is a Wolof concept that describes a wife who is attentive to her husband's needs, going above and beyond in many ways to please him. The verb *mokk* is used to describe culinary actions of blending as well as to signify a person's mastery of knowledge or actions among others.

2. Here, I am using the orthography as it is presented in the official titles of the shows.

3. The neighborhood of Medina, or "native quarter" (Betts 1971), where Jéynaba lived was one of the original fringe quarters where Black Senegalese were sent by the French colonial administration. As part of segregation from the French and in response to a reoccurrence of the bubonic plague in 1914, Medina served to separate Black Senegalese from the French (Betts 1971). Those from Medina referred to themselves based on their *rue*, or street. Jéynaba lived on rue 6 between the main street, Blaise Diagne, and the seaside. When greeting a fellow Medina resident, the street name sufficed to establish residential affiliation and therefore identity in a specific spatial milieu. The houses often were separated by a shared wall, and so the neighborhood was characterized by close quarters.

4. See https://ich.unesco.org/en/RL/ceebu-jen-a-culinary-art-of-senegal -01748.

5. I use the spelling *Jongué* when referring to the commercial product and *jongé* when speaking about the term in general following the orthographic guidelines laid out at the beginning of the book.

6. "Yaa baax" literally means "you are good" but can be translated differently given the context. Here, it is praise for a woman's action of giving or looking nice. In this way, the concept of doing good things is a process that makes someone good.

7. The suffix -si in Wolof means an action that is directed back to a specific location. For example, "dellosi naa sama kër" means "I came back to my house."

8. Njékke leegi ak njékke bu njëkk du benn. Xam nga bu njëkk ba, maam yi ñoo doon wut njekke yi. Dañu respecterwoon seen njékke. Sunu yaay, sa soeur-u jëkkër dañu koy fóotal, dañu koy toggal, dañu koy neexal parce que danga bëggul mu mer. Parce que su mere ëlëg say doom duñu baax. Loolu lanu wax parce que aada la. Mais leegi, Su ñu amee dañuy may seeni sœur-u jëkkër wàlla seeni ràkku jëkkër parce que dañu bañ ñu dugg ci séy bi famille bi tasaaroo. Soo jóge sa këru yaay, dañuy teg benn basaŋ ñu jox la conseils, sa bàjjen, sa pàppa, sa nijaay mu wax la « su sa jëkkër ji wax: na nga toggal lu neex sa jëkkër, nga fonk sa këru jëk-kër, nga respecter leen. Lu ñu bëgg nga bëgg ko. Sa yaay dina la wax "boo demee sa këru jëkkër dootuloo fi dellusi." Xam nga waxiñ la rekk, sa yaay fu mu nekk dinga dem foofu. Conseil la pour boo deme seen kër, ngeen juboo. Bu njëkk ba mag ñi dañu fonkoon loolu. Mais leegi am na changement. Leegi looy gis mooy xale yi, ku nekk dangay dem beru, nga am sa appartement bopp. Moo tax gis nga leegi divorce ye bare. Parce que dañuy dem beru, te leegi mag ñi nekkuñu foofu pour wax sa jëkkër "danu lay wax indi ko du pour nga maltraiter ko. Leegi am nga jabar nga wañni sa dox" Xam nga conseils lañu. Te boo bëggee gen ñu wax la sa jëkkër nekku fi xar ko. Mais dañu bëgg liberté, lu ñu moom ñu moom ko, moo tax ñu préférer seen appartement bopp.

2. Sénégalaisement and the Politics of Personality

1. Interview with Ndey Sukkey Géy, May 2, 2017, Géejaway, Dakar, Senegal. Un représentant d'Abdoulaye Wade m'a appelé disant que le Président voulait que j'aille à New York pour la conférence annuelle des femmes des Nations Unies, et que je devais représenter officiellement le Sénégal. J'ai été choquée quand ils ont dit que nous serons seulement quatre femmes. Donc, j'ai demandé une audience avec le Président pour lui demander qu'aillent plus de femmes pour pouvoir bien représenter le Sénégal, surtout parce que nous sommes le pays de la Teraanga. Je suis arrivée au palais présidentiel avec un grand groupe de femmes et je lui ai dit directement que si on va aller à New York, on devait le faire à la sénégalaisement ou on ne va pas aller du tout. Il faut qu'on aille avec de la grandeur. Il était d'accord. Quand on est arrivées sur scène tout le monde était content, avec un grand sourire et ils nous ont applaudi. On était toutes belles avec nos vêtements traditionnels de yére Wolof, on avait sañse. Tout le monde nous a écouté. Quand on est retournées à Dakar, le Président nous a invité à aller

le voir. Il était tout content de la façon comme on a representé le Sénégal qu'il a voulu nous teral, et il nous a donné une enveloppe avec de l'argent. L'argent est la manière dont les Sénégalais montrent l'appréciation pour les autres.

2. Although *sénégalaisement* as an adverb does not distinguish between feminine and masculine structures, given the context in which the term is being used to denote femininity—and anthropologists' compulsion to play with words—I am highlighting a gendered form of *sénégalaise*, which is in fact the feminine form.

3. Coming from the Wolof word *jeeg* to mean woman or wife that we saw in chapter 1.

4. Dans ce pays-là, les femmes sont fatiguées. Dieu seul sait que c'est elles qui dépensent autant d'argent, et elle peut être répudiée deux jours après. À travers les problèmes, ses belles-sœurs peuvent faire en sorte que l'homme divorce de son épouse. . . . Moi, c'est ma belle-mère qui m'a rendue la vie difficile. Tu ne peut même pas imaginer. Devant tout le monde, elle m'a crié dessous et j'avais accepté d'aller rejoindre le domicile conjugal chez elle. . . . La norme sociale qui exige qu'on donne des cadeaux à sa belle-sœur, à sa belle-mère, à son mari, à l'ami de son mari, jusqu'à là ça existait mais ce n'était pas de l'argent. L'argent était uniquement pour le transport. Maintenant, on dit le fóot. Le fóot ça éxistait avant mais pas de cette manière parce que la belle-soeur qui arrive, elle est dans l'obligation d'amener du savon de la poudre des serviettes du parfum et voilà. Et une fois elle peut ajouter un peu d'argent. Maintenant qu'est-ce que vous voyez? Les valises, des bijoux en or, on en est arrivé à des moments où la belle-mère elle amène même des meubles. Elle amène de l'or. Où est ce qu'elle a trouvé tout ça? C'est la question fondamentale.

5. Jataayu tey bii la jigéen ñépp ragal, ba lu ñu am, jox seeni goro booleek li gën a metti, di toroxlu ci seen kanam, di leen dawal aka ak a raamal, di jaamu seeni mbokki jëkkër: maam, ndey, baay, mag, ràkk, nijaay, bàjjen, ndey-ju ndaw, doomu ndey, doomu baay, képp ku seen jëkkër xam, ba ciy xaritam. Lu jigéen am ci bés bii, jëfam sax a ko koy may: jabar ju bëgge, juy moy, ju tële gan, njékke du laal boppam, waxumaak di ko gërëm.

6. Un jour, il y avait personne dans la maison. C'était moi qui faisait sa chambre. J'ai mis du cuuraay, et j'ai fermé la porte à clé. "Assis-toi," je lui ai dit. "Depuis quand vous me faîtes du mal? Ça fait plus de dix ans. Vous ne m'avez pas vu mourir; je ne suis pas aveugle; je ne suis pas devenue folle. Vous croyez que vous verrez quelque chose sur moi? Vous avez de la chance, vous avez de la chance vous et votre fils. Je peux la sortir [une lettre] mais je ne le ferai pas parce que je regarde mon mari et je t'adore. Je vais vous dire une chose: je ne quitterai jamais cette maison tant que je suis en vie. Je vous vois aller voir les marabouts, moi tous mes grands-pères sont des marabouts. Moi-même, je peux le faire pour vous. Attend rekk, vous allez voir ce qui va arriver. Je vais te démontrer de quel

bois je souffle." Alors elle a vu et elle a perdu sa tête, "aahh ehhh" quand mon mari est arrivé elle lui a dit, "Ndey Sukkey m'a fait ceci elle m'a dit que tu vas voir." Mon mari a dit "elle a raison. Pourquoi tu lui crées des problèmes?" Le lendemain je suis allée au marché c'était aussi la tabaski. Je lui ai acheté une valise pleine de robes, tous ce qu'elle voulait j'ai acheté la poudre, le truc qu'elle met j'ai tout acheté. Je lui ai acheté les bijoux en or, j'ai tout acheté. Je revenais de mission on m'a payée et je suis allée au marché, alors c'est moi qui a mis la valise sur la tête et je chantais, je chantais et je dansais quand je suis arrivée, sa fille était là-bas qui venait de Thies, alors j'ai pris la valise j'ai dansé, j'ai chanté pour elle ses louanges. J'ai posé la valise, je l'ai embrassée, elle dit "eh eh eh," elle pleure, mon mari pleurait et sa grande soeur qui est sortie de sa chambre lui a dit, "tu as honte aujourd'hui."

7.   Mon amie que tu as rencontrée, Alimatou, sa petite soeur Penda, moom dafa dem seyi këru goroom. Te seen famille dañu am xaalis. Bi mu ñëwee, dañu doon ngente. Trois millions la yoroon. Penda, loolu la terale belle-famille bi. Keneen ki, bi mu ñëwee xam nga ñaata la yore? Sept millions! Ba pare goro bi di ko léebu, di wax ne "amuma goro bu bon mais diiw lay gërëm," ku ko jox sept millions. Alors que amul sax un an kii dafa ko joxoon trois millions, te ne na dafa tuuti.

8.   Les Cérémonies Familiales, véritables entreprises au Sénégal.

9.   Xam nga boo ko xolee ci beneen côté ci yaay ji. Doom bu góor rekk la am. Te sonn na ci moom, nga fayal ko mu jàng te kooku mën na baña am jabar, ba Yàlla def ni takk na jabar. Leegi lu muy defal jabar ji dootu la defal yaw. Parce que kooku moom la nekkal di faj soxlaam, Yaay ji weer wu dee rekk la koy jox xaalis. Loolu rekk lañu am ci seen doom bu góor. Donc, jour u xew rekk la am pour mu rembourser ko, en quelques sortes.

10.   Par exemple nun, sunu càmmiñ, sunu frère yi, danu nekkando ak ñoom di màggando di sonn di dimbalante. Manaam, yaa ngi fenn di toog ak say frère, peut-être "amuma cigarette," ñu laaj la 100 francs. Leelee nga jëndal leen chemise. Leelee "sama gel bi day ñëw defal ko jus." Ngeen nekkando di màggando, donc benn bes boo amee jabar, ça serait bien que jabar ji intégrer ci famille bi, xam nga ñépp nekk benn. Mu bokk ci.

11.   See Article 166 in the Code de la Famille Sénégalais elaborated by the Senegalese government.

12.   Li ma ci fàttaliku mooy mës nañu ko daan tere. Ba léegi, boo amee xew ca jamano ju yàgg yooyu dangay dug sa biir néeg di fa genne xaalis jox sa njékke, doom di jox say goro, dangay tëj sa buntu di nëbbatu, parce que booba bu la police gisee dañu lay jàpp yóbbu la. Booba ak leegi mat na 40 ans. Dangay tëj sa buntu ngir jox sa goro wu doom teeranga, piis, xaalis, ak ndawtal.

13.   Booba ndawtal gi gëna bare moo doon 1000 francs ak legoos six yards, wàlla 12 yards piis. Moom lanu doon boole ak 1000 francs joxe. Wàlla nu boole ko ak 500. Jamano yi nu tollu leegi ci la xaalis bu bare di génn di ko yàq di ko maye.

Moment bii, tey bu nu xewlewoon tey, dangay gis ku ñëw ndawtal ma 500,000, yaa ngiy dégg? Ndawtal ma 300,000 wàlla 200,000. Ndeyale, indi un million ak ay materiels, bazin riche, ganila, ou brodé. Leegi, bu nu ma joxee sama ndawtal ak sama ndeyale, dinaa dem ci géew gi xool sama liste di compter ñaata lañu ma joxoon, ma dajale ak li ma dencoon togg nak di maye. Di jox sama goro yi un million, te ñeneen di leen jox 500,000, ay 300,000 ay 200,000 ay 100,000 ba xaalis bi jeex. Leegi bu ma demee ci yeneen xew, dinaa joxe le double.

14. Li am leegi bokkul ak la amoon. Am na différence yu bare sax. Ndax bu njëkk loo amoon lu mu tuuti-tuuti danu ko doon fonk. Xam nga loolu mooy lan? Rëyal ko ba mu koy jox tuuti Soo joxee 5,000 francs, ki nga koy jox day kontaan. Bu tey, booy joxee 5,000 ki nga koy jox da la koy deloo. Du ko jël. Difference boobu lanu am. Leegi ki nga daan jox 5,000 boo ko joxoon un million, du ko jël, day bañ. Booba, nit ñi muusuñu comme ni ñu muuse leegi. Booba, ku njëkka def teraanga, am na mille chances. Parce que booba nit ñi ci jàmm lañuwoon. Ku amulwoon ni, développement amul itam démocratie amulwoon. Booba, nit ki loo ko jox rekk kontaan na ci. Leegi, démocratie dafa yàq réew mi. Démocratie baaxul. Dafa yàq réew mi. Moo tax lu mu neex nit ñi dugg ci xel. Ku nekk danga naan maa moom sama alal, lu ma neex def ci. Te déedéet demewulwoon noonu. Bu njëkk, lu ma moom moom, dama koy teg ci yoon. Leegi, démocratie moo tax tegatunu dara ci yoon. Ku nekk na wax ne, maa ko liggéey lu ma neex def ci. Difference boobu moo am.

15. Limiter li ngay joxe, denc li ci des. Leegi, danuy xey wuti di ñaan lu nuy jënde ndekki. Xam nga loolu baaxul. Lu njëkk moo gënoon leegi de! Lan lanu doon def bu njëkk ba sunu ko continuerwoon Sénégal passe na fii!

3. From Associations to Parliament

1. At the time of this opinion piece, Kofi Annan was the Secretary-General of the United Nations.

2. I spell it ngenté elsewhere. In the standard Wolof spelling, it should be ngente (naming ceremony).

3. The author's attempt to replicate the sentiment of the newspaper article written in French.

4. Here she is referring to Marie-Angélique Savané, feminist intellectual and wife of major opposition leader Landing Savané.

5. A daayira is a specifically religious association where members gather to study the Qur'an, share ideas, and pool resources for religious events.

6. A police officer.

7. This is a tip of my hat to Oyèrónké Oyěwùmi's *The Invention of Women*.

8. L'AFEPES a installé sa mutuelle d'épargne et de crédit.

9. Quote from Soukeyna Bâ Ndiaye from the same *SudQuotidien* article.

10. La revolution silencieuse des groupements féminins.

11. J'ai eu un travail comme secrétaire de la Chambre de Commerce de Boon mais depuis que Abdou Diouf a distribué notre société, je ne peux plus trouver du travail alors que j'ai cherché partout. C'est depuis 1989 ou 90 que j'ai laissé tomber et j'ai décidé de vendre du poisson séché. Tu vois, amul liggéey, amul xaalis. Le chômage est épuisant et tout le monde vend, et on ne diversifie pas les produits et ils sont tous les mêmes.

12. Je pense que le gaspillage est mauvais, ils pensent que pour qu'un pays se développe il a besoin d'argent, on a besoin d'épargner. Quand c'est une question d'être social et non une cérémonie, je comprends. Moi aussi je peux être sociale. Je veux donner à ma belle-mère un cadeau. Je peux lui acheter une robe et lui donner ça. Ce n'est pas un problème. Ce n'est rien en comparaison à quand j'offre un cadeau dans une cérémonie parce que j'achèterai une robe qui coûte 20,000 CFA, et lui donner 25,000 cash, et je ne m'arrête pas là. Je dois lui donner 10 à 15 plus de robes, de l'argent, boles, musóor, kuruus, et sandales. Seulement à elle. Si elle avait des sœurs, je dois leur donner en plus si mon mari a des soeurs ou tantes, je dois donner. Bien sûr les griots gagnent le plus. Je suis obligée de faire tout cela. Souvent quand j'entends qu'il y aura une cérémonie dans le coin, subitement je ne veux pas aller. Le gouvernement a besoin de nous mettre tous en prison pour qu'on arrête de gaspiller.

13. Gassame, interview on August 5, 2017.

14. Archives d'Outre-Mer, 1 mars 1945, Dakar, lettre de Lamine Gueye addressée au Monsieur le gouverneur Général.

15. Archives d'Outre-Mer, 9 mars 1945, Saint-Louis, lettre de Khalilou Ka au Ministre des Colonies—Affaires Politiques.

16. Archives d'Outre-Mer, 5 mars 1945, Saint-Louis, renseignement du chef du Service de la Législation et des Affaires Civiles.

17. Avant, les femmes étaient confinées au second plan. Elles applaudissaient et accompagnaient les hommes. Avant, elles n'avaient aucune rôle. Elles n'étaient pas élues. Mais, c'était elles qui élisaient les hommes. Avant, elles n'avaient rien à voir avec la politique. Elles restaient à la maison, s'occuper des enfants et de leurs maris. Et puis les gens ont commencé à aller à l'école, et les femmes sortaient pour faire de la politique. Mais, actuellement nous sommes troisième en Afrique en matière de parité et huitième au niveau mondial. Parce que, actuellement on a 64 députées sur les 150. En ce moment que je vous parle, pratiquement chaque femme sénégalaise est dans la politique ou s'intéressent à la politique.

18. Sénégal, boo xoolee amunu problème ci jigéen buy def politig. Parce que, depuis temps- wu Senghor, avant, ba leegi, nit ñi dañu mayoon place jigéen ci politig parce que dañoo yorewoon lepp ci organisation, bu meeting waree am ñooy genee nit ñi, ñooy teg chaise yi. Animation bi jigéen yi ñoo ko yorewoon. Avant indépendance, jigéen yaa ngi politig. Jigéen ci politig poser-wuñu

problème, mais jigéen ji gédd, chaque societé c'est différent. Par exemple, les sociétés qu'on appellé matrimoniales, comme les Lébu, wàlla nga dem Waalo, foofu
ay jigéen ay buur lañuwoon. Ci Lébu yi lañu gëna jox droit jigéen ci wàllu koom-
koom. Bu de itam ci autorité, jigéen di nekk Lingéer comme Ndaté Yàlla. Danga
am jigéen yoo xam ne dañu nekk buur. Donc pouvoir de décision ci Afrique de
manière générale jigéen yi dañu ci bokkoon. Mais ñu dem ba ci biir, ba indépendance bi dugg, modernité bi dugg jigéen yi dañu ñëw taxaw, rôle bu utile lañu def
am taxaway bu rafet bi nu wara taxawee, mais bu desee dem ci sphère de décision
yiy doggal, duñu leen jox place bu important bi ñu leen wara jox. Ñenneen ñi
leena bëgga confiné ci kër gi, bëgg leena gëmloo ni loolu la diine ji wax.

19. Je travaille en tant que consultante, formatrice en genre et leadership,
genre et développement. Je travaille également dans le domaine de l'éducation
parce que je suis diplômée en science de l'éducation de l'Université de Paris 8.
Je suis membre de plusieurs organisations, notamment le Conseil Sénégalais
des Femmes mais également l'institution qu'on appelle le Conseil National de
Gouvernance. C'est qu'on a constaté ces organisations de la société civile et des
organisations de femmes qui ont été créés en 1994–95, notre objectif c'est déjà
de promouvoir le leadership des femmes. La parité a été un processus qui a commencé comme quelque chose qui ne s'appelait pas la parité. Mais le travail pour
moi c'était un travail fait par nos aînées depuis très longtemps. Elles se sont bat-
tues. Ça ne s'appelait pas parité mais seulement impliquer les femmes, entre guillemets les libérer pour qu'elles puissent occuper les postes de décisions, qu'elles
puissent participer à la vie de la nation. C'était ça au départ. Donc ce furent les
femmes sénégalaises qui ont voulu que nous faisions un diagnostique de la participation des femmes dans les instances de décisions. On a constaté qu'il y avait
un grand déficit des femmes dans ces postes.

20. En 1996/97 le COSEF a fait un diagnostic et a mise en place un conseil. Son
objectif principal c'était de promouvoir la participation des femmes dans des instances de décisions. Surtout au niveau gouvernemental ou institutionnel, même
dans les autres secteurs comme les collectives locales. Donc après ce travail de
diagnostic il fallait faire le tour pour voir des politiciens, les leaders politiques,
voir des autorités religieuses et coutumières et savoir quelle était la perceptions
de la femme au sein de la prise de décision. On a d'abord commencé avec des
leaders du parti parce qu'à cette époque il y avait que des grands partis.

21. Avant, daan nañu utiliser jigéen bi ñu soxlawoon mbooloo, waaye bu ñu
wara jël décisions dañu teg jigéen ca ginaaw. Sama jëkkër, Mouhamet Seydoou
Bâ ci membre fondateur yi MRDS la. Ba ñu daan def seeni réunion, fii lañu
daan daaje. En 2001, 2002 ñu lancer parti bi te ñu bëgg nag ma nekk responsable
des femmes nationales. Imam Mbaye Niang président wu parti lawoon te man
leader-u jigéen ñi laawoon 14 ans.

22. Il y a des hommes qui refusent que leurs femmes fassent de la politique ou restent tard dans les réunions. Il y a des hommes qui l'acceptent. Je prends mon cas, comme j'ai l'habitude de dire que je l'ai négocié dès le mariage.

23. On a fait beaucoup de progrès. Même avant que la loi ne soit adoptée on avait fait beaucoup de pas importants. Ça veut dire que les femmes quittent la maison à elles étaient confinées, et elles ne pouvaient pas aller travailler et participer en politique. La parité a aidé à consolider ça. Mais il y a toujours beaucoup de maisons à il est difficile que les femmes participent. Dans les zones rurales, les hommes ont vraiment tendance à dire que la place de la femme est dans le foyer. Elle doit s'occuper de la nourriture, des enfants et de leur éducation. Maintenant on a des formations même pour que les hommes comprennent qu'en dehors de la maison les femmes peuvent aussi contribuer beaucoup dans les espaces publics. Et que si elles arrivent à faire quelque chose de positif, ce n'est pas seulement pour elles mais pour leur famille. Si c'est un foyer avec très peu de recsources, et elles arrivent à gagner quelque chose, elles ont contribué.

24. Boo jàngul sa diine wàlla nga nekk ak koo xam ni jàngale na la ko, yaw ku jigéen dinga xalaat lu la diine ji wax. Waaye du loolu. Parce que bu nu xoolee histoire-u Islam gis nanu importance bi Sunu Yaay Khadiija amoon. Mooy première-u jabaru sunu prophète Mohammet. Nekkoon na jigéen, commerçante bu amoon xaalis lawoon. Nu ñëwaat gis beneen exemple Yaay Aicha jabaram bi gëna ndaw. Maashaa Allah, géeju xam-xamam lawoon. Yoneent bi dafa doon wax, seen génn wàllu xam-xam dangeen ko jële ci ndawsi, parce que li mu doon def yépp, Sunu Yaay Aicha moo ko jàngoon. Bu ñu la bëgge wax diine moo ne jigéena war nekk ci kër gi nii, nu ne déedéet parce que soxnay Yoneent bi salaatu wa salaam ñu ngi doon def commerce, ñenneen doon jàng ni góor ñi di jànge. Jigéen bu wara jëriñ société bi dafa ko wara jëriñ. Su fekkee jàngul te amoo accès ci texte yi, nanguwuñu la jangal dañu lay dominé toujours. Dañuy wax lu sa diine ji waxul.

25. In the next chapter, I highlight how the wives of the Prophet Muhammad are important references for Muslim women as they argue for place in economic and political activities of the nation.

26. En général ce sont des jaloux. Beaucoup d'hommes pensent que ce sont les femmes qui les barrent. Qui les empêchent de tourner en rond. Ils n'ont aucune raison d'être contre la parité. Il y a des gens qui disent qu'il y a des femmes qui ne sont pas capables. Il y a des femmes qui ne sont pas capables mais aussi il y a des hommes pas capables, alors ils cachent leur incapacité et s'attaquent à l'incapacité des femmes. C'est vrai que les femmes surtout manquent de formation, mais jusqu'à présent on lutte pour qu'elles aient cette formation. Il y a des hommes qui ne peuvent pas accepter la parité et luttent contre.

27. Oui, Emily, je pense qu'il est l'heure pour les femmes de faire plus qu'organiser les gens au sein du parti. Souvent, elles sont là pour la mobilisation

sociale, le folklore, mais les femmes sont prêtes pour s'engager dans leurs partis et aussi au parlement.

Biographies of the Women of the Teraanga Republic

1. Man, Aysatu Mbóoj laa tudd, wànte li gëna bari Ayda Mbóoj lañu ma gëna xame . . . ci état civil Aysatu moo ci nekk. Maa ngi juddoo ci kër goo xam ne kër gu yaatu la . . . dama juddoo rekk ci environnement politique, parce que man sama yaay dafa nekk ci jigéen yu rare yi di def politique. Elle est née en 1928. Sama pàppa, dama juddu rekk gis ko ci UPS (Union Progressiste Sénégalaise). Sama pàppa, Alaaaji Amadu Mbóoj mu ngi juddu 1891. Ci ay caatam laa bokk. Sama pàppa ak sama yaay yépp Waalo-Waalo lañu. Sama pàppa mbokku sama yaay la. Ñu sànt Mbóoj ci Waalo lañu jóge dans le nord du Sénégal, famille princière yi maanaam famille yi nga xam ne ay buur lañu. Sama pàppa moom bi mu jógee foofu booba xale la. Dañu ñewoon Tuubaa ci temps booba dafa ñew wax leen nan ñoom ñi nekk taaw ci famille, nañu leen di yóbbu leen école des fils du chef.

2. Waaw dañu wax ne jigéen du wax age-am mais, dinaa wax sama age parce que xayna nga soxla ko, nga xam sama génération. Je suis née le 20 mars 1957 à Bambey. Sama yaay en 1945 bi Senghor waree wër réew mi, le tour du pays, sama yaay moo ko téyewoon Bambey. Mënulwoon bind, waaye leader lawoon. Sama pàppa sax daan na politig, di faral Lamiin [Géy] bi mu àndee ak Senghor. Sama yaay moo faraloon Senghor. Bambey, dëkk bu amoon importance te Pierre Senghor, frèrem, moo nekkoon premier maire de Bambey.

3. Sama ñoomu yaay ñooñu dañu kontaanoon, am seeni góor. Il était impensable yaw jigéen ngay politig yaw kenn. Dangay am sa góor. Dinga affirmer-wu ci sa groupe-u jigéen pour nekk leader. ci seen biir mais doo nekk maire wala tête de liste departamentale ci élections legislatives yi comme sama cas en 2007 bi ma nekke tête de liste te góor moo toppoon sama ginnaaw.

4. Am na jigéen yoo xam ne dañu juddu rekk nekk femmes leaders. Am na jigéen yiy def politique de développement di mobiliser ay nit di organiser ay nit di leen définiral yoon. Pour man, loolu politig la. Parce que ñu ngi def politique de développement. Nekk ay relais ci prévention ci santé, ci éducation, di encourager nit ñi pour ñu dugal seeni xale ci école yi, surtout xale yu jigéen yi. Pour man, politig la. Mais politig dugg ci partie loolu aussi dañu ko wara dug. Am na ñoo xam ne xamuñu sax seeni turu partie est-ce que liberalisme la wàlla socialisme. Senegaal xamuñu loolu. Dañuy dug ci politig parce que dañu naan man, Suleymaan[1] sama caat bi te Suleymaan danu yàgg. Suleymaan man maay njékke jabaram. Sama yaay mooy yaayam, donc Suleymaan dafay politig. Nun politig lanu mën. Il faut que ma politig. Surtout jigéen yi nak. Wax naa leegi nak pour que jigéen ñi affirmer-wu, am position, ñeme nekk en face l'homme comme ni ma defe, dañu lay xeex. Dafa metti.

5. Je pense que li am solo mooy jàng, am xam-xam moo am solo. Jàng naa araab aussi. Mais comme fi ci Senegal langue bi nuy liggéeye mooy, langue officielle mooy faranse, ci laa def sama certificat d'études. Te xam nga, mag yi ñewoon ne ma ma dem seyi. Mais bi ma dellusee di liggéey dugg ci politig ba Yàlla def ni ma jiite parti Jëf Jël comme présidente nationale des mouvements de femmes de l'Alliance Jëf Jël bu Talla Sylla foofu laa militewoon. En 2002, ci laa nekk conseillère municipale de Hann Bel-Air. En 2007 ma nekk députée. En 2009, ma nekk adjoint au maire de la commune de Hann Bel-Air, te en 2012 population bi renouvelewaat seen confiance ci man.

6. Sama maam bu góor daan na politig ak Léopold Sédar Senghor, leader bu mag lawoon. Icon lawoon, Amadu Gaye Ndickou. Amoon na charisme. Nekkoon na chef du village. Mais, tamit sama maam bu jigéen bi jur sama yaay meeru dëkk ba, maire wu jigéen yi, di jitte seen mbootaay yi mais aussi doon jàppale boroom këram ci lu mu daan def. Mais aussi jigéen yi dañu daan jàppale rekk. Dañu wax ne damay jàppale sama càmmiñ wàlla sama boroom kër mooy politig ma di ko jàppale . . . mais sama maam boobu dafa amoon solo. Dafa nekkoon non seulement politician, mais chef de village de Jaxaaw Gay. Mu ngi ci wetu Ndand. Diggànte Jaxaaw, Kabu, Taaleen, Njaxaxaan. Moo nekkoon ku ñu tudde boroom dëkk bi.

7. Du ñépp la Yàlla may ñu jaar ci associations féminines comme man. J'ai crée beaucoup d'associations. Je les ai crées ba mu dox quand même ma bàyyi leen ñu doxal ma dem ci leneen. Première association bi ma crée mu ngi tudd Association des Femmes de Sicap Urbam en 1993. Boobu sama taaw sax juuduwul, parce que sama taaw mu ngi juudu ci 1994. Après ma crée Kaay Baax après ma dem liggéey ci mouvement A3J (Ànd, Jàppoo, Jëf ci Jàmm).

8. This interview was done in English.

9. She refers to French school here, which is the national education standard.

10. Il y a la femme en politique, il y a la femme africaine en politique, et il y a la femme sénégalaise en politique. Et dans ces trois-là je crois que nous pouvons dire des choses. Ma vie elle professionnelle ne commence pas par la politique. Ma vie professionnelle commence par l'avocat. Je suis née dans une famille maraboutique, et c'est pour cela que je vous dis qu'il faut parler de la femme sénégalaise dans la politique. Je viens d'une famille conservatrice dont même les hommes ne vont pas à l'école. Ils font les études coraniques. Ils sont marabouts. Donc, quand les femmes vont à l'école, c'est vraiment une exception. Et nous on a eu de la chance d'avoir un papa qui nous a dit qu'on va à l'école. Et dans notre famille nous sommes 11 enfants. Neuf filles et seulement deux garçons. Et mon père a compris très tôt que les garçons et les filles, c'est la même chose. Il faut pas distinguer les filles et les garçons et on peut dire qu'au Sénégal, c'est quand même exceptionnelle. Tous les papas ne sont pas comme ça. Donc, j'ai été dans l'école avec ces conditions. Et à Podor la société est très conservatrice. La femme a sa

place et elle reste à sa place. Le reste ce sont les autres qui conduisent. Je me rappelle même avec les condoléances les femmes allaient la nuit accompagnées par un petit fils, parce que dans la journée la femme ne doit même pas marcher le jour ni pour travailler, ni pour faire de la politique. Alors, c'est d'où je viens, et c'est dans ces conditions que j'ai fait mes études.

11. Mon grand-père qui était le marabout disait tous les jours à mon père: "Il faut sortir les filles de l'école . . ." Et mon père disait: "Non, non, non, elles sont brillantes. Elles ont de bonnes notes. Il faut continuer." Et on a continué jusqu'au baccalauréat, et mon grand-père disait: "bon, ces femmes-là sont foutues. Elles ne vont pas se marier. Il faut les faire des nonnes et les mettre dans un couvent." Bon, c'était une façon de parler de la part de mon grand-père . . . Et arrive maintenant de l'université, et je dis à mon père que je veux faire des études de droit. Là commence la discussion avec mon propre père. Mon père ne veut pas que je fasse des études de droit, il veut que je fasse des études de lettres. Après, je vais devenir professeure. Il pense que c'est plus tranquille. Après, je vais me marier, avoir des enfants, avoir trois mois de vacances, que c'est plus tranquille comme ça pour une femme. Moi, je ne le voyais pas comme ça. Je me voyais destinée pour faire du droit. Mais, si j'insistais, mon père aurait arrêté la discussion. Donc, j'ai fait un compromis que je ferai administrateur civil, quelque chose comme gouverneur de région. Et après ça, mon père savait que je vais être avocate parce que je savais mettre des choses l'un après l'autre. Les gens racontent que même quand j'étais toute petite, j'avais peut être trois ans, quand quelqu'un parlait je répondais tout de suite. Que j'avais un talent naturel pour ça . . . ça fais 30 ans que je suis avocate, et chaque fois que je gagne un dossier, que ça soit un petit dossier, je suis contente, heureuse, je rebondis de joie comme une petite fille à qui nous avons donné une sucette. Le fait de gagner ou le fait de persuader quelqu'un pour moi, c'est quelque chose extraordinaire.

12. En réalité, j'ai eu un dossier, un dossier très dur, que j'ai gagné. Et quand je l'ai gagné le Ministre de la Justice a voulu donner des instructions au Procureur pour faire le contraire de mon jugement. On voulait presque prendre ma victoire. Et je me suis révoltée parce que ce sont des choses que je n'accepte pas. J'ai fait une lettre très sévère au Président Abdou Diouf. Très sévère, où je dénonçais ça. Et que s'il côtionne ça, je le dénoncerai partout où il sera possible de ce dénoncer. Le président a reçu la lettre, et dans la lettre je lui ai demandé de me recevoir. Pour que je vienne lui expliquer ce qui s'est passé parce que je suis sûre que son Ministre de la Justice ne lui a pas expliqué les choses. Il a demandé à un de ses conseillers de me recevoir. J'ai refusé parce que lui il avait déjà reçu l'autre parti. Vous avez reçu l'autre parti, vous devez me recevoir . . . mais tu sais, le Chef de l'État n'aime pas qu'on lui refuse. Après, il a compris que j'ai refusé. Un jour il reçoit une de mes cousines et il demande si on est parenté, et ma cousine lui dit que si. Trois mois après il avait besoin de faire un renouvellement des ministères.

Il a dit, "je veux que tu sois mon Ministre de la Communication et Porte-parole de mon gouvernement. Je me souviens que tu parles bien le français, tu l'écris bien, et moi j'ai besoin de visage neufs surtout une femme." J'ai réfléchi un peu, j'ai parlé avec mon père pour avoir son avis et j'ai accepté. Je suis devenue ministre à 18 mois de l'élection présidentielle. C'était en 1998.

13. Déjà, être une femme dans la politique est très difficile. Même en Occident. Regard Madame Clinton, tout le monde dit que c'est la candidate idéale et qu'elle va passer. Et finalement elle n'est pas passé. Et quand tu demandes aux hommes, "pourquoi vous n'avez pas voté pour elle?" Ils te disent que Madame Clinton est une femme trop forte. Elle a perdu parce qu'elle est sortie du registre de la femme. Tout le monde était sûr qu'elle va passer. Elle représente des choses trop fortes, et elle a été victime de ce qui signifie une femme forte.

4. Patronas and Hustlers

1. From *Nawetaan* in the Wolof standard spelling.

2. Quand on parle de pouvoir économique et la femme en islam, la première femme du prophète Mohammet, paix soit sur lui, Khadija, était une businesswoman avec beaucoup de succès et très riche. Non seulement elle était plus âgée que lui, mais elle était aussi sa patronne.

3. *Leket* and *calebasse* are the Wolof and French words for a gourd-like basket used to carry water, catch the hair shaved from a baby's head during its naming ceremony, or collect money during association meetings. The baskets have numerous other uses and are symbolic of ceremonies and other social spaces and consequential life moments.

4. Ndand is a small town on the road north to Saint Louis before reaching Kébémer.

5. Maa ngi juddoo Tamba en 1965, jaar Ndande samay këru maam boobu daan politig. Moo jur sama yaay. Ma jóge fa dem Tuubaa jàngi Alxuraan. Bi ma jóge Tuubaa dellusiwaat Ndand. Ci laa jóge fekksi sama yaay Géejawaay nekk ak moom, commencer di def cours de vacances ci faranse.

6. Am na ñu destin di nekk leader, dangay gis jigéen dañuy créer quelque chose ci seen quartier ñu ngiy def ay tontine di def ay basañ lu ñuy defe ci seen xew yi. Ñoom ay femme leader lañu. Ñun ñiy politig dañuy dem ci femme yooyu. Dañuy bëgg femme yooyu nekk responsable groupement de GPF yi te def politig.

7. Lépp loo yendoo war ngaa xam fi mu tàmbale ak fi muy jëm. A3J mooy, Ànd Jàppoo Jëf ci Jàmm, muy association boo xam ne sunu honorable Mously Jaxate moo ko sos ci 2011. Mooy jigéen bu am jom, mu créer FADES muy Fonds d'Appui au Développement Économique et Social. Réseau A3J day politig mais ginnaaw politig day def développement communautaire durable. Loolu mooy lan? Mooy suqali sa am-amu bopp. Ba nu ko falee 2012 mënoon na faluwaat ne

la "li ma am dama koy bokk ak samay mbokk," waaye deful loolu. Tey réseau A3J mu ngi am 250 associations ci biir Senegaal ak à l'international, du noonu? FADES mooy fonds di def renforcement de capacité, manaam ñi mënul bind seen tur nu jàngal leen na ñuy bindee. Mu wëlbatiku def formation micro-jardinage nañuy béye ci sunuy kër.

8. Sama association bi [A3J] c'est mix homme-femme, mais quand même des femmes sont dominantes parce que dama leen yërëm. Parce que sonn nañu ci association yi, ci tuur yi, ci mouvement yi, ci parti yi, alors que les revenus demewuñu noonu. Alors que les banques nu ngi leen di bëgga rey parce que institutions financières yu bare seen taux de pourcentage chère na, durée bi gàtt na. Alors que les femmes sénégalaises am nañu courage bu mag-a-mag pour yor seen famille yi. Même ñu fi am jëkkër presque ñoo yor seen famille à 80%.

9. La Première Dame moo nu wax ne commune bu nekk dañu recevoir trois million cfa, ñu bokk ci biir mbootaay yi, te 10 communes lañu. Maa ne ko déedéet, defal cinq millions CFA. Mu ne waaw te may na 50 millions CFA te li ci desoon ci ministre des femmes lay jóge ba mu nekk 95 millions CFA ba ñu seddale ko. Affaire bi mooy Cambérène commune bu bokk lépp. Mënoo joxe benn nit te joxoo keneen. Leneen bi mooy, Cambérène am na mbootaay yu bare ak daayira yu bare, kon bi ma woote mbootaayu Cambérène, 48 lañuwoon, duwoon 10. Am na jigéen yoo xam ne bokk nañu ci mbootaay yu bare ngir gagner plus. Xam nga këru Mbaye Seck? Jotunu ñepp ci biir, xamuma ñaata lanuwoon.

5. Good Women, Good Deeds

1. Éditeur yi jaay nañu quelque uns ci Ministère de la Culture, li ci desoon maa leen di maye. Def naa ko ngir génération bi topp ci man ñu mëna gëm seen bopp. Am na solo ne nit ñi xam nañu fu ñu jogé ak fu ñu jëm. Su ma amoon possibilité imprimer yeneen dinaa leen may université yi ak lycée yi comme ça ku bëgg nekk sama place dañu xam ne naka lañu wara comportewu.

2. Man députée Sëriñ Abdu Lahad laa. Liggéey bi samay waa-jur doon liggéey di taxaway askan wi, di sama maam ba sama baay ba ci man, mission boobu lay eggale. Te loolu lépp ci Sëriñ Abdu Lahad la.

3. Màggalu Tuubaa dañu koy def de manière exceptionnelle par rapport ak yeneen, waaye pour nun jaamu Yàlla la. Ag jaamu Yàlla moo tax bu yegsee ak li nu mën lepp ak li nu mënul danuy dimbali sunuy dëkkandoo yoo xamantene seen loxo jutul seen ginnaaw te bes bi lañu bokk. Te lu gëna am solo mooy boo dee sànt Yàlla danga koy sànt won ko ne ci doomu adamam yi nga xamantene moo leen sàkk te yemalewul. Ñàkkam lay ñakka def tane nga li nga leen tane ci sa alal li mu bon-bon nga jox leen ko, nga bokk ak ñoom won leen ni yeena ko bokk, yeena ko moom sax. Ndaxte ginnaaw sabaab bi nuy def ak rendi li nuy def la ca des doomu adaama lanu koy jox.

4. Xoolal sama géer gi Ayda Mbóoj! Mu bomb cere ji. Teg ko ci leket bi. Lii cosaan la, Mbóoj! Dafa jël cere ba mu mokk def ko sauce. Mu raay ca loxom, bomb bu baax, bomb ba mu dëgër. Def ci njaga ji, def ci raisin bi, daldi ko bomb. Def ci haricot def ci sauce nak. Lepp a ngi ci biir, AH! Ayda, jàngal nga ma cere, jigéen ñi nañu xool ci yaw. Ku ko def, sa reer bi dina normal. Nga yekkal sa goro, sa goro gi di la ree di la dëkk di la ñaan. Nga yekkal jigéen mu xam li mu doon, cere a ngi nii. Sama géer gi maa ngay cere Mbóoj, law la cat ci lii! Mais lii du tey, démb la. Mbóoj li nga tuutiwoon nga commencer, jàngal la liggéey, teg ko ca temps, dem ecole ba, am sa diplôme. Doomu jigéen, jàng ba normal. Nga jang liggéeyu jigéen ni la ko bëgge. Ku dégg Ayda Mbóoj, nga xam ko. Dangay mën te ligéey kontaan naa ci lii.

5. The Bac, as it is commonly referred to, is short for Baccalauréat, the competitive end of a high school exam in the Francophone educational system. The S1 refers to the mathematics and physical sciences strand and the S2 is for experimental sciences.

6. J'aimerais contribuer en tant que vice-président et en tant que religieux sur la question de la parité. Parce que très souvent j'entends à la radio que les gens s'opposent sans fondement scripturel, sans fondement dans le coran, sans fondement dans la Sunna. Avant-hier j'ai présidé une cérémonie de remise de diplôme aux éleves de l'école coranique Seydi Djamil qui ont appris le coran par cœur. Sur 19 laurèats, 11 étaient des filles. Et parmi ces 11 5 viennent d'avoir le Bac S1 et S2. Donc c'était l'exemple le plus vivant de voir des filles à la fois performante au lycée mais aussi performante dans les daaras. Dama bëgga wax benna aaya. Yàlla dafa wax ne [spoken first in Arabic], ils se trouvent parmi les musulmanes des gens qui ont rempli le contrat qu'ils ont avec Dieu. Et je disais aux étudiants qu'on ne peut pas parler du dôn sans parler de rujula. Il y a deux concepts dans l'islam. On parle de dhukura qui est la virilité biologique. Soo gisee góor nga xam ne góor la, soo gisee jigéen nga xam ne jigéen la. Il y a rujuula qui pour moi est la plénitude d'une perfection humaine, sexuellement indifférencié, masculinité mën na ko incarner, fémininité itam mën na koo incarner. Ma doon wax xale yi, tey laa dora dégg aaya boobu, parce que le contrat que vous avez avec Dieu, cette à dire que la lettre qu'Il vous a envoyé vous l'avez maîtrisée, vous l'avez rempli. Donc, aay bi kenn mënul wax ne fiire góor. C'est la plénitude d'une personne sexuellement indifférenciée.

7. C'est très culturel. Ça date de très longtemps, même avant Aline Sitoe Diatta jusqu'aux femmes de Nder, donc nous avons beaucoup de références. Il y a jigéen ju mën góor, ou on dit ki méngale na ak góor. Dans mon opinion, ça a été instrumentalisé contre nos objectifs. Parce que une jigéen ju mën góor est une femme qui a dépassé les hommes en termes de comportement et autorité. C'est-à-dire que notre société nous dit que ces caractères agressifs ne sont pas d'elles, mais des hommes. Si une femme veut réussir à un certain niveau, la

société lui fait comprendre que si elle veut une chaise à la table, il faut qu'elle soit un homme. Et ce comportement agressif a marché au début quand les femmes commençaient à avoir de l'autorité. Les femmes qui nous ont représenté au début elles sortaient les biceps. Elles se comportaient comme les hommes et les hommes disaient, "oui, ce sont des lionnes." La référence aux lions veut dire qu'elles se comportent et parlent comme cet animal-là. Et ce n'est pas un animal subtil, mais agressif. C'est pour cela que je ne suis pas d'accord avec cette phrase parce que les femmes devront prendre des référence d'elles-mêmes et n'ont des hommes.

8. *Baol* is the French transcription of the region of Bawol in Wolof, corresponding to present-day Diourbel.

9. "Le double standard est, ils disent au moins que vous n'êtes pas comme nous, vous ne pouvez pas être à notre niveau. On vous reconnaîtra si vous êtes comme nous, mais si vous nous dépassez on ne vous reconnaîtra pas."

10. Jigéen ju baax lañu doon waxtaane. Danu faral di wax, jigéen ju mën góor, waaye su ñu bëggee benn exemple, danuy indi Soxna Jaara. Soxna Jaara, xarbaaxi Yàlla la. Kenn mënu ko roy. Amul benn jigéen ci àdduna ku ko gën. Ku mëna muñ di xaar boroom këram ci ngelaw ak taw bi ba bët set. Su nu bëggee indi ku roy xeyna Soxna Anta Njaay Mbakke. Ñeppa ko xamewoon ngir jëf yu rafet yi te fiitam. Bu benn jigéen ci këram waroona seyi benn góor gi jogé famille bu gëna suufe. Jigéen jooju dafa daw te Soxna Anta moo seyi ak góor googu ngir cëram te fay na ndawtalam. Góor gi amulwoon allal yu bare.

11. Maa ngi leen di nuyu yeen ñépp, góor ñi ak seeni soxna, ñi ñëwooon jangsi ci leket bi. Sëriñ Mansour, li nga wax ci jigéen ñi dëgg la. Jigéena wara nekk ci këru góor. Sama pàppa moo ma ko jàngal. Responsabilité nga am ci sa néegu séy moo ma ko jàngal. Li ma ci dolli mooy, mu ne bu la sa jëkkër ji xoolee la xelam dem ci yaayam nga dalal xelam. Responsabilité la jigéen ji am, fexe ba mu baax. Te loolu terewul dara lu parité bi wax. Bi ma njëkke xeex ngir parité, cow lu bare amoon te sous-préfet bi moo ma woo di wax ne "yaa ngiy indi ay problémes diggënte góor ak jigéen, jëkkër ak ay soxnam te leegi jigéen yi ngi wax duñu def dara ndaxte fayunu leen." Mësuma wax loolu. Te benn bes ñew nañu sama kër di gis maa ngi doon servir sama jëkkër di ko toppatoo. Dama sañsewoon. Yàlla mo santane sunu diggënte. Danu wax liggéyu ndey. Am na explication bu scientifique ci waxiñ boobu. Sunu wareef ci société bi mooy am doom te toppatoo leen. Na nu ñewaat ci parité bi. Cheikh Sidy Makhtar yonné na tawam, Moustapha Mbakke, di ma setsi. Sama xarit la. Dafa ñew ndaxte cow boobu di ma laajale. Dama ko wax ne, su benn jigéen am ndam ci lenn, dina am ci jëkkër itam. Su jigéen amee cër ci politig, jëkkëram day am également. Jigéen day yeg auto, góor itam. Danu bokk investissement. Waaye dëgg la, am na contextam. Nu ngiy waxtaan parité ci politig. Waxunu parité ngir bañ diine. Waxtaanunu parité ngir corrompre sunuy taalibé. Waxunu parité ngir remplacer sunuy jëkkër. Séy dafa am solo. Yàlla moo ko santane. Sama séy yaqul samay jàng wàlla sama opportunité nekk leader. Au

contraire. Dama bëgga nekk un modèle ba waxtu julli jot, ma julli. Dama jox sama jëkkër cëram di ko toppatoo. Ba bu ñu amee gan, dañu xam kan mooy boroom kër ga.

12. Xam nga, taalibe laa. Loolu moo tax c'est important. Dafa bokk ci yaaru yoonu Murīd laa jànge. Parce qu'une autre dimension de l'éducation Murīd c'est l'humilité. Dañu lay wax nga wàcce sa bopp, koo woolu nga duggal ko ci sa bopp. Parce que koo duggal ci sa bopp moom tam it mu bëgg la te sopp la. Beneen leçon booy def politig.

13. Dafay difficile pour ñu considérer jigéen. Ci religion, dañuy wax ne jigéen li gëna metti mooy li nga xam ne jànguñu bu baax. Par exemple mosquée bu Sacré Coeur am na benn imam Cisse, dafay wax anglais di wax wolof di wax français. Il est tres ouvert. Benn bes dafa amoon les Qadirs mooy vingt-septième nuit ci weeru koor. Mu inviter ma. Bi mu ma invité, booba maa ngi nekk ministre mu yóbbu ma ci mindar bi. Am na ñu fa doon casser, di protester, di wax "xoolal muy jël jigéen di ko teg foofu. Kii moo bëgg xaalis. Ni mu amee folie de grandeur." Moom, dégg na leen après mu génn suuraat bi. Ne na am na suraat boo xam ne "Yàlla daf ne, bu jigéen demee ba nekk ci benn station de pouvoir, ma ne Yàlla maa ko def, parce que pouvoir Yàlla moo ko moom. Kon ma ne Yàlla moo ko may ci sama wàllu pouvoir bu jigéen boobu dañu ko émanciper ba mu mëna toog ak góor yi. Parce que kooku dafa jàng, culturam moo ko may ouverturam moo ko may."

14. Coalition bi mu ngi tudd Ànd, Saxal Liggéey . . . ndaxte liggéey lanu gëm, te danu bëgga def politique autrement. Politique autrement boobu mooy ni nu doon tàcculoo jigéen yi mu jeex. Danu bëgga saxal liggéey. Saxal liggéey mooy liggéey bu fi nekk nu wara koo saxal. Nun danuy liggéey fu nu mësa nekk. Mësunu taxaw. Ay ligéeykat lañu moo tax nu tuddee ko noonu te pour jigéen ñi politique autrement. Politig boo xam ne dafa jël ci seen autonomisation. Affairu duggal jigéen ci kars, tàcculeen mu jeex fi. Danuy leen di wutal moyen ñu am pour seen fass yëf. Ak politique bi encadrer jeune yi ba am encadrement de développement social ba am prise en charge des plus vulnerables.

6. Political Economies of Teraanga

1. Bi ma nekkee xale dama daan ngente xar yi. Xar bu juddu ma ngente ko maa inviter ñépp, xale ci coin bi yépp, inviter leen. Danu daan def semblant di togg. Après ñu laal basin bi. Donc déjà sama jikko di diriger doon na feen.

2. Sama yaay mu ne, jàng rekk taxul nga nekk leader. Sa leadership da nga koy juddowaale en suite say jikko, sa éducation, sa générosité, luy tax daal nga mëna dajale jigéen ñépp seen position yepp ci yaw, après nga taxaw, taxawaay fi . . . parce que, am na ñu bare ñoo xam ne bu ñu ñëwee Bambey nekk foofu ay jeunes marriés ba ñooñu tey am na ñu nekk ay membres. Sama yaay moo tax ñu mëna

toog ci seen séy. Da leen di yedd, di leen wax muñ leen, su ñu amee problème ak seeni jëkkër, bu amee lu ko nàqari ñu ñëw ci moom. Moom itam mu wax leen waruloo def lii, daldi wax jëkker ji defal lii. Su la waree dimbali itam, dimbali la. Yenn say yi, danga gis ku jëkkëram liggéeyul mu jàppale la ba nga yor sa njaboot. Amoon na ay nit ñoo xam moo leen dimbali ba ñu wax ñeeneen ñi "demal ci Ajaa Aminta sunu yaay, nga teral ko parce que su ma toogee fii ba nga mel nii moom moo tax." Te loolu jëriñ na ma ci sama politique. Bi ma ñëwee di politig dans le départemnt wàlla fépp fu ma demee dangay gis benn nit ñëw ne ma dama lay jàppale spontanément. "Dama lay jàppale parce que sama pàppa ne na sa yaay moo doon njëkke sama yaay. Donc yaw sama pàppa, sa nijaay la." Après man itam, maay kaf ak kooku, "yaw sama sàng nga wàlla sama doomu ndey nga parce que sama yaay sa xaritu yaayu ku jigeen yooyu" daal. Gis nga sax benn xale bu góor démb bu ñëwoon di ma filmer sama bureau, bi nu enregistreremission bi. Mu ne "xamuloo ne sa yaay moo ma uuf, moo ma ngente."

3. Political Declaration of Madame Aminata Touré, Prime Minister of Senegal, to Parliament, October 28, 2013.

4. Le système de justice moderne, entre guillemets, n'est pas très bien vu par les Africains, et au Sénégal en particulier. Pourquoi je particularise toujours le Sénégal? Parce qu'il y a toujours la religion qui intervient dans les choses. Donc, la justice en général elle est très mal vue. Elle est très mal vue parce qu'elle applique les règles que personne ne comprend. Nous, nos règles de droits sont héritées de la tradition française qui elle les a héritées de la tradition romaine, et c'est complètement aux antipodes de nos cultures et de nos civilisations africaines. Donc les gens pensent que la justice et un jeu tout à fait étranger que jouent les personnes qui ne comprennent pas le fait social dans lequel les gens sont en train de vivre. Parce que pour nous, c'est quoi la justice? Pour nous, pour les Africains, la justice est un régulateur de tension sociale. Ce n'est pas un arbitre et encore moins un juge, c'est essayer de toujours pondérer, c'est de la médiation. Ce n'est pas de la justice. Moi quand je fais du tort, on nous appèlle, par exemple, encore moi je suis plus âgée que vous devant nous on va pas dire que Aysata tu as tort. On va dire "bon, après tout, Emily, Aysata est ta grande sœur. Il y a des choses que tu dois accepter. Il y a des choses que tu dois comprendre." Maintenant, quand tu sors de la pièce, on va dire "bon, Aysata tu as quand même déconné." Parce qu'il y a des choses plus importantes, par exemple le droit d'aînesse, c'est le droit qu'on donne à l'ancien. Ça c'est plus important que donner une justice à Emily.

5. Bu fekkantane mayee teraanga mooy corruption, corrupte laa! Ay waa société civile yooyu di wax naan oui il y a la corruption dans la politique xamuñu. Xamuñu teraanga ngay joxe, dangay def teraanga, def teraanga, def teraanga, bes boo soxlaa kooku nak, ah dama koy jàppale Ayda Mbóoj vraiment xawma naka laa koy def . . . parce que dafa ma defal teraanga. Du corruption, teraanga la, dangeen koy defaante, même soo politikulwoon nga jox ko ko. Yaw itam bes

boo bëggee politig nga ñëw ci moom mu jàppale la. Xam nga boo bëggee wax ne ci politig wàlla ci xaritoo wàlla ci séy teraanga, teraanga rekk la. Su dee politig la, war nga yaw responsable bi ak kiy politig ngeen séq teraanga. D'autant plus, pour wax la du corruption, yaw mii responsable bi, boo demee nga dem ci kër ki ngay defando politig comme nii may def tournée nii, may dem ci communauté rurales yi, dangay gis ñu defal la teraanga, di la jox ay xar, ay ginaar, ay geerte, ay ñebe. Di la jox lu nekk nga def sa oto. Xam nga loolu teraanga la. Leegi, su nu ñëwee Bambey, maa toggal leen ceeb ñu lekk. Bu nuy dem ma jox leen paas. Loolu teraanga la. Donc, teraanga ñaari nit ñoo koy séq. Su de séy nga, gis sa yaay jëkkër wàlla sa magu jëkkër, nga defal ko teraanga. Moom itam, su ñëwee, bu fa fekkee sa doom wàlla dara mu defal la teraanga, wàlla boo amee tissu bu rafet, wàlla mu am cadeau bu rafet mu may la, mu defal la teraanga. Leegi tissu bi ma may maymouna teraanga la. C'est pas parce que yaayu jëkkëram moo ma wara defal. Man tam it dama koy may. Loolu itam teraanga la. Teraanga mooy toujours échange de civilité moo am ci ñaari nit.

7. Is Senegal Ready for a Female President?

1. J'ai vu ce lundi 28 janvier beaucoup de rêves s'effondrer. D'abord, celui de beaucoup de femmes, peu ou très politisées, qui voyaient en Me Aysata Tall Sall l'incarnation la plus élégante, la plus éloquente et la plus républicaine de ce que devait être la femme sénégalaise en politique.

2. Sarine, January 29, 2019.

3. Osez est venu de nos expériences communes. J'ai compris très tôt que l'une des choses plus importantes dans la politique c'est le courage. Quand on n'a pas le courage on ne peut pas s'engager dans la politique, surtout comme une femme. C'est pour cela que les femmes vous parlent du courage parce qu'elles savent qu'il faut transgresser une barrière. Il y a une barrière sociale et il faut aller au-delà pour osez faire de la politique. Parce que tout ce que la politique demande, la société le refuse aux femmes. Être fort, une femme ne doit pas être forte, c'est mal vu. Si c'est de pouvoir parler au public, une femme ne doit pas parler au public, c'est très mal vu. Si c'est de diriger, une femme doit pas diriger, c'est très mal vu. Si c'est de chercher le pouvoir, une femme doit pas chercher le pouvoir. C'est pour cela quand une femme s'engage en la politique, la première critique qui vient à leur esprit c'est le courage parce qu'elle quitte un monde qui a été tracé pour elle et fait tomber une barrière pour entrer dans un autre monde qui n'est pas fait pour elle. Qui n'est fait que pour les hommes, par les hommes. Le jeu politique est défini par les hommes. En plus, quand on veut réussir dans la politique il faut jouer comme un homme toute en restant une femme. Sinon, on ne peut pas. Il faut être complètement comme eux et si on est comme eux, on n'est plus une femme. Or l'on doit rester femme parce que physiquement, c'est ce

qu'on est. C'est compliqué et les femmes sont complexées de faire de la politique. Pour tout cela, c'est un acte de courage. D'où vient "osez." Osez s'adresse aussi aux hommes pour qu'ils aient le courage de rompre avec le passé. C'est ce courage qu'on demande aux hommes. Parce que vous les hommes jusqu'à présent voilà comment vous avez fait de la politique. Maintenant, c'est l'heure de faire de la politique autrement. Il s'agit de la faire plus sérieusement. Il est question de la faire pour apporter quelque chose à notre pays, d'où vient l'idée de la générosité. On ne fait pas de la politique pour avoir des postes. On ne fait pas de la politique pour être star. Si tu veut être une star, tu fait comme Neymar. Tu signes le contrat, tu joues au ballon, tu fais un show. C'est ça être une star. On ne fait pas de la politique pour les postes. On ne fait pas de la politique pour avoir de l'argent. Si on voulait de l'argent, on ouvre notre propre business. On fait de la politique parce qu'on croit qu'on peut changer des choses. C'est ça l'idée de la générosité. C'est de se dire, moi je considère que j'ai ma vie, je peux la vivre tranquillement, mais moi je ne le ferai pas comme ça. Je ne serai pas tranquille. Je vais sortir de mon petit confort. Je vais sortir de mon petit luxe et je vais donner une chance à ceux qui n'ont pas eu ce que j'ai. D'où l'idée de générosité d'oser. Donc, après le courage, il y a la générosité. Mais la générosité sans la participation des gens c'est la charité. La politique, ce n'est pas la charité. La politique c'est une participation collective à une œuvre collective parce qu'on pense qu'il va servir tout le monde. D'où vient le courage, la générosité, et la participation de notre campagne Osez l'Avenir. Parce que l'avenir c'est un inconnu. On ne sait pas ce qu'il y a dedans. Mais on est sur d'une chose, si on ne travaille pas pour aller vers l'avenir, l'avenir sera un échec. Donc il faut avoir le courage de se lever, de se mobiliser, d'agir, se battre pour l'avenir. On voulait un slogan pour mobiliser les gens enfin qu'ils rompent avec le passé et avoir le courage d'affronter l'avenir.

4 Amul problème. Am na ay préjugés. Waaye jigéen day def lu góor di def. Aux temps, kenn du xalaat jigéen buy def politique. Mais leegi, ce temps-là est révolu. Les gens ont évolués. Ils ont mûr . . . regarde, mon village Gede, ci département de Podor la bokk, et la mairesse de la ville de Podor jigéen la, mon leader Aysata Tall Sall. Te moom, def na ñaari mandats.

BIBLIOGRAPHY

Literature Sources

Achebe, Nwando. 2020. *Female Monarchs and Merchant Queens in Africa*. Athens: Ohio University Press.

Adebanwi, Wale. 2024. *How to Become a Big Man in Africa: Subalternity, Elites, and Ethnic Politics in Contemporary Nigeria*. Bloomington: Indiana University Press. Kindle.

Adjamagbo, Agnès, Philippe Antoine, and Fatou-Binetou Dial. 2004. "Le dilemme des Dakaroises: entre travailler et 'bien travailler.'" In *Gouverner le Sénégal: entre ajustement structurel et développement durable*, edited by Momar-Coumba Diop, 247–72. Paris: Karthala Éditions.

Akamonye, Felix O. 2019. "Can Ubuntu Philosophy Inaugurate and Sustain Modern Development in Africa?" *Nnadiebube Journal of Philosophy* 3 (1): 180–206.

Alidou, Ousseina. 2005. *Engaging Modernity: Muslim Women and The Politics of Agency in Postcolonial Niger*. Madison: University of Wisconsin Press.

Allerton, Catherine. 2012. "Making Guests, Making 'Liveliness': The Transformative Substances and Sounds of Manggarai Hospitality." *Journal of the Royal Anthropological Institute* 18:49–62. https://doi.org/10.1111/j.1467-9655.2012.01760.x.

Andrewes, Janet. 2005. *Bodywork, Dress as a Cultural Tool: Dress and Demeanor in the South of Senegal*. Leiden: Brill.

Bâ, Mariama. 1981. *So Long a Letter*. African Writers Series 248. London: Heinemann.

Babou, Cheikh Anta. 2007. *Fighting the Greater Jihad: Amadu Bamba and the Founding of the Muridiyya of Senegal, 1853–1913*. 1st ed. Athens: Ohio University Press.

Barry, Boubacar. 1985. *Le royaume du Waalo: Le Sénégal avant la conquête*. Paris: Éditions Karthala.

Bass, L., and Fatou Sow. 2006. "Senegalese Families: The Confluence of Eth-
     nicity, History, and Social Change." In *African Families at the Turn of the 21st
     Century*, edited by Y. Oheneba-Sakyi and B. K. Takyi, 83–102. Westport, CT:
     Praeger.
Bastian, Misty. 2013. "Dressing for Success: The Politically Performative Quality of
     an Igbo Woman's Attire." In *African Dress: Fashion, Agency, Performance*, edited
     by Karen Tranberg Hansen and D. Soyni Madison, 15–29. London: Bloomsbury.
Baum, Robert M. 1999. *Shrines of the Slave Trade: Diola Religion and Society in Pre-
     colonial Senegambia*. Oxford: Oxford University Press.
Bayart, Jean-François. 1989. *L'État en Afrique: la politique du ventre*. Paris: Fayard.
Bayart, Jean-François. 1993. *The State in Africa: The Politics of the Belly*. Harlow:
     Longman Group United Kingdom.
Beck, Linda. 2003. "Democratization and the Hidden Public: The Impact of Pa-
     tronage Networks on Senegalese Women." *Comparative Politics* 35 (2): 147–69.
———. 2008. *Brokering Democracy in Africa: The Rise of Clientelist Democracy in
     Senegal*. New York: Springer.
Bernal, Victoria. 1994. "Gender, Culture, and Capitalism: Women and the Remak-
     ing of Islamic 'Tradition' in a Sudanese Village." *Comparative Studies in Society
     and History* 1:36–67.
Bertolt, Boris. 2018. "Thinking Otherwise: Theorizing the Colonial/Modern Gen-
     der System in Africa." *African Sociological Review* 22 (1): 2–17.
Betts, Raymond F. 1971. "The Establishment of the Medina in Dakar, Senegal,
     1914." *Africa* 41 (2): 143–53.
Bienen, Henry. 1974. *Kenya: The Politics of Participation and Control*. Princeton, NJ:
     Princeton University Press.
Boone, Catherine. 1992. *Merchant Capital and the Roots of State Power in Senegal:
     1930–1985*. Cambridge, UK: Cambridge University Press.
Buggenhagen, Beth A. 2011. "Are Births Just 'Women's Business'? Gift Exchange,
     Value, and Global Volatility in Muslim Senegal." *American Ethnologist* 38 (4):
     714–32.
———. 2012. *Muslim Families in Global Senegal: Money Takes Care of Shame*.
     Bloomington: Indiana University Press.
Burrill, Emily. 2015. *States of Marriage: Gender, Justice, and Rights in Colonial Mali*.
     Athens: Ohio University Press.
Butler, Judith. 1999. *Gender Trouble: Feminism and the Subversion of Identity*. 1st ed.
     London: Routledge.
Camara, Fatou K. 2008. "La Parité au Sénégal, Une Exigence de l'état de Droit
     Moderne Conform au Droit Constitutionel Précolonial." In *Rapports Sociaux de
     Sexe-Genre et Droit: Repenser le Droit*, edited by Louise Langevin, 85–102. Lyon:
     Éditions des archives contemporaines.

Candea, Matei, and Giovanni Da Col. 2012. "The Return to Hospitality." *Journal of the Royal Anthropological Institute* 18 (s1): 1–19.

Castaldi, Francesca. 2006. *Choreographies of African Identities: Négritude, Dance, and the National Ballet of Senegal*. Chicago: University of Illinois Press.

Chanock, Martin. 1985. *Law, Custom, and Social Order: The Colonial Experience in Malawi and Zambia*. African Studies Series 45. New York: Cambridge University Press.

Comaroff, John L., and Jean Comaroff. 1997. *Of Revelation and Revolution, Volume 2: The Dialectics of Modernity on a South African Frontier*. Chicago: University of Chicago Press.

———. 2009. *Ethnicity, Inc.* Chicago: University of Chicago Press.

Cooper, Barbara M. 1997. *Marriage in Maradi: Gender and Culture in a Hausa Society in Niger, 1900–89*. Suffolk: Currey James.

———. 2010. *Evangelical Christians in the Muslim Sahel*. Bloomington: Indiana University Press.

Cooper, Frederick. 2014. *Citizenship between Empire and Nation: Remaking France and French Africa, 1945–1960*. Princeton, NJ: Princeton University Press.

Cornwall, Andrea, Elizabeth Harrison, and Ann Whitehead. 2008. *Gender Myths and Feminist Fables: The Struggle for Interpretive Power in Gender and Development*. Oxford: Blackwell.

Coulon, Christian. 1992. "Avant-propos: La démocratie sénégalaise, bilan d'une éxperience." *Politique africaine* 45 (1): 2–8.

Coulon, Christian, and Donal B. Cruise O'Brien. 1989. "Senegal." In *Contemporary West African States*, edited by Donal B. Cruise O'Brien, John Dunn, and Richard Rathbone, 145–64. Cambridge, UK: Cambridge University Press.

Creevey, Lucy. 2004. "Impacts of Changing Patterns of Women's Association Membership in Senegal." In *The Power of Women's Informal Networks: Lessons in Social Change from South Asia to West Africa*, edited by Bandana Purkayasha and Mangala Subramaniam, 61–67. Oxford: Lexington.

Creevey, L., R. Vengroff, and I. Gaye. 1995. "Devaluation of the CFA Franc in Senegal: The Reaction of Small Businesses." *Journal of Modern African Studies* 33 (4): 669–83.

Cruise O'Brien, Donal B. 1975. *Saints and Politicians: Essays in the Organisation of a Senegalese Peasant Society*. Cambridge, UK: Cambridge University Press.

———. 1998. "The Shadow-Politics of Wolofisation." *Journal of Modern African Studies* 36 (1): 25–46.

Cruise O'Brien, Donal B., M. Diop, and Mamadou Diouf. 2002. *La construction de l'état au Sénégal*. Paris: Karthala Editions.

D'Alisera, Joann. 2001. "I ♡ Islam: Popular Religious Commodities, Sites of Inscription, and Transnational Sierra Leonean Identity." *Journal of Material Culture* 6 (1): 91–110.

Dell, Jeremy. 2018. "Unbraiding the Quran." *Islamic Africa* 9 (1): 55–57.

Derrida, Jacques. 1993. *Aporias: Dying–Awaiting (One Another at) the "Limits of Truth" (Mourir—s'attendre Aux "Limites de La Vérité")*. Palo Alto: Stanford University Press.

Derrida, Jacques, and Anne Dufourmantelle. 2000. *Of Hospitality*. Palo Alto: Stanford University Press.

De Sardan, Olivier. 1999. "A Moral Economy of Corruption in Africa?" *Journal of Modern African Studies* 37:25–52.

Diakhaté, Moukhsinatou. 2011. *Du Daara à l'Hémicycle*. Dakar: Nègre International.

Diallo, Ibrahima. 2012. "Qur'anic and Ajami Literatices in Pre-colonial West Africa." *Current Issues in Language Planning* 13 (2): 91–104.

Diaw, Aminata. 1998. *Femmes, Éthique et Politique*. Dakar: Friedrich Ebert Stiftung.

———. 2004. "Les femmes à l'éprouve du politique: permanences et changements." In *Gouverner le Sénégal: entre ajustement structurel et développement durable*, edited by Momar Coumba Diop, 229–46. Paris: Karthala Éditions.

———. 2009. "La femme entre ordre et désordre publics." *Diogenes* 228 (4): 50–59.

———. 2010. "The Woman between Public Order and Disorder: The Ambiguities of Modernity." *Diogènes* 57 (4): 37–45.

Dieng, Bassirou. 1993. *L'Épopée du Kajoor*. Dakar: Khoudia-ACCT.

———. 2008. *Société Wolof et discours du pouvoir: analyse des récits épiques du Kajoor*. Dakar: Presses universitaires de Dakar.

Diop, Abdoulaye-Bara. 1981. *La société Wolof: tradition et changement*. Paris: Karthala Editions.

———. 1985. *La famille wolof: Tradition et changement*. Paris: Karthala Éditions.

Diop, Momar Coumba, ed. 2004. *Gouverner le Sénégal: entre ajustement structurel et développement durable*. Paris: Karthala Éditions.

Diop, Momar Coumba, and Mamadou Diouf. 1990. *Le Sénégal Sous Abdou Diouf: État et Société*. Paris: Karthala Éditions.

Diouf, Mamadou. 2013. "Introduction: The Public Role of 'Good Islam': Sufi Islam and the Administration of Pluralism." In *Tolerance, Democracy, and Sufis in Senegal*, edited by Mamadou Diouf, 1–35. New York: Columbia University Press.

Diouf, Aly. 2011. "Cérémonies Familiales: Ayda Mbóoj déplore la persistance des gaspillages." *Agence de Presse Sénégalaise*, July 4, 2011. Société-Fêtes édition, sec. Société.

Diouf, Jean-Léopold. 2003. *Dictionnaire wolof-français et français-wolof*. Paris: Karthala Éditions.

Djibo, Hadiza. 2001. *La participation des femmes africaines à la vie politique: Les exemples du Sénégal et du Niger*. Paris: L'Harmattan.

Doligez, François, François S. Fall, and Mansa Oualy. 2012. *Expériences de microfinance au Sénégal*. Dakar: Karthala Editions; Paris: CRES.

Edmann, Gero, and Ulf Engel. 2007. "Neopatrimonialism Reconsidered: Critical Review and Elaboration of an Elusive Concept." *Commonwealth and Comparative Politics* 45 (1): 95–119.

Ekeh, Peter. 1975. "Colonialism and the Two Publics in Africa: A Theoretical Statement." *Comparative Studies in Society and History* 17:91–112.

Ellerson, Betty. 1991. "Decolonizing research: A Study of the Indigenous Research Efforts of AAWORD/AFARD- the Association of African Women for Research and Development/Association des Femmes Africaines pour la Recherche sur le Developpement." Diss., Howard University.

Elyachar, Julia. 2005. *Markets of Dispossession: NGOs, Economic Development, and the State in Cairo.* Durham, NC: Duke University Press.

Escobar, A. 1995. *Encountering Development: The Making and Unmaking of the Third World.* Oxford: Princeton University Press.

Esteva, Gustavo, Salvatore Babones, and Philipp Babcicky. 2013. *The Future of Development: A Radical Manifesto.* Bristol: Policy Press.

Evans, Ruth. 2015. "Working with Legal Pluralism: Widowhood, Property Inheritance, and Poverty Alleviation in Urban Senegal." *Gender and Development* 23 (1): 77–94.

Fall, Anta. 2021. Goorgoorlou. YouTube video, 12 July. https://www.youtube.com/watch?v=aZJC3Pf-oms&t=988s.

Fall, Babacar. 2005. "Senegalese Women in Politics: A Portrait of Two Female Leaders, Arame Diène and Thioumbé Samb 1945–1996." In *African Gender Studies: A Reader*, edited by Oyèrónké Oyěwùmi. New York: Palgrave Macmillan.

Fallon, Kathleen M. 2004. "Using Informal Networks to Seek Formal Political Participation in Ghana." In *The Power of Women's Informal Networks: Lessons in Social Change from South Asia to West Africa*, edited by Bandana Purkayasha and Mangala Subramaniam, 75–88. Oxford: Lexington.

Fassa, Farinaz, and Marta Roca i Escoda. 2016. "Fatou Sarr, sociologue féministe. Parcours de la loi sur la parité au Sénégal." *Nouvelles Questions Féministes* 35 (2): 96–107.

Fatton, Robert. 1986. "Clientelism and Patronage in Senegal." *African Studies Review* 29:61–78.

———. 1987. *The Making of a Liberal Democracy: Senegal's Passive Revolution, 1975–1985.* Boulder, CO: Rienner Publishers.

Ferguson, James. 2015. *Give a Man a Fish: Reflections on the New Politics of Distribution.* Durham, NC: Duke University Press.

Flynn, Peter. 1974. "Class, Clientelism, and Coercion: Some Mechanisms of Internal Dependency and Control." *Journal of Commonwealth and Comparative Politics* 12 (2): 133–56.

Foucher, Vincent. 2007. "Blue Marches. Public Performance and Political Turnover in Senegal." In *Staging Politics: Power and Performance in Asia and Africa*, edited by Julia Strauss and Donal Cruise O'Brien, 111–31. London: I.B Tauris.

François, Doligez, François Seck Fall, and Mansa Oualy. 2021. *Expériences de microfinance au Sénégal.* Dakar: Karthala Editions; Paris: CRES.

Glovsky, David N. 2021. "Medina Gounass: Constructing Extra-National Space in a West African Borderland." *African Studies Review* 64 (3): 569–94.

Graeber, David. 2001. *Toward an Anthropological Theory of Value: The False Coin of Our Own Dreams.* New York: Palgrave Macmillan.

Gueye, Marame. 2011. "Ode to Patriarchy: The Fine Line between Praise and Criticism in a Popular Senegalese Poem." In *Gender Epistemologies in Africa: Gendering Traditions, Spaces, Social Institutions, and Identities,* edited by Oyèrónké Oyěwùmí, 63–83. New York: Palgrave Macmillan. https://doi.org/10.1057/9780230116276_4.

Hannaford, Dinah, and Ellen E. Foley. 2015. "Negotiating Love and Marriage in Contemporary Senegal: A Good Man Is Hard to Find." *African Studies Review* 58 (2): 205–25.

Heath, Deborah. 1992. "Fashion, Anti-Fashion, and Heteroglossia in Urban Senegal." *American Ethnologist* 19 (1): 19–33.

Hill, Joseph. 2011. "Languages of Islam: Hybrid Genres of Taalibe Baay Oratory in Senegal." *Islamic Africa* 2 (1): 67–103.

Hodžić, Saida. 2014. "Feminist Bastards: Toward a Posthumanist Critique of NGOization." In *Theorizing NGOs: States, Feminisms, and Neoliberalism,* edited by Inderpal Grewal and Victoria Bernal, 221–47. Durham, NC: Duke University Press.

———. 2017. *The Twilight of Cutting: African Activism and Life After NGOs.* Berkeley: University of California Press.

Hoffman, Barbara. 2000. "Griots and Griottes: Masters of Words and Music." *African Arts* 33 (3): 16–17.

Imam, Ayesha M. 2004. "Introduction: Intégrer le genre aux sciences sociales africaines." In *Sexe, genre, et société: Engendrer les sciences sociales africaines,* edited by Ayesha M. Imam, Amina Mama, and Fatou Sow, 1–47. Paris: Karthala Éditions.

Jackson, John L., Jr. 2001. *Harlemworld: Doing Race and Class in Contemporary Black America.* Chicago: University of Chicago Press.

Jones, Hilary. 2005. "From Mariage à La Mode to Weddings at Town Hall: Marriage, Colonialism, and Mixed-Race Society in Nineteenth-Century Senegal." *International Journal of African Historical Studies* 38:27–48.

———. 2020. "Women, Family and Daily Life in Senegal's Nineteenth-Century Atlantic Towns." In *African Women in the Atlantic World,* edited by Mariana Candido and Adam Jones, 233–47. Suffolk: James Currey.

Josephides, Lisette. 1985. *The Production of Inequality: Gender and Exchange among the Kewa.* London: Tavistock.

Kandiyoti, Deniz. 1988. "Bargaining with Patriarchy." *Gender and Society* 2 (3): 274–90.

Kane, Oumar, and Hawa Kane. 2018. "The Origins of the Feminist Movement in Senegal: A Social History of the Pioneering Yewwu-Yewwi." *African Sociological Review* 22:18–30.

Kang, Alice J., and Aili Mari Tripp. 2018. "Coalitions Matter: Citizenship, Women, and Quota Adoption in Africa." *Perspectives on Politics* 16:73–91.

Kâ, Omar. 2009. *Nanu Dégg Wolof: A Multidimensial Approach to the Teaching and Learning of Wolof as a Foreign Language*. Madison, WI: NARLC.

Karim, Lamia. 2011. *Microfinance and Its Discontents: Women in Debt in Bangladesh*. Minneapolis: University of Minnesota Press.

———. 2014. "Demystifying Microcredit: The Grameen Bank, NGOs, and Neo-liberalism in Bangladesh." In *Theorizing NGOs: States, Feminisms, and Neoliberalism*, edited by Inderpal Grewal and Victoria Bernal, 193–218. Durham, NC: Duke University Press.

Kelly, Catherine Lena. 2019. *Party Proliferation and Political Contestation in Africa: Senegal in Comparative Perspective*. New York: Springer.

Keese, Alexander. 2015. *Ethnicity and the Colonial State: Finding and Representing Identifications in a Coastal West African and Global Perspective (1850–1960)*. Leiden: Brill.

Kilimo, M. J. 2022. "'You can't do politics without money': female politicians, matronage, and the limits of gender quotas in Kenya." *Africa* 92(2):210–229.

Kitane, Alassane Khodia. 2010. *Le Sénégal sous Abdoulaye Wade: Cahiers d'une démocratie sans démocrates*. Paris: L'Harmattan.

Kouyaté, Bassi, and Vincent Zanetti. 1993. "La nouvelle aaw génération des griots." *Cahiers d'ethnomusicologie. Anciennement Cahiers de musiques traditionnelles* 6:201–209.

Lang, Sabine. 1997. "The NGOization of Feminism." In *Transitions, Environments, Translations: Feminism in International Politics*, edited by Joan W. Scott, Cora Kaplan, and Debra Keates, 101–20. New York: Routledge.

Leymarie-Ortiz, Isabelle. 1979. "The Griots of Senegal and Change." *Africa: Rivista trimestrale di studi e documentazione dell'Istituto Italiano per l'Africa e l'Oriente* 34 (3): 183–97.

Lo, Marieme. 2011. "Self-Image and Self-Naming: A Discursive and Social Analysis of Women's Microenterprises in Senegal and Mali." In *Gender Epistemologies in Africa*, edited by Oyèrónké Oyěwùmi, 155–78. New York: Palgrave Macmillan.

Lombard, Jérôme, Pape Sakho, and Catherine Valton. 2019. "Le Nouvel Horizon Sénégalais: Peuplement et Urbanisation Des Campagnes Occidentales Aux Périphéries." *L'Espace Géographique* 4 (48): 306–28.

Mahadeen, Ebtihal. 2016. "Arabizing 'Masculinity.'" *Journal of Middle East Women's Studies* 12 (3): 450–52.

Mahmood, Saba. 2005. *Politics of Piety: The Islamic Revival and the Feminist Subject*. 2nd Revised. Oxford: Princeton University Press.

Masquelier, Adeline. 2009. *Women and Islamic Revival in a West African Town.* Bloomington: Indiana University Press.

Maurer, Bill. 2006. "The Anthropology of Money." *Annual Review of Anthropology* 35:15–36.

———. 2009. "Afterword: Moral Economies, Economic Moralities, Consider the Possibilities!" In *Economics and Morality: Anthropological Approaches,* edited by Katherine E. Browne and B. Lynne Milgram, 257–70. Lanham, MD: AltaMira Press.

Mauss, Marcel. 1990. *The Gift: Forms and Functions of Exchange in Archaic Societies.* New York: W. W. Norton.

M'Baye, Babacar. 2019. "Representations of the Gôr Djiguène [Man Woman] in Senegalese Culture, Films, and Literature." In *Gender and Sexuality in Senegalese Societies,* edited by Babacar M'Baye and Besi Brillian Muhonja, 77–106. Lanham, MD: Lexington.

Mbembe, Achille. 2001. *On the Postcolony.* Berkeley: University of California Press.

Mbow, Penda. 2008. "Senegal: The Return of Personalism." *Journal of Democracy* 19 (1): 156–69.

McClintock, Anne. 1995. "No Longer in a Future Heaven: Women and Nationalism in South Africa." *Transition* 51:104–23.

McLanahan, Sara S., and Erin L. Kelly. 2006. "The Feminization of Poverty: Past and Future." In *Handbook of the Sociology of Gender,* edited by Janet Saltzman Chafetz, 127–45 New York: Springer.

McLaughlin, Fiona. 2008. "Senegal: The Emergence of a National Lingua Franca." *Language and National Identity in Africa* 7:79–97.

———. 2009. "Senegal's Early Cities and the Making of an Urban Language." In *The Languages of Urban Africa,* edited by Fiona McLaughlin, 71–85. London: Bloomsbury.

McNee, Lisa. 2000. *Selfish Gifts: Senegalese Women's Autobiographical Discourses.* Albany: State University of New York Press.

Melly, Caroline. 2018. *Bottleneck: Moving, Building, and Belonging in an African City.* Chicago: University of Chicago Press.

Meneley, Anne. 1996. *Tournaments of Value: Sociability and Hierarchy in a Yemeni Town.* Toronto: University of Toronto Press.

Mikell, Gwendolyn. 1997. *African Feminism: The Politics of Survival in Sub-Saharan Africa.* Philadelphia: University of Pennsylvania Press.

Mills, Ivy. 2011. "Sutura: Gendered Honor, Social Death, and the Politics of Exposure in Senegalese Literature and Popular Culture." Diss., University of California, Berkeley.

Moya, Ismaël. 2015. "Unavowed Value: Economy, Comparison, and Hierarchy in Dakar." *HAU: Journal of Ethnographic Theory* 5 (1): 151–72.

Munyaka, Mluleki, and Mokgethi Motlhabi. 2005. "The African Concept of Ubuntu/Botho and its Socio-Moral Significance." *Black Theology* 3 (2): 215–37.

Ndiaye, Khadidiatou 2012. "Le 'scoring' en microfinance: Un outil de gestion du risque de crédit." In *Expériences de microfinance au Sénégal,* edited by François Doligez, François Seck Fall, and Mansa Oualy, 105–13. Paris: Karthala Éditions.

Ngom, Fallou. 2016. *Muslims beyond the Arab World: The Odyssey of 'Ajami and the Murīdiyya.* AAR Religion, Culture, and History. Oxford: Oxford University Press.

Nugent, Paul. 2010. "Do Nations Have Stomachs? Food, Drink, and Imagined Community in Africa." *Africa Spectrum* 45 (3): 87–113.

Ong, Aihwa. 2006. *Neoliberalism as Exception: Mutations in Citizenship and Sovereignty.* Durham, NC: Duke University Press.

Oyěwùmi, Oyèrónké. 1997. *The Invention of Women: Making an African Sense of Western Gender Discourses.* Minneapolis: University of Minnesota Press.

———. 2011. "Introduction: Gendering." In *Gender Epistemologies in Africa: Gendering Traditions, Spaces, Social Institutions, and Identities,* edited by Oyèrónké Oyěwùmi, 1–8. New York: Palgrave Macmillan.

Panzacchi, Cornelia. 1994. "The Livelihoods of Traditional Griots in Modern Senegal." *Africa* 64:190–210.

Parkin, David. 1987. *Transformations of African Marriage.* Manchester: Manchester University Press.

Perutz, Sidney S. 2008. *Strange Reciprocity: Mainstreaming Women's Work in Tepoztlán in the "Decade of the New Economy."* New York: Lexington.

Pierce, Steven. 2016. *Moral Economies of Corruption: State Formation and Political Culture in Nigeria.* Durham: Duke University Press.

Pina-Cabral, João. 2020. "Introduction." In *Elites: Choice, Leadership and Succession,* edited by João Pina-Cabral and Antonia Pedroso de Lima, 1–8. Oxford: Berg Press.

Pitcher, Anne, Mary H. Moran, and Michael Johnston. 2009. "Rethinking Patrimonialism and Neopatrimonialism in Africa." *African Studies Review* 52 (1): 125–56.

Ralph, Michael. 2015. *Forensics of Capital.* Chicago: University of Chicago Press.

Riley, Emily. 2016. "Teràanga and the Art of Hospitality: Engendering the Nation, Politics, and Religion in Dakar, Senegal." Diss., Michigan State University.

———. 2019. "The Politics of Teràanga: Gender, Hospitality, and Power in Senegal." *PoLAR: Political and Legal Anthropology Review* 42:110–24.

Robinson, David. 2000. *Paths of Accommodation: Muslim Societies and French Colonial Authorities in Senegal and Mauritania, 1880–1920.* Athens: Ohio University Press.

Rosen, Jennifer. 2017. "Gender Quotas for Women in National Politics: A Comparative Analysis across Development Thresholds." *Social Science Research* 66: 82–101.

Sahlins, Marshall. 1965. "Exchange Value and the Diplomacy of Primitive Trade." In *Essays in Economic Anthropology: Dedicated to the Memory of Karl Polanyi,* edited by American Ethnological Society, 95–129. Seattle: University of Washington Press.

———. 1972. *Stone Age Economics*. 1st ed. Chicago: Aldine and Atherton.

Sall, Cheikh Tidiane. 2010. "Les gaspillages dans les cérémonies familiales au quartier Santhiaba Ndiobène de Rufisque." Mémoire de fin d'études. Dakar: École Nationale des Travailleurs Sociaux Specialisés.

Sankara, Thomas. 2007. *Women's Liberation and the African Freedom Struggle*. Liverpool: Pathfinder Press.

Sarr, Fatou. 1998. *L'Entrepreneuriat Féminin Au Sénégal: La Transformation Des Rapports de Pouvoirs*. Paris: L'Harmattan.

———. 2011. *Ndate Yalla Reine Du Waalo 1846–1855*. Dakar: Laboratoire de Genre et Recherche Scientifique de l'IFAN, Université Cheikh Anta Diop de Dakar.

———. 2013. *La 12éme Législature au Sénégal: Les Premières Héritières de la Loi sur la Parité*. Dakar: Laboratoire Genre et Recherches Scientifique de IFAN; Fondation Friedrich Ebert.

Schaffer, Frederic C. 1998. *Democracy in Translation: Understanding Politics in an Unfamiliar Culture*. Ithaca, NY: Cornell University Press.

Schulz, Dorothea E. 1997. "Praise without Enchantment: Griots, Broadcast Media, and the Politics of Tradition in Mali." *Africa Today* 44:443–64.

———. 2012. *Muslims and New Media in West Africa: Pathways to God*. Bloomington: Indiana University Press.

Scott, Joan Wallach. 2005. *Parité!: Sexual Equality and the Crisis of French Universalism*. Chicago: University of Chicago Press.

Sebidi, L. J. 1988. "Towards a Definition of Ubuntu as African Humanism." Unpublished paper. Private collection.

Seck, Abdourahmane. 2010. *Question musulmane au Sénégal: Essai d'anthropologie d'une nouvelle modernité*. Paris: Karthala Editions.

———. 2015. "Après le développement : détours paradigmatiques et philosophie de l'histoire au Sénégal." *Presence Africaine* 192:13–32.

Seck, Fatoumata. 2018. "Goorgoolou, the Neoliberal *Homo Senegalensis:* Comics and Economics in Postcolonial Senegal." *Journal of African Cultural Studies* 30 (3): 263–78.

———. 2022. "La sutura dans l'intercase. Goorgoorlou et le travail des femmes." *Africana* 539 (2): 291–318.

Seesemann, Rüdiger, and Benjamin F. Soares. 2009. "'Being as Good Muslims as Frenchmen': On Islam and Colonial Modernity in West Africa." *Journal of Religion in Africa* 39:91–120.

Shryock, Andrew. 2004. "Other Conscious/Self Aware: First Thoughts on Cultural Intimacy and Mass Mediation." In *Off Stage/On Display: Intimacy and Ethnography in the Age of Public Culture*, edited by Andrew Shryock, 3–30. Palo Alto: Stanford University Press.

———. 2008. "Thinking about Hospitality, with Derrida, Kant, and the Balga Bedouin." *Anthropos* 103 (2): 405–21.

———. 2012. "Breaking Hospitality Apart: Bad Hosts, Bad Guests, and the Problem of Sovereignty." *Journal of the Royal Anthropological Institute* 18 (June): 20–33.

Simioni, Elena. 2019. "Se débrouiller à Dakar: langue(s) et culture(s) urbaines dans la bande dessinée Goorgoorlu de T.T Fons." *Il Tolomeo* 21 (2019): 207–30.

Smith, Étienne. 2006. "La nation 'par le côté': Le récit des cousinages au Sénégal." *Cahiers d'études africaines* 184 (4): 907–65.

Smith, Maya Angela. 2019. *Senegal Abroad: Linguistic Borders, Racial Formations, and Diasporic Imaginaries.* Madison: University of Wisconsin Press.

Souleles, Daniel Scott, Matthew Archer, and Morten Thaning. 2023. "Introduction to Special Issue: Value, Values, and Anthropology." *Economic Anthropology* 10 (2): 162–68.

Sow, Fatou. 1980. *"Femmes, socialité et valeurs africaines. Notes africaines": Bulletin d'information et de correspondance.* Dakar: Institut Français d'Afrique Noire.

———. 1985. "Muslim Families in Contemporary Black Africa." *Current Anthropology* 26 (5): 563–70.

Strathern, Marilyn. 1988. *The Gender of the Gift: Problems with Women and Problems with Society in Melanesia.* Berkeley: University of California Press.

Strauss, Julia, and Donal B. Cruise O'Brien. 2007. *Staging Politics: Power and Performance in Asia and Africa.* London: I.B. Tauris.

Sylla, Assane. 1978. *La Philosophie morale des Wolofs.* Dakar: Sankoré.

Sylla, Seynabou N. 2001. *"Femme et Politique au Sénégal": Memoire de D.E.A.* Paris: Université de Paris 1 Pantheon Sorbonne.

Tamale, Sylvia. 1999. *When Hens Begin to Crow: Gender and Parliamentary Politics in Uganda.* Oxford: Westview Press.

———. 2020. *Decolonization and Afro-Feminism.* Québec: Daraja.

Telingator, Susan, and Sindiso Mnisi Weeks. 2019. "Catalyzing Stagnant Norms: Female Parliamentarians' Creative Impact on Weary Public Institutions." In *Gender and Sexuality in Senegalese Societies: Critical Perspectives and Methods,* edited by Babacar M'Baye and Besi Brillian Muhonja, 227–56. Lanham, MD: Lexington.

Temple, Dominique. 2008. "Les niveaux de réciprocité." http://dominique.temple .free.fr/reciprocite.php?page=reciprocite_2&id_article=68.

Tøraasen, Marianne. 2019. "Gender Parity and the Symbolic Representation of Women in Senegal." *Journal of Modern African Studies* 57 (3): 459–81.

Toulabor, Comi, Achille Mbembe, and Jean-François Bayart. 2008. *Le Politique par le bas en Afrique noire.* Paris: Éditions Karthala.

Tidjani, Bassirou. 1998. "African Unions Under Structural Adjustment Programs." *Relations Industrielles/Industrial Relations* 53 (2): 278–99.

Toliver-Diallo, Wilmetta J. 2005. "'The Woman Who Was More Than a Man': Making Aline Sitoe Diatta into a National Heroine in Senegal." *Canadian Journal of African Studies/Revue Canadienne Des Études Africaines* 39:340–62.

Tripp, Aili Mari, Isabel Casimiro, Joy Kwesiga, and Alice Mungwa. 2009. *African Women's Movements: Changing Political Landscapes.* Cambridge, UK: Cambridge University Press.

UNFPA. 2024. "World Population Dashboard—Senegal." https://www.unfpa .org/data/world-population/SN.

Van Eerdewijk, A. 2007. *The ABC of Unsafe Sex: Gendered Sexualities of Young People in Dakar.* Paris: Calman-Lévy.

Weber, Max. 1947. *The Theory of Social and Economic Organization.* Translated by A. M Henderson and Talcott Parsons. Edited by Talcott Parsons. New York: Free Press.

——— 1968. *On Charisma and Institution Building.* Chicago: University of Chicago Press.

Yamaguchi, Masao. 1991. "The Poetics of Exhibition in Japanese Culture." In *Exhibiting Cultures: The Poetics and Politics of Museum Display,* edited by Ivan Karp and Steven D. Lavine, 57–67. Washington, DC: Smithsonian Institution Press.

Yuval-Davis, Nira. 1997. "Women, Citizenship and Difference." *Feminist Review* 57 (1): 4–27.

Interviews

Ba, Mame Mbayame Gueye Dione, May 26, 2017, Liberté 6 Extension, Dakar, Senegal.

Biaye, May 30, 2017, Point E, Dakar, Senegal.

Codou, Daba, June 21, 2019, Yarax-Dakar, Senegal.

Dia, Aysatu Daouda, November 5, 2013, Lac Rose, Senegal (not recorded).

Diakhaté, Moukhsinatou, May 5, 2017, Hann Bel-Air, Dakar, Senegal.

Dièye, Cécile, June 5, 2013, Yeumbeul, Dakar, Senegal.

Gassama, Rokhyatou, August 2 and 5, 2017, Point E, Dakar, Senegal.

Gaye, Rokhaya, July 5, 2010, Liberté 6, Dakar, Senegal.

Géy, Ndey Sukkey, May 2, 2017, Géejawaay, Dakar, Senegal.

Ka, Awa, May 24, 2017, Cambérène, Dakar, Senegal (not recorded).

Kouyate, Jéynaba, September 4, 2013, Medina, Dakar, Senegal.

Laye, Aysatu, October 10, 2013, Amitié 2, Dakar, Senegal.

Mbóoj, Ayda, December 18, 2013, Sacré Coeur 3, Dakar, Senegal.

Mbóoj, Ndey, June 29, 2017, Amitié 2, Dakar, Senegal.

Sall, Aysata Tall, August 7, 2017, Plateau, Dakar, Senegal.

Samb, Uley, October 10, 2013, Amitié 2, Dakar, Senegal.

Sarr, Fatou, August 1, 2017, Sacré Coeur 2, Dakar, Senegal.

Seck, Penda, May 17, 2017, National Assembly, Dakar, Senegal.

Sow, Mareem, August 4, 2017, Amitié 3, Dakar, Senegal.

Tine, Elène, July 5 2017, Hann Bel-Air, Dakar, Senegal.

Touré, Aminata, January 14, 2021, by telephone.

Archival and News Sources

2STV. 2020. "Corruption au Sénégal, La source du mal." YouTube video, 6 de Septembre. https://youtube.com/live/iIbzoHRHnLM?si=lgVb6yhzZd4WmA_F.

Agence de Presse Sénégalaise. 2010. "Femmes priée de ne pas imposez la parité dans l'espace familial." *Agence de Presse Sénégalaise*, 18 août.

AiichaBamba. 2019. Twitter Post. January 29, 4:53. https://x.com/AiichaBamba /status/1090201275516571648?t=H10tNsvsREM5b-Ekfsd79A&s=19.

Aljazeera. 2023. "Senegal's Ousmane Sonko Charged with Fomenting Insurrection." *Aljazeera*, 30 July. https://www.aljazeera.com/news/2023/7/30/senegals -ousmane-sonko-charged-with-fomenting-insurrection.

Allou. 1966. "Yacine Boubou: un acte de foi, un émouvant sacrifice." *AWA: La revue de la femme noire*, 40–43.

APA News. 2024. "Senegal's ex PM Aminata Touré Bounces Back." African Press Agency, August 28. https://apanews.net/senegals-ex-pm-aminata-toure -bounces-back/.

Ba, Mehdi. 2020. "Sénégal—Aminata Touré: 'En Politique, l'ambition n'est pas un Délit.'" *Jeune Afrique*, 26 décembre.

Benga, Marie-Louise. 1996. "La révolution silencieuse des groupements féminins." *Le Soleil*, mars.

Camara, Mouhamed. 2024. "Aissata Tall Sall: 'Un Jour, Une Femme Sera Présidente de La République Du Sénégal.'" *Seneweb*, March 8.

Carayol, Rémi. 2013. "Sénégal: Aminata Touré, forte tête." *Jeune Afrique*, 16 septembre.

Daour, Adama Yacine. 2009. "Grave conséquences pour la lutte d'égalité des sexes et la parité dans les sociétés occidentales." *Le Soleil*, 4 novembre.

Dianko, M'Bodé. 2000. "Marches Nationale et Mondiale des Femmes: Sénégalaises y participeront à New York." *Le Soleil*, 12 septembre.

Diedhiou, Maguette Gueye. 2014. "Application des lois en faveur des femmes: L'ONP préconise une collaboration avec le gouvernement et le secteur privé." *Le Soleil*, 15 mai.

Dieng, Babacar. 2000. "Opératrices économique, les avantages de la micro-finance." *Le Soleil*, samedi 1 et dimanche 2 juillet.

Dieng, B., and S. Diamanka. 2000. "Opératrices économique, les avantages de la micro-finance." *Le Soleil*, 1 et 2 juillet.

———. 2019. "Après l'avoir brocardée pendant longtemps: Me Aysata Tall ose la transhumance." *Leral Net*, January 28. https://www.leral.net/Apres-l-avoir

-brocardee-pendant-longtemps-Me-Aissata-Tall-ose-la-transhumance-_a242056
.html.

Dione, Babacar. 2006. "Hommage des femmes à Me Wade: Le Pacte de confiance
consolidé." *Le Soleil*, 27 mars.

Diop, Seynabou. 1991. "Groupements de promotion féminine: Aïssa Guèye Diène
contre-attaque." *Le Soleil*, 20 novembre.

Drame, Moussa. 2012. "Sédhiou: Rôles et Places de la Femme dans le Processus
Électoral. L'Enjeu de la Parité." *Sud Quotidien*, Mardi 5 juillet.

Faye, Hady. 2000. "Marie Angélique Savané: La victoire de l'alternance c'est celle
des femmes." *Le Soleil*, June 26.

Gonzales, Abdurahmane Sarr. 2001. "L'union des femmes commerçantes de Thiès:
'un espace de solidarité tourné vers le développement.'" *Le Soleil*, 24 avril.

Gueye, Marame. 2024. "Between Woman and Nation." *Africa Is a Country*, 6 May.

Gueye, Saër. 2000a. "Diourbel, un prêt de 12 millions aux associations féminines."
Le Soleil, 21 et 22 octobre.

———. 2000b. "Un prêt de 12 millions aux associations féminines." *Le Soleil*, 21 et
22 octobre.

Hann TV. 2020. "Magal Touba 2020_Mously Diakhaté." Hann TV, 7 octobre.
https://www.youtube.com/watch?v=tMee7uePVPI&t=134s.

Hawoye, Aïssata. 2019. Twitter Post. January 29, 5:51. https://x.com/HawoyeAissata
/status/1090215764920098818?t=l8dp-vcmRSU86_GsN9yy3A&s=19.

Hazard, Domitille. 1991. "La Federation Devenue ONG: Ouverture aux Finance-
ments Exterieurs." *Le Soleil*, 20 novembre.

Jean-Bart, Anne. 1990. "Les femmes dans l'histoire." *Le Soleil*, 29 aout.

Kane, Coumba, and Théa Ollivier. 2022. "Adji Sarr, the Woman Who Accused Senegal's Leading Opposition Figure of Rape." *Le Monde*, April 7, 2022.

Kibangula, Trésor. 2013. "9 choses à savoir sur Aminata Touré, nouvelle Première
Ministre du Sénégal." *Jeune Afrique*, 3 septembre.

Laye, Aïssatou. 2009. "Les Cérémonies Familiales, véritables entreprises au Sénégal." *La Gazette*, May 7, 2009.

Le Soleil. 1993. "Systeme D. et Tontine." 8 mars.

———. 2000a. "Me Wade lors de la journée internationale de la femme: 'la solution à vos problèmes c'est l'alternance.'" 9 mars.

———. 2000b. "Promotion de l'entrepreneuriat féminin: Des manuels de formation en langues nationales." novembre.

———. 2001. "Ministère de la famille et de la petite enfance: 200 machines à coudre offertes aux groupements de femmes." 7 novembre.

———. 2004. "Madame Mareem Ndiaye." 1 avril.

Marone, S. 2000. "Accès des femmes au crédit: La FAFS entame la promotiono
d'un système décentralisé." *Le Soleil*, 14 novembre.

Mbengue, Alioune Badara, dir. 1967. "Édition Speciale: La loi de 1967." *Radio Télévision Sénégalais*, 26 février.

Mbóoj, Aïssatou. 2015. "Lancement de sa campagne de lutte coontre la détention arbitraire: mémorandum d'Ayda Mbóoj." *Dakaractu*, 04 Août.

MLB. 1999. "Federation des Groupements de Promotion Féminine: Khady Ndao, nouvelle présidente." *Le Soleil*, 3 et 4 juillet.

Ndao, Fary. 2019. Twitter Post, January 29, 4:04. https://x.com/ndaofary/status /1090188850239029248?t=fOYlS5fr10WAtAn-PrMQ6A&s=19.

Ndao, Madine. 2000. "1 million de francs offert aux femmes de Podor." *Le Soleil*, 4 septembre.

Ndiaye, Le Soleil S. D. 1998. "Femmes: faut-il imposez des quotas?" *Le Soleil*, 5 août.

Ndiaye, Maurice. 1999. "Élus et Conseillers Locaux: Le Devenir de la femme en question." October 13.

Ndiaye, Momar Seyni. 1998. "Politicorama: Femme, puissance et pouvoir." *Le Soleil*, 5 mars.

Ndiaye, Papa Mater. 2019. "Après sa transhumance, Aysata Tall Sall se fait lynchée sur les réseaux sociaux." *Kéwoulo: Journal d'Investigation*, Janvier 29.

Samb, Babacar. 1988. "IIéme Assemblée Generale de l'Association des Femmes de l'Afrique de l'Ouest (AFAO): Cadencé de l'Initiative Privée Féminine." *Le Soleil*, vendredi 28 octobre.

Sarine. 2019. Twitter Post. January 29, 8:47. https://x.com/Sarinedie/status /1090244994672328707.

Sarr, Abdurahmane. 1999. "Federation Nationale des Groupements de Promotion Feminine: La presidente Khady Ndao installé." *Le Soleil*, 17 novembre.

Sarr Fall, Amy. 2019. *Le jour où une femme sera Présidente du Sénégal*. Seneweb. https://www.seneweb.com/news/Contribution/le-jour-ou-une-femme-sera -presidente-du-_n_273882.htm.

Sow, Bassirou. 1998. "Mobilisation pour la promotion de la femme sénégalaise." *Sud Quotidien*, 24 novembre.

Sow, El Bachir. 1996. "Journée International de la Femme: Cérémonies Familiales, A nouveau, le gaspillage." *Le Soleil*, 8 mars.

Sow, Fatou et al. 2022. "'Il est temps que les Sénégalaises cessent d'être traitées comme des citoyennes de seconde zone': Un collectif de féministes s'inquiète de la remise en cause de la loi sur la parité." *Le Monde Afrique*, 03 juin 2022, sec. Tribune.

Sow Ba, Aida. 2002. "Femme et politique : Le pouvoir local est rebelle à la féminisation." *Le Soleil*, 9 mars.

Sud Quotidien. 2000. "Marie Angélique Savané: La victoire de l'alternance c'est celle des femmes." 25 mars.

Sy, Mamadu. 2006. "Développement Économique et Social: le leadership féminine, un puissant levier." *Le Soleil*, 23 mars.

Sylla, Mariama. 2001. "Associations Féminines: 'Non aux femmes députés alibi!'" *Le Soleil*, 16 février.

Tabara, Kiné. 2000. "Bric-à-Brac." *Le Soleil*, 2 et 3 décembre.

Talla, Amadu. 2000. "Mutuelles d'épargne et de crédit: Les banques des femmes." *L'info 7*.

Thiam. 2014. "Causes et Clauses du Divorce." Seneplus, July 17. https://www.seneplus.com/article/causes-et-clauses-du-divorce.

Thiam, C. 2000. "L'AFEPES a installé sa mutuelle d'épargne et de crédit." *Le Soleil*, 20 décembre.

Touré, Aminata. 2016. "Sénégal: 'Saluons l'audace du chemin parcouru contre la corruption.'" *Le Monde*, 30 juin.

"UNESCO—Ceebu Jën, a Culinary Art of Senegal." n.d. Accessed March 6, 2024. https://ich.unesco.org/en/RL/ceebu-jen-a-culinary-art-of-senegal-01748.

Unknown. 1987. "Congrès Constitutif de la Fédération Nationale des Groupements Féminins: Une Note d'Espoir." *Le Soleil*, 23 octobre.

———. 1999. "Amsatou Sow Sidibé, Pr. Agrégée de Droit privé." *L'info*, 2 décembre.

———. 2000. "Femme Développement Entreprise en Afrique (FDEA): La micro-finance pour le renforcement des capacités d'action des opératrices économiques." *SudQuotidien*, mercredi 3 mai.

———. 2001. Ministère de la Famille et de la Petite Enfance: 200 machines à coudre offertes aux groupements de femme.

———. 2020. "Zoo sur Soukeyna Konaré, l'une des épouses de Alboury Ndiaye et première femme politique au Sénégal." *Leral TV*. 24 séptembre. https://www.leral.net/Zoo-sur-Soukeyna-Konare-l-une-des-epouses-de-Alboury-Ndiaye-et-premiere-femme-politique-au-Senegal_a283699.html.

"World Bank Open Data." 2024. "Personal Remittances, Received (% of GDP)—Senegal." https://data.worldbank.org/indicator/BX.TRF.PWKR.DT.GD.ZS?locations=SN.

Xalima News. 2012. "Me El Hadji Diouf tire encore sur la loi instituant la parité." Xalima News, 7 août. https://www.xalimasn.com/me-el-hadji-diouf-tire-encore-sur-la-loi-instituant-la-parite-ces-feministes-qui-prennent-le-pays-en-otage-sont-finances-par-des-lobbies/.

INDEX

Emily Jenan Riley is Associate Professor and Researcher in the Center for Asian and African Studies at El Colegio de México. She holds a PhD in Cultural Anthropology and lives in Mexico City.

For Indiana University Press

Sabrina Black, Editorial Assistant
Tony Brewer, Artist and Book Designer
Anna Francis, Assistant Acquisitions Editor
Anna Garnai, Production Coordinator
Katie Huggins, Production Manager
Darja Malcolm-Clarke, Project Manager/Editor
Bethany Mowry, Acquisitions Editor
Dan Pyle, Online Publishing Manager
Pamela Rude, Senior Artist and Book Designer
Stephen Williams, Assistant Director of Marketing